JOHN IN THE COMPANY OF POETS

Studies in Christianity and Literature 6

EDITORIAL BOARD

John in the Company of Poets

The Gospel in Literary Imagination

Thomas Gardner

BAYLOR UNIVERSITY PRESS

Cover Design by Dean Bornstein
Cover Image: "St. John the Evangelist" (oil on canvas) by Batoni, Pompeo Girolamo (1708–87). Basildon Park, Berkshire, UK/The Iliffe Collection/National Trust Photographic Library/John Hammond/The Bridgeman Art Library

Library of Congress Cataloging-in-Publication Data

Gardner, Thomas, 1952–
 John in the company of poets : the Gospel in literary imagination / Thomas Gardner.
    p. cm. -- (Studies in Christianity and literature ; #6)
 Includes bibliographical references and index.
 ISBN 978-1-60258-315-3 (hardcover : alk. paper)
 1. American poetry--History and criticism. 2. English poetry--History and criticism. 3. Christian poetry, American--History and criticism. 4. Christian poetry, English--History and criticism. 5. Bible. N.T. John--In literature. 6. Christianity in literature. 7. Christianity and literature--United States--History. 8. Christianity and literature--Great Britain--History. 9. Bible. N.T. John--Criticism, interpretation, etc. I. Title.
 PS310.R4G37 2011
 811.608'03823--dc22
                                2010052543

Printed in the United States of America on acid-free paper with a minimum of 30% pcw recycled content.

For my students

CONTENTS

ACKNOWLEDGMENTS

Esther Richey has been part of this project from its very beginning, encouraging me, reading drafts, helping me to see what I had written. I am very grateful. I have been fortunate to read the Gospel over the years with John and Linda Tyson, Chris and Kirstan Hutchinson, David Poteet, and others. Chris Hutchinson, Laura Gardner, William and Marion Gardner, Fritz Oehlschlaeger, John Wheatcroft, Fred Carlisle, and Robert Siegle read the manuscript and offered useful suggestions. Carolyn Rude, my Department Chair during the writing of this book, has been a constant source of support and encouragement. Roger Lundin, Carey Newman, and two anonymous readers from Baylor University Press helped shape the book in important ways.

I have dedicated this book to my students at Virginia Tech for a number of reasons. Years ago, I first saw the possibility of such an approach to the Gospel in a class I was teaching on biblical and classical backgrounds to literature. More recently, and more soberly, I was privileged to experience in the final classes I taught after the terrible events of April 16, 2007, in Blacksburg, in which thirty-two students and faculty were killed and many others wounded, the power of poetry to lead us through our inner lives. How fortunate my students and I felt, after passing through that almost unspeakable series of events, to have in common a number of poems that allowed us to draw close and speak and begin to find ourselves again. Imagine, if you would, the great gift it was to turn to Emily Dickinson's "After great pain, a formal feeling comes— / The Nerves sit ceremonious, like Tombs—," to know that poem in advance and be able to walk through its drama once again at such a time and in such company. I have written this book with those classes in mind, seeking to make the various dramas I unfold as clear as possible, trusting them to speak into contexts I cannot on my own even imagine.

I am grateful for permission to reprint the following material:

"Directive" from *The Poetry of Robert Frost*, edited by Edward Connery Lathem. Copyright © 1947, 1969 by Henry Holt and Company. Copyright © 1975 by Lesley Frost Ballantine. Reprinted by permission of Henry Holt and Company, LLC.

"Noli Me Tangere" from *The End of Beauty* by Jorie Graham. Copyright © 1987 by Jorie Graham. Reprinted by permission of HarperCollins Publishers.

"Mass for the Day of St. Thomas Didymus: Agnus Dei" by Denise Levertov. From *The Selected Poems of Denise Levertov*. Copyright © 1982 by Denise Levertov. Reprinted by permission of New Directions Publishing Corp. Additional permission from Bloodaxe Books, Denise Levertov, *New Selected Poems* (Bloodaxe Books, 2003).

"Pietà" from *Deaths & Transfigurations* by Paul Mariani. Copyright © 2005 by Paul Mariani. Used by permission of Paraclete Press.

"Judas" from *If I Had Wheels or Love: Collected Poems of Vassar Miller*. Copyright © 1991 by Vassar Miller. Reprinted by permission of Southern Methodist University Press.

"La Vierge Romane" from *Journey: New and Selected Poems, 1969–1999*, by Kathleen Norris, copyright © 2001. Reprinted by permission of University of Pittsburgh Press.

"The Answer" from *Collected Poems 1945–1990* by R.S. Thomas. Copyright © 1993 by R.S. Thomas. Reprinted by permission of Weidenfeld and Nicolson, an imprint of The Orion Publishing Group, London.

"A Wedding Toast" from *The Mind-Reader*, copyright © 1972 by Richard Wilbur, reproduced by permission of Houghton Mifflin Harcourt Publishing Company. This material may not be reproduced in any form or by any means without the prior written permission of the publisher.

Excerpt from "A Journal of the Year of the Ox" from *The World of the Ten Thousand Things: Poems 1980–1990* by Charles Wright. Copyright © 1990 by Charles Wright. Reprinted by permission of Farrar, Straus and Giroux, LLC.

Poems Examined

Introduction

In an essay entitled "Psalm Eight," the novelist Marilynne Robinson focuses on the words Jesus greets Mary Magdalene with on the morning of his resurrection. Mary, in John's account, has come to the tomb while it is still dark and found the stone blocking its entrance rolled away. She runs and tells two of the disciples, who hurry to the place, explore the empty tomb, and then return to their homes. Mary, who has followed along, is left alone, standing outside the tomb and weeping. When she senses someone behind her, she turns and sees Jesus but does not recognize him, taking him for the gardener. "Woman, why are you weeping?" (20:15),[1] he says. Recalling that phrase from a childhood sermon, Robinson returns to it in this essay, struck by a sense that the "words in some exceptional sense [were] addressed precisely to me."[2] Why did Jesus approach Mary with such deference? she asks. Why, in this moment of almost inexplicable glory, would he take the time to quietly tease her into awareness? Hearing the words as if they were also addressed to her across an almost unimaginable distance, Robinson writes in order to make out their meaning.

What I argue in this study is that Robinson's response to the Gospel is not unique. John writes in order to draw readers into a confrontation with the words of Jesus, structuring his Gospel so that the reader is drawn deeper and deeper into the struggle to make out the meaning of his rich, enigmatic words. What Jesus says is both strikingly simple—"I am life"—and almost impossible to immediately take in. He knows this and accompanies this claim with a series of invitations, phrased to give those who hear him a way to imagine and think through the implications of his words. "I am life," he says. "Come to me and rest." "I am life—don't cling to me." Jesus forces

1

those who hear his words to work them out themselves. As I see it, John does not so much talk us into believing as set up spaces where the words and illustrations of Jesus address us, drawing us into the struggle to taste and see and understand. John writes at the close of his Gospel that he has drawn into sequence some of the "signs" that Jesus performed precisely for this purpose. Jesus said and did many things, he writes, "but these have been written that you may believe that Jesus is the Christ, the Son of God; and that believing you may have life in His name" (20:31).

What I offer here is a literary reading of the Gospel, paying particular attention to the way John's structural patterns, chiming repetitions, and narrative interventions draw the reader into an engagement with Jesus' elusive but down-to-earth descriptions of himself. As I unfold the way John sets up opportunities for the words Jesus uses to address us, I turn at regular intervals to the work of some twenty poets who dramatize what hearing his words looks like. Poets are our best readers, and it is no surprise that each of them responds in a similar way—hearing themselves addressed, they each work out, through their own experiences, ways of approaching and considering his words. What we find in poems, Wallace Stevens writes, is "the mind in the act of finding / What will suffice," and as we follow these various minds pondering, considering, leaping forward, or coming to a halt, we see dramatized the sort of work to which John's readers are called.[3] Following along as these poets imagine what it would mean to eat the flesh of Jesus or drink his blood, we gain access to a way of thinking everywhere called for by the text but not fully articulated in exegesis alone. To illustrate this thinking, I draw mainly from poetry I regularly teach and write about—twentieth-century and twenty-first-century British and American poetry, with a few well-known selections from crucial, earlier writers—but my approach here is not limited to recent poetry. It is simply the work that was most available to me—a sort of second tongue—as I searched for ways to unfold the inner work to which John's language seemed everywhere to be calling me.[4]

It is this sort of reading that Robinson performs when she returns to Jesus' words to Mary, seeking not so much to explicate them as to hear them, under the assumption that they are, at some level, addressed to her. This is no simple thing, for, like much of the Gospel, this text speaks and yet "remains almost entirely elusive. So I must come back to hear it again; in the old phrase, to have it opened for me again."[5] The way Robinson works her way back to the text seems at first quite circuitous. We first find ourselves back in a memory of her Idaho childhood and its mountain meadows:

Because of the altitude, or the damp, or the kind of grass that grew in such places, they were radiant, smoldering, gold with transparency, accepting light altogether. Thousands of florets for which I would never learn names, so tiny even a child had to kneel to see them at all, squandered intricacy and opulence on avid little bees, the bees cherished, the flowers cherished, the light cherished, visibly, audibly, palpably.[6]

A beautiful scene, stunning in its celebration of the light's attention, but to a child acutely aware of her vulnerability before the mountains' "great constant silence . . . some intention too huge even to notice my fragile flesh," it was "a parable brilliant with strangeness, cryptic with wisdom, disturbing as a tender intention full of the frightening mercy of foreknowledge."[7] What it said to her, disturbingly, darkly, was that her life was always exposed and visible, never fully her own.

That memory then brings to mind a second scene, also involving flowers. She remembers her grandfather, dressed in his oldest suit to honor the occasion, working in his garden:

His gardening was uncanny. The flourishing he set in motion brought admirers from other counties. I remember once following him down a row of irises, not sure whether I was invited, whether the irises were being shown to me. He would hold one blossom and another in the tips of his fingers, at arm's length, and tilt his face up and back to look at them. It was an old man's method of scrutiny, but to me it seemed as if he were revealing prodigy or sleight, the way a magician opens his hand to reveal a dove. I looked carefully at every blossom he appeared to commend to me, noting how they were made of cell and capillary, whisker and freckle, frail skin tented on white bone, and how they were chill to the touch, and how they curled on themselves like smoke, and how, till the life was wrung out of it, each one accomplished a small grandeur of form.[8]

The second memory grows out of the first. Both are parables about flowering and intention, about a loving or demanding attention, but at this point in the essay it is not clear what they have to do with the words Jesus speaks to Mary on Easter morning. For now, Robinson simply lets them gather and rise, like clouds on an afternoon's horizon.

But once those memories are alive in her head, she is ready to consider the words of Jesus. When he spoke to Mary that morning, Robinson writes, Jesus spoke to her "in something like the ordinary manner of a friend," "teasing her toward delight and recognition." Although he was "a figure of unutterable holiness," he quietly drew near, in the form of an ordinary man: "From whatever cosmic grandeur the moment claims for him, he speaks to the friend of his humanity with joy and kindness, but also with deference, honoring her."[9] Jesus, that is, spoke to Mary with the attentive deference Robinson had first experienced in her grandfather's approach to his irises. Rather than cloaking himself in the barely restrained intensity Robinson had experienced in her childhood, Jesus had bent down to Mary and gazed at her in love and wonder. The two memories allow Robinson to hear. They give her a way to weigh the words and make them her own. "What is man, that thou art mindful of him?" Robinson responds in wonder, quoting Psalm 8. What is man that God would go to the almost inconceivable lengths of taking on flesh and dying a criminal's death in order to gaze at Mary, honoring her and drawing her near? Someone whom he loves, Robinson writes—someone in whom he sees his own likeness. Robinson finds that a thing of "astonishing beauty," hearing, by means of the image of her grandfather gardening in his oldest suit, the tone of voice with which Jesus addressed Mary and understanding, through that tone of voice, what the crucifixion had accomplished.[10] She hears the words as if they had been spoken to her, "commend[ing]" her "commonplace, ineffable humanity" as a thing of almost inexplicable worth to God and coming to life under his gaze.[11]

In what follows, I trace the way John's arrangement of his material draws readers deeper and deeper into the claim that Jesus is life itself—that through his death his Father offers life to the world. Linking scene to scene in what could be thought of as a series of spiritual exercises, John prepares the reader to hear himself or herself addressed by the words of Jesus. Bringing out one pattern and linking it to another, he draws the reader ever closer to the cross and what God is "saying" through it. What I attempt to do here is "re-enact" the narrator's steps, making visible the dramatic arc and the inner logic of the way he organizes his material.[12] The poets I turn to along the way powerfully respond to this organization. Like the Robinson essay, they slow us down and walk us through the process of taking in or turning away from Jesus' strikingly phrased claims.

In chapter 1, I focus on John's Prologue (1:1-18) and his claim that Jesus was life itself. In bringing life to a dark world, he brought light to darkness, and John includes himself among those who took that light in. He writes from the perspective of having had his eyes opened, acknowledging that there were those who did not comprehend the light, but offering himself as an example of someone who came to life in Christ's "fullness." T. S. Eliot's "Gerontion" lets us hear how unsettling this claim might be. The poet hears John's opening assertion that, when the light of life came to the dark world, "the darkness did not comprehend it" (1:5), and responds, through the chastened words of his invented speaker, that this was indeed the case—he did not take it in. What John's words draw out of him are reasons for this failure, excuses. Blaming history, the times, language itself, Eliot's speaker dramatizes, in a way that simply unfolding the Prologue's argument does not, the exhausting, life-sapping circles that someone still in the dark might find himself tracing out.

My second chapter (1:19-51) examines the flurry of early encounters with Jesus with which John begins his narrative. "Look," says John the Baptist, "the Lamb of God who takes away the sins of the world." "We have found the Messiah," says Andrew, after spending a day with Jesus. "We have found Him of whom Moses in the Law and also the Prophets wrote," Philip reports. Much of what led to these identifications takes place away from the eyes of the reader, but as these titles ring out, what the reader hears is "Come and see"—come and see for yourself. Denise Levertov's "Agnus Dei" lets us experience the moment when these claims first begin to draw someone. Not fully settled, but her skepticism beginning to melt away, Levertov's speaker, much like those in the first chapter of John, hears the Baptist identify Jesus as "the Lamb of God who takes away the sins of the world" and is pierced through by the thought and bewildered. Without a theology to explain or smooth out the idea, Levertov feels her way into the words by thinking about her own experience with lambs, unfolding for the reader the very moment it dawned on her that the omnipotent God had "tossed [all] away," reducing himself "to a wisp of damp wool." She hears the words for herself, exactly as the Gospel calls its readers to do.

In the passages I examine in chapter 3 (2:1–4:54), the struggle to comprehend begins in earnest. Jesus begins to describe himself, offering those gathered around him ways of thinking about the life God is offering the world. Picture it this way, he says. I am a new wine, replacing the water of ritual; a new temple, replacing the empty satisfactions of buying and selling. Turn to me and live, drink of me and never thirst again, trust in me and have your greatest treasure restored—in each of the scenes in this powerful sequence, Jesus describes himself and then calls those who hear and see to take him in through these images. The reader is included among those who are asked to visualize these things and weigh them out internally. The poems I turn to in chapter 3 capture the struggle all those who hear his words go through. Richard Wilbur, for example, uses the occasion of toasting his own son's marriage to puzzle out why Jesus, at the Cana wedding, produced not just wine but gallons and gallons of it. "It made no earthly sense," he says, then thinks about that phrase. The miracle made a different kind of sense, he realizes, a spiritual one—love itself, in all its abundance, was blessing the marriage, offering to "pour its plenty out for such as you." In a similar manner, it made no earthly sense to Nicodemus, in one of the Gospel's early chapters, when Jesus invited him to turn to him for life. What sort of life was he talking about, Nicodemus asks, at which point Jesus points to the invisible wind moving in the trees, completely outside of Nicodemus' ability to know or control. Charles Wright hears those words and puts himself into the same position, watching the wind moving through his own backyard and trying, and failing, to put into words something just at the range of his consciousness, an "unalterable music" forever affecting him but always "untouched, / Moving as certainly as the wind does, / invisible in the trees."

In chapter 4 (5:1–10:42), I look at passages where, faced with mounting opposition, Jesus continues to describe the life he has come to offer, but now asks people to visualize that life through visualizing need. Approach me through your need, he says. "You are blind, but I am sight. Let me give you eyes." "You are crippled, but I am wholeness. Let me raise you up." "You are enslaved, but I am freedom. Let me release your bonds." As the narrator links these scenes together, the reader inevitably begins to explore his or her own blindness or inability to hear. What do I not get? we ask. What am I blind to? The poets I examine ask the same questions. John Donne, for example in "Holy Sonnet XIV," hears Jesus say in John 8 that he is speaking to those enslaved by sin, and explodes in recognition. It is *my* heart you're talking about, he says—so deeply bound that it cannot free itself. "Batter" it, he exclaims: break it into pieces and make it new. The intensity of his response lets us hear how deeply he is pierced by these words. Tear down my walls, he goes on, rip away the knots in which I have bound myself. Similarly, when Jesus says in John 10 that he is speaking to those who are lost and need a shepherd, he is challenging those who hear him to acknowledge their own wandering and in that acknowledgment to hear him calling them home. Hearing this, George Herbert in "The Collar" responds by loosening the tongue of his speaker and letting his words run as free and as wild as their self-absorbed wandering might take them. When his Lord's voice suddenly breaks in with the only word that matters—"*Child*"—we hear the deep security of that name all the more powerfully against the backdrop of the speaker's wild raving.

With chapter 5 (11:1–12:50), the narrator pulls us away from those opposing Jesus and back into the inner circle of those who have proved receptive to the claims he has been making about himself. The talk is suddenly all about glory and death—the glory of the death confronted in tears at the tomb of Lazarus or celebrated when Mary anoints his feet or shouted about when Jesus enters Jerusalem in triumph. His death as our life—what had been withheld from the reader now begins to be spelled out. The poets I examine respond to these passages by describing moments when this particular notion of death as glory began to make sense. Gerard Manley Hopkins, for example, exquisitely details that moment of awakening in "The Windhover." One moment, he says, he was stirred to ecstasy by the grand sweeping gestures of a falcon, mastering a morning sky, and the next, when the bird's flight suddenly "buckled" and the morning light flashed off him at a new angle, he found himself overwhelmed with a beauty "a billion / Times told lovelier [and] more dangerous"—Christ's beauty, true glory, flashing out of his brokenness.

The focus becomes even tighter in chapter 6 (13:1–17:26) as we listen to Jesus speak to his disciples on the night before he dies, preparing them to see that event, in all its horror, as life. Once again, he is appealing to their imaginations, asking them to visualize his words internally: think of my death as washing you clean, preparing a place for you, making your joy full. They will not be able to understand this until after it has happened, he says, but when it does, they are to love one another, expressing through that love what they have come to understand about God's love for them. Like the disciples, the reader hears these things and waits, understanding the words without yet being able to take them in. Elizabeth Bishop, for example, hears the promise that, as the King James Version puts it, "in My Father's house are many mansions" but can only imagine such a thing in earthly terms. Responding, in "Squatter's Children," to children on a distant Brazilian hillside being called in to their parents' "soluble, / unwarrantable ark" of a house as a thunderstorm approaches, Bishop searches for an image to describe the larger freedom that she desperately wishes to offer them and recalls these words of Jesus. They are standing, she writes, on the threshold of the storm, among the unseen mansions of "a bigger house" than they could possibly imagine. Nature itself is "lawfully" theirs, she asserts, a house in which they need never be thought of as squatters. And yet, even as she holds out to the children the words of the Gospel, she is careful to draw a line—all she can really offer, she acknowledges, are "soggy documents," melting away "in rooms of falling rain."

In the account of the crucifixion and resurrection examined in chapter 7 (18:1–20:31), the narrator quite deliberately begins to interpret, explaining how it is that in the humiliating death of Jesus, God's own glory, reaching out to those incapable of reaching out to him, was displayed. What had been withheld or pictured or anticipated is now before us, and John powerfully steps forward and lets us see what he has seen. Jesus is the Passover lamb, sacrificed in our place; he is the image of "Man" in all his shame and glory; he is God himself, pierced for our sins. The reader is swept up into this, details suddenly falling into place, and when John steps back again and describes the resurrection in a series of simple recognition scenes, putting aside theological explanation and concentrating on three quite varied human struggles to make sense of what has happened, the sequence all but invites the reader to step into the struggle and use what he or she had visualized to see with and believe. It is very deftly done. "Behold, the Man," John says of the crucifixion and resurrection, and the poets I draw from do exactly that. John Berryman's "Ecce Homo," its title the Latin version of these words first uttered by Pilate as he presented the broken body of Jesus to the crowd, is a particularly striking example. I finally did, Berryman writes. I saw him for years as an extraordinary man, "*almost* beyond humanity," but still a man. Once, perhaps, in a museum, I caught a glimpse of him as divine, not human at all. But now, he writes, musing over a photograph, I have seen him as both God and man—most powerfully God in that very human death, thin arms held out "in unconquerable beseeching." What each of these poets gives us is the moment when the words of the Gospel broke through, the moment they beheld through them the man, either turning to him or turning away. They dramatize its words becoming flesh in specific, individual imaginations.

My final chapter touches briefly on John's Epilogue (21:1-25) where, some days after these events, Jesus appears to a group of disciples who have returned home and are fishing. Intimate, domestic, quiet, restorative—the Epilogue occurs in something very like the reader's own world. This, John seems to say, is where the light reaches, and this is what it seeks to restore. Here, in your daily walk, you are known and loved and forgiven. Can you see that? he seems to say. Can you make it out for yourself?

* * *

In approaching the Gospel in this way, I am building on a significant body of work, much of it focused on the literary means John employs to establish and draw his readers into an engagement with his portrait of Jesus. Over the past twenty-five years, biblical scholars have become increasingly interested in reading the text in what Richard Bauckham calls a "horizontal" rather than a "vertical" manner, focusing not on "accumulated layers of evidence" of various composing hands but on what can be seen when the Gospel is read "sequentially and as a whole."[13] To those alert to the ways literary texts work, "many of what seemed aporias to the source and redaction critics appear no longer to be so."[14] Instead, argues Bauckham, if we focus on the way the Gospel unfolds its materials, explaining some elements while leaving others, for a time, undeveloped, it seems clear that the Gospel is designed to "lead its readers and hearers progressively into a greater understanding of its themes by initiating them step by step into its symbolic world."[15] Consider the "figurative or enigmatic sayings of Jesus," the ways in which he describes himself and points toward his coming death.[16] Bauckham convincingly argues that, in slowly unfolding the full implications of Jesus' words, John is deliberately seeking to "stir readers into a desire to understand," adopting "a literary strategy that drives readers both to think about their meaning and to read on in hope of discovering their meaning, . . . [These] enigmas are meant to tease initially uncomprehending readers into theological enlightenment . . . by [not] giving too much help too soon."[17]

We see the same focus on the reader when we turn to the issue of plot. Alan Culpepper, one of the earliest biblical scholars to take a literary approach to the Gospel, notes that both individual scenes and the Gospel as a whole have the same shape—what we could describe as recognition and response. He writes, "[T]he Gospel is constructed around a series of recognition (or nonrecognition) scenes. Belief and unbelief, recognition or nonrecognition of Jesus as the Revealer, is the fundamental opposition on which the plot is developed."[18] This opposition drives the Gospel forward, ultimately bringing Jesus to Jerusalem and the cross, and it continually keeps before us John's central theological point—that as God's Word, Jesus speaks for or reveals the heart of his Father. Culpepper writes, "Each episode repeats the story of Jesus as the Revealer calling others to faith, while the varying responses allow us as the readers to consider the responses to Jesus we might make."[19] Noting how the elements of the plot echo and work together makes it clear that the Gospel has its eyes on the reader: "While the Gospel tells the story of Jesus, it also draws us as readers into it and seeks to move us along the continuum of responses to a higher level of response to Jesus as the Revealer."[20]

At about the same time that biblical scholars began foregrounding literary questions, literary scholars began training their eyes on the Bible. Robert Alter's *The Art of Biblical Narrative* (1981) was perhaps the crucial early text here, a close analysis of the way linked words and scenes guide readers to the issues most significantly at play in the Genesis passages he examines.[21] Frank Kermode's chapter on John in the volume he edited with Alter, *The Literary Guide to the Bible* (1987), is a good example of what might be gained by asking not about the "conceptual grid" behind the Gospel but about what the reader can discover through "close attention to the words as they stand in the text."[22] Focusing on the Gospel's Prologue, Kermode asks what this opening poem, "in its internal relations—in its language and also its connection with the subsequent narrative—means to us, now, reading it as Augustine said we have to, in accordance with our restricted capacities."[23] For Kermode, discovering meaning is something that John's "method imposes upon his readers," densely interweaving the Prologue and the episodes that follow along a linguistic/symbolic axis that the reader is charged with noticing and unfolding the implications of.[24]

What Kermode notices is that the Prologue is built on the opposition or tension between the Greek words for *being* and *becoming*. He calls this the *ēn* (was) / *egeneto* (became) axis.[25] Verse 1, for example, uses versions of *ēn* three times: "In the beginning was the Word, and the Word was with God, and the Word was God." Verse 3 uses three versions of *egeneto*: "All things were made (became) by him; and without him was not any thing made that was made." He comments, "So we have three 'becomings' to set against the triple *was* of eternity."[26] This tension between being and becoming is played out again in the Gospel's central declaration in 1:14 that "the Word which *was*, in that special poetic sense, now *became*—became flesh."[27] And then it is repeated in the episodes that follow—"The Word transcends the curative powers of the pool of Bethesda, just as the living water transcends the still water of Jacob's well, the wine of the Messiah the inferior wine or water of the Law, the bread of life the manna of mere existence"—making them "not only elements in a sequence but self-contained exempla" of the Gospel's central concerns.[28] What a reader with Kermode's eye notices is that the Prologue's artful use of language has given him or her a way to engage with and make sense of the Gospel's "deepest purpose, which is the representation of the eternal in relation to the transient, of the manifestation of being in a world of becoming."[29]

In the readings I provide here, I build on work such as this and a number of excellent commentaries, most notably D. A. Carson's *The Gospel According to John* (1991), developing my own observations but sharing a similar commitment to drawing out connections and tensions made visible when the Gospel is read as a literary whole.[30] In turning at regular intervals to poets who have heard themselves addressed by the Gospel, reading in their company, I am, however, attempting to introduce a second way of responding to that call.[31] If Jesus speaks about himself in figures of speech, he must be encouraging those who hear him to not just translate those images into ideas but to use them to explore his claims. His words and actions make the Word spoken by God flesh. They make it something we can handle and visualize and take into ourselves, as we are able. Poetry teaches us how to do this. It is another way of thinking, a second way of responding. It encourages us not simply to think abstractly and theologically about what the words of Jesus might mean to us, though surely we must do that. It also encourages us to re-enact them—to hear what he is saying by taking them in through our own senses and experiences and fears and desires.[32]

Emily Dickinson makes exactly this point in a poem in which she works her way into the debate in John 6 over Jesus' claim that those who eat his flesh and drink his blood will live forever. Jesus establishes the context for these words in a famous scene by feeding over 5,000 people with five small loaves and two fish and then claiming that *he* is the "bread of life" through which God is about to feed the world. The miracle is a sign, an image giving those who experience it a way to think about what God was offering the world. But Jesus' language about flesh and blood ups the ante. "How can this man give us his flesh to eat?" (6:52), those who hear him complain. It is a real question and cannot be fully answered until after the crucifixion and resurrection, but both Jesus and John want those who hear these words to begin wrestling with them now. Dickinson begins to do so, but quite tentatively. How can this man give us his flesh to eat? He must have been talking about belief, she proposes—belief, for a person of her doubts and intense privacies, being a matter one would hesitate to put into words: "A word made Flesh is seldom / And tremblingly partook / Nor then perhaps reported."[33] In proposing this, she translates the image of eating his flesh into an idea—a brilliant idea, since eating and believing, as we shall see, are consistently linked in the Gospel. But then she starts up again, reaching for a different way of thinking about these words, focusing on the image of eating itself:

> But have I not mistook
> Each one of us has tasted
> With ecstasies of stealth
> The very food debated
> To our specific strength—

If I am not mistaken, she writes, each of us *has* tasted the Word, *has* eaten his flesh. Jesus spoke of himself in such an abrupt, offensive way because he was challenging them, presenting them with a strong taste and then daring them to take it in. Focusing on eating, approaching his words through visualizing what it means to take something in and what it means to choke, gives Dickinson a second way of considering his words, seeing them as a challenge to think and taste deeply—to take in as much of the Word as her own individual "strength" and needs and imagination would permit. Jesus *was* talking about belief—belief that his bloody, bodily sacrifice would be a source of life to this who turned to it in faith—but what Dickinson also sees is that his figurative way of speaking was designed to encourage an individual encounter, one exploring and drawing on her own "specific strength." This is an encounter each of us has expertise in and about which each of us can freely speak.

The issue of individual expertise brings me to the question of whom we are referring to when we speak of the Gospel's author. It is not a simple question. The title "according to John" was added in the second century. The Gospel's concluding verses, 21:24-25, claim that the figure commonly known as the Beloved Disciple was the writer:

> This is the disciple who bears witness of these things, and wrote these things; and we know that his witness is true. And there are also many other things which Jesus did, which if they were written in detail, I suppose that even the world itself would not contain the books which were written.

The Beloved appears as a character late in the Gospel: at the Last Supper (13:23), at the cross, where Jesus gives him to his mother and her to him (19:26-27), at the empty tomb (20:2-9), and in Galilee, in the Gospel's Epilogue (21:7, 20-23). The traditional view is that the Beloved is the Apostle John, who is otherwise unnamed in the Gospel and has chosen, perhaps out of humility and an overwhelming sense of being loved, to represent himself in this way. Other names have been suggested, including Lazarus and a figure known as John the Elder. A number of commentators prefer to leave the author unnamed. Virtually every book written on the Gospel surveys this question and can be easily consulted.[34]

For my purposes, I am most concerned with the fact that the Gospel's narrator speaks quite directly to the reader in the Prologue, then steps aside for the bulk of his story, only occasionally reminding us of his presence. When, in the passage I have quoted above, he quietly identifies himself at the end of his story as someone who has come to know himself as God's beloved, he is testifying to the effect the words and actions of Jesus have had on him, returning us to his description of himself in the Prologue as someone who has received life from "His fullness" (1:16). Having tasted "the very food debated" to his "specific strength," the narrator's arrangement of the words of Jesus are his report on what he has "tremblingly partook." Whether we can know the author's name with certainty is less important to me than that he is making an individual claim to be someone beloved of God. Without pressing the point, I will refer to him as both the narrator and John, and, near the end of the text, when it becomes appropriate, as the Beloved. Seeing for oneself, I would argue, is what poets model for us and is why their various and sometimes idiosyncratic ways of testing and responding to the words of the Gospel should be of deep interest to anyone caught up in its claims to stir and unsettle and speak, to bring to a halt and quietly draw near.

1

Prologue (John 1:1-18)

John's Prologue raises the issue of understanding who Jesus was and what he was saying in a very powerful way. It falls into three parts, which, much like the three stanzas of a poem, work together to focus the reader's eye on the claims John wants us to consider. John lays many of his positions out in advance, giving us a kind of outline to be filled in later, but he crucially leaves one question unanswered—how Jesus gives life to the world. When we hear ourselves addressed by the Gospel in the narrative that follows, it is that question to which it will be formulating an answer.[1]

1:1-18

The first part of the Prologue describes Jesus from the broadest perspective imaginable, positioning us outside of space and time:

> In the beginning was the Word, and the Word was with God, and the Word was God. He was in the beginning with God. All things came into being by Him, and apart from Him, nothing came into being that has come into being. In Him was life, and the life was the light of men. And the light shines in the darkness, and the darkness did not comprehend it. (1:1-5)

As most readers notice, John is deliberately echoing the first verses of Genesis here. Rather than name Jesus directly, he begins with a way of thinking about him. "In the beginning God created the heavens and the earth," Genesis 1:1 reads. The earth was "formless and void, and darkness was over the surface of the deep." Into that darkness and emptiness, God spoke and life was created—"Let there be light" being the first words uttered. What

John now claims is that when God spoke, the Word through which he created all things was actually a separate being, there with him from before all
time, co-eternal, a part of his identity.[2] This Word, capitalized in all transla-
tions to show his standing, was both separate from God ("with" him before
all things began) and the same as him (he "was" God).

This is an extraordinary claim, of course, and arguments for and against
the divinity of Jesus will rage throughout the Gospel. But just as extraordinary is the metaphor itself—hardly a metaphor at all—the title that John
uses: Word. Two things stand out. First, John is claiming that Jesus represents God. Just as our words spell out and make visible our thoughts and
intentions, so Jesus speaks God forth and makes visible his very nature, first
of all to himself. Our words, of course, constantly disappoint—they do not
fully represent what we actually think, or they represent something not there
at all, and so forth. John's point is that in Jesus God spoke himself forth
fully—he was separate from God, as our words are from our hearts, let us
say, but at the same time he "was" God. When God spoke Jesus to the world,
Jesus was everything he intended to say. He spoke forth his whole heart. Second, and this is why John begins with the Genesis reference, as God's Word
spoken once again into the unformed darkness of the world, Jesus had within
himself the power to create life. John spells this out. "In Him was life," and
"by Him" all things that "came into being" were given form and shape
and existence. What was once true is true again, for now, says John, God has
spoken into a deeper darkness—a spiritual darkness—but with exactly the
same intent: to create life where there was none, bringing into existence an
inner responsiveness to God.

These two ideas come together in the last verses of this first section of the
Prologue. When God spoke Jesus into the world, he said, "Let there be light,"
bringing life to darkness. But, John adds, what God said and did through
Jesus had to be "comprehended" in order for that life to come about. That
gives us the charged fifth verse: "And the light shines in the darkness, and
the darkness did not comprehend [or *overcome*] it." The light that God spoke
into the world through Jesus still "shines," John remarks. It still makes visible God's heart. It is still the way he shows himself to the world. And this is
true even if the darkness "did not comprehend it," past tense. John writes in
order to call attention to that light, creating a space whereby what was once
misheard or misrepresented, distorted or ignored, might be understood and
taken in.

In the second part of the Prologue (1:6-13), John works through all of
this again, positioning us in a specific time and place and making each of his

claims more tangible. "The true light," he writes, came into the world, potentially "enlighten[ing] every man" (1:9)—bringing light to darkness, opening minds to what God had done. There were witnesses—the first was John the Baptist—who understood what God was doing and called attention to it. But for the most part, the light entered the world and was not comprehended: "He was in the world, and the world was made through Him, and the world did not know Him" (1:10). He was not recognized, even by Israel, whom God had called to himself as his own people: "He came to His own, and those who were His own did not receive Him" (1:11). One can hear just how difficult it must have been to take him in—even his own did not understand.

But then John backtracks a bit. There were some who understood—some who received the light, took in the Word, and believed what God had said. In doing so, they were brought to life as surely as the dark and formless void of Genesis had been. Here is what that looked like:

> But as many as received Him, to them He gave the right to become children of God, even to those who believe in His name, who were born not of blood, nor of the will of the flesh, nor of the will of man, but of God. (1:12-13)

Receiving him was like being born a second time. What once had been dark was now light. What once had been dead was now alive. Those who had been cut off from God—dead, in the dark, unaware of him—were given the right to be called "children of God." All it took, says John, though again he is leaving much unsaid, was "receiving" what God had said, "believing" that in his life and death, Jesus had enacted the "name" of God fully and completely. Such a birth is not physical, John insists. It is not brought about by inheritance or desire or the human will. It is spiritual—brought about by God, breaking as light into human darkness.[3]

The third section of the Prologue is denser and more personal. John once again reworks his core ideas, this time in the first person, drawing the reader who is enacting his thoughts after him significantly closer. The first verse in this section is powerfully compressed. Not only has God spoken life into the world and light into darkness, he has done so in the flesh and blood of his one-and-only ("only begotten") offspring:

> And the Word became flesh, and dwelt among us, and we beheld His glory, glory as of the only begotten from the Father, full of grace and truth. (1:14)

"We beheld His glory," says John. God's life-giving Word became flesh and walked among us. They touched him, ate with him, watched him suffer and die. In time, they understood and accepted all that God had said through him—which is to say, they beheld his glory, glory (*doxa*) being an intensification of light, the "true light" shining in the world's darkness.

John builds his remarkable testimony in verse 14 on a series of echoes drawn from the book of Exodus. The first occurs with his use of the word *dwelt*: "the Word became flesh, and dwelt among us." The Greek word here means "tented" or "tabernacled."[4] John is thinking about the way God's glory dwelt with his people in the tabernacle (Exod 25:8) or tent of meeting (Exod 33:7) as Moses led Israel through the wilderness after they had been freed from captivity in Egypt. In the same way, John writes, in Jesus, God's glory took residency among them in a tent of human flesh.

A second echo occurs when John says that the glory he beheld in Jesus was "full of grace and truth." These terms are also drawn from Exodus. Early in the journey out of Egypt, desperate for a sense that God would not abandon him after discovering the people worshipping a golden calf, Moses pleads for a sense of God's reassuring presence. "I pray Thee, show me Thy glory" (Exod 33:18), he says. God replies that Moses, being a man, could not survive such an encounter: "You cannot see My face, for no man can see Me and live" (Exod 33:20). Instead, God hides Moses in the cleft of a rock, covers him with his hand, and passes by, proclaiming his name and giving him an indirect, but reassuring sense of his presence: "The Lord, the Lord God, compassionate and gracious, slow to anger, and abounding in lovingkindness and truth" (Exod 34:6). *Lovingkindness* and *truth* are translated as *charis* (grace) and *alētheia* (truth) in the Greek version of Exodus John would have known, the very words he uses in 1:14 to describe Jesus—abounding in grace and truth. It is a fascinating allusion. John saw in Jesus the very glory that God proclaimed to Moses, but he saw it, in the flesh, and he was not destroyed. He saw God's grace, his love for the undeserving, and his truth, his faithfulness to his holy nature, combined in the words and actions of a single man. As he puts it later in this third section of the Prologue, John saw in Jesus God's nature not simply proclaimed but realized and lived out: "For the Law was given through Moses; grace and truth were realized through Jesus Christ" (1:17). What Moses could not see, Jesus has now, in the flesh, unfolded or explicated: "No man has seen God at any time; the only begotten God, who is in the bosom of the Father, He has explained Him" (1:18).

As in the first two sections of the Prologue, John declares that in comprehending or receiving this explanation, in taking in the glory of what God accomplished through Jesus, he was brought to life. John the Baptist bore witness to the glory of Jesus, saying, "This was He of whom I said, 'He who comes after me has a higher rank than I, for He existed before me'" (1:15), and

John responded. As he puts it, "For of His fullness we have all received, and grace upon grace" (1:16). In him was the fullness of God—life itself—and of that fullness John received an endless outpouring, grace piled upon grace, seemingly without end. In concluding by pointing to his own experience, John is suggesting that the encounter with what God has said through Jesus must always be a personal one. He places his testimony before the reader as a challenge, leaving us to puzzle out, as we read, how it is that Jesus' manifestation of "grace and truth"—God's very nature—had the power to bring to life hearts utterly turned away from him to death.

T. S. Eliot, from "Gerontion"

In his 1919 poem "Gerontion," T. S. Eliot places himself before the words of John's Prologue and, as I have been arguing, considers them, attempting to make them out. Although he was in his mid-thirties when he wrote the poem, Eliot adopts the voice of an old man, as if, in order to take on the full weight of John's words, he had to acknowledge by exaggeration the spiritual position in which he found himself. Gerontion—the name means "little old man"—identifies himself as "an old man in a dry month," someone who had shriveled up as life had passed him by. Writing some eight years before his conversion, Eliot hears John's claim that the Word had become flesh and dwelt among us but can only shake his head. Perhaps it had, Eliot writes, but if so, it had been spoken into a world that could not comprehend it. Speaking after the possibility of life had passed him by, Eliot's speaker lets us feel the full impact of John's words in 1:5: "And the light shines in the darkness, and the darkness did not comprehend it." Perhaps it still shines, says Gerontion, but all I can see is that I could not take it in. Focusing on his failure to comprehend, vividly unfolding its history and implications, Gerontion's anguished words let us hear the crucial role comprehension plays in the Gospel, offering us something that a straightforward rendering of the term cannot touch.

Here are the central stanzas of the poem:

Signs are taken for wonders. 'We would see a sign!'
The word within a word, unable to speak a word,
Swaddled with darkness. In the juvescence of the year
Came Christ the tiger

In depraved May, dogwood and chestnut, flowering judas,
To be eaten, to be divided, to be drunk
Among whispers; by Mr. Silvero
With caressing hands, at Limoges

Who walked all night in the next room;
By Hakagawa, bowing among the Titians;
By Madame de Tornquist, in the dark room
Shifting the candles; Fräulein von Kulp
Who turned in the hall, one hand on the door.
    Vacant shuttles
Weave the wind. I have no ghosts,
An old man in a draughty house
Under a windy knob.

After such knowledge, what forgiveness? Think now
History has many cunning passages, contrived corridors
And issues, deceives with whispering ambitions,
Guides us by vanities. Think now
She gives when our attention is distracted
And what she gives, gives with such supple confusions
That the giving famishes the craving. Gives too late
What's not believed in, or is still believed,
In memory only, reconsidered passion. Gives too soon
Into weak hands, what's thought can be dispensed with
Till the refusal propagates a fear. Think
Neither fear nor courage saves us. Unnatural vices
Are fathered by our heroism. Virtues
Are forced upon us by our impudent crimes.
These tears are shaken from the wrath-bearing tree.

The tiger springs in the new year. Us he devours. Think at last
We have not reached conclusion, when I
Stiffen in a rented house. Think at last
I have not made this show purposelessly
And it is not by any concitation
Of the backward devils.
I would meet you upon this honestly.
I that was near your heart was removed therefrom
To lose beauty in terror, terror in inquisition.
I have lost my passion: why should I need to keep it
Since what is kept must be adulterated?
I have lost my sight, smell, hearing, taste and touch:
How should I use them for your closer contact?[5]

In the first stanza quoted here, Eliot thinks about John's Word made
flesh, coming as light to a dark world. His response is riddling and abrupt:

Signs are taken for wonders. 'We would see a sign!'
The word within a word, unable to speak a word,
Swaddled with darkness.

Behind these lines is a Christmas 1618 sermon by Lancelot Andrewes on the birth of Christ. Once we understand the background, the sad resignation of Eliot's lines becomes strikingly clear. Meditating on a demand that Jesus produce a sign to authenticate his preaching ("Master, we would see a sign," Matt 12:38), Andrewes noted on that Christmas day that the birth of Christ was just such a wonder. How extraordinary, that the Word that spoke all creation into existence became for a time wordless and silent:

> Signs are taken for wonders. "Master we would fain see a sign," that is a miracle. And in this sense it is a sign to wonder at. . . . *Verbum infans* [the infant Word], the Word without a word; the eternal Word not able to speak a word.[6]

For Andrewes, that the "eternal Word" who created all things became for a time a helpless infant was a marvel almost beyond description. But when Eliot picks up these lines, he changes them slightly. Andrewes' "Word *without* a word; . . . not able to speak a word," the child, becomes for Eliot the "word *within* a word, unable to speak a word." Eliot's Word loses its capital letter and becomes merely human, held captive by the words that speak for it. Always spoken for, never able to speak, Eliot's Word is born into a world where it is "swaddled with darkness." The dilemma as he phrases it seems almost insolvable. If the Word became flesh, that could only mean that it had become silent and voiceless, any possibility of it carrying life within itself seemingly negated by its involvement with the distorting forces of time and language.[7]

This is what Gerontion is getting at in the second stanza quoted here when he describes a kind of lifeless, ritualized consuming of "Christ the tiger," who, although he may have once come with power in the youth ("the juvescence") of all things, has now been reduced to something eaten, divided, and drunk "among whispers." The international cast of characters—Mr. Silvero, Hakagawa, Madame de Tornquist, Fräulein von Kulp—busy bowing and pacing and shifting candles, is simply another expression of the modern world swaddling the Word and rendering it speechless and powerless. They are "vacant shuttles," moving back and forth without understanding, weaving only the wind. They bequeath to Gerontion a world without "ghosts" or spirit, leaving him nowhere to turn for life: "An old man in a draughty house / Under a windy knob."

In the third stanza I have quoted, Gerontion looks back on his failure to receive the swaddled, speechless Word with real anguish. "After such knowledge," he acknowledges, "what forgiveness?" But how could it have been otherwise? Gerontion looks at the history he has lived through and sees that it has been filled with "cunning passages, contrived corridors / And issues" that have drawn him away from any straightforward confrontation with the Word's claims. Gerontion lives in a time in which, even when History presents us with something extraordinary, outside the daily press of events, "She gives when our attention is distracted / And what she gives, gives with such supple confusions / That the giving famishes the craving," leaving her bewildered recipients hungrier than before they began. Gerontion's analysis is lacerating. If History lets us glimpse the divine, that glimpse comes "too late," when it is no longer "believed in" or, if it "is still believed," is believed "In memory only, reconsidered passion." Or she "Gives too soon," when one's hands are too "weak" to hold what has been given and one thinks the revelation "can be dispensed with" and set for a time aside. Now Gerontion understands the situation he is in, but, old man, dry brain in a dry season, there is nothing he can do with that knowledge. He simply surveys what remains: none of his acts of refusal have "save[d]" him; even his moments of "fear" and "courage" seem now like "unnatural vices," "forced" on him by a failure to comprehend.

The most powerful moment in the poem occurs in the fourth stanza I have quoted, in which Gerontion reaches toward an unnamed "you," speaking out of an unsettling sense of having let something deeply important slip away. The "you" could be a lover, once near to the speaker's heart but now far from him, but the poem most powerfully suggests it is "Christ the tiger," the "word within a word," unable to speak in a way that Gerontion could comprehend:

> I would meet you upon this honestly.
> I that was near your heart was removed therefrom
> To lose beauty in terror, terror in inquisition.
> I have lost my passion: why should I need to keep it
> Since what is kept must be adulterated?

I "was removed," Gerontion laments, in the passive voice. He did not choose; it was simply done to him by the situation in which he found himself, by some misfit between the world of spirit and the world of flesh. All he knows is that what had once seemed beautiful—John calls it "glory"—has become now, in its remote inaccessibility, a source of "terror." And worse than that, what had once seemed terrible, has now become the endlessly circling accusations filling out this poem. How could I have known? What was it I sensed? What if I had responded? Gerontion is left with questions but no "passion." Passion, like his "sight, smell, hearing, taste and touch," has been adulterated, watered-down, shrinking away because there is nothing to call it out of itself. I take the reference to the senses to be a nod to the way Jesus continually calls those around him to see and eat and touch the life God has offered the world through him. If so, one can sense Gerontion's dilemma: even if Christ were there, calling out and urging "closer contact," Gerontion's spiritual senses have all atrophied; they are as worn away as the "decayed house" in which he mutters out the last of his days.

How interesting, then, to find these same words from John's Prologue and the Lancelot Andrewes Nativity sermon returning in "Ash Wednesday" (1930), a poem written eleven years later, after Eliot's 1927 conversion. Clearly, the image of the silent but living Word, uttered into an uncomprehending darkness, continued to unsettle him.[8] In "Ash Wednesday," section V, Eliot returns to this problem, but now, instead of being bound within and tormented by the world's incomprehension, the speaker has arrived at a much different position. He pictures himself in this poem as a pilgrim caught between "dying and birth," trying to quiet himself enough to hear the Word, while still acknowledging that he writes from within Gerontion's whirling world of time and language:

> If the lost word is lost, if the spent word is spent
> If the unheard, unspoken
> Word is unspoken, unheard;
>
> Still is the unspoken word, the Word unheard,
> The Word without a word, the Word within
> The world and for the world;
>
> And the light shone in darkness and
> Against the Word the unstilled world still whirled
> About the centre of the silent Word.[9]

I have broken these riddling lines into stanzas so we can hear their quiet assurance more clearly. Andrewes' Word, we remember, was silent and unable to speak, as was Gerontion's, although for completely different reasons. Now, in the first lines quoted here from "Ash Wednesday" we read that even "*If* the lost word is lost, *if* the spent word is spent / *If* the unheard, unspoken / Word is unspoken, unheard; / *Still*" something remains.

This is a remarkable change in perspective, as the next lines explain. Even if, in our "darkness," the Word is unspoken because there are no longer words to voice it and unheard because there are no longer ears capable of taking it in, "Still is the unspoken word, the Word unheard, / The Word without a word, the Word within / The world and for the world." Even if unspoken and unheard, the Word is still "within / The world and for the world." This is a declaration of faith, perhaps as forceful and personal as the one John ends his Prologue with. Even if unheard, the Word, for Eliot, still "shines in the darkness" (1:5). "[W]ithout a word" (Eliot has returned to Andrewes' original phrasing), defenseless as a child, the Word has given itself to the world. It is "within" and "for" it. And if the world is uncomprehending, then that is the greatest wonder of all—that God would take on even that, willingly emptying himself out against that black incomprehension. Calmly, Eliot returns to John's words to once more describe the world we inhabit. "[T]he light shone in darkness" and against the "Word the unstilled world still whirled," but even as it whirled, focused on its own empty clatter, it whirled "About the centre of the silent Word." What Eliot sees, through the lens of his own failure to comprehend, is the still-vibrant Word at the world's core.[10] How live a document John's Prologue becomes, when lived with this intensely.

COME AND SEE (JOHN 1:19-51)

John twice notes in his Prologue that God began the process of opening eyes to the glory of Jesus by sending a witness—John the Baptist. His glory is not obvious, which is why someone must be called to direct eyes to him. Nor are the words obvious that the Baptist uses to describe what he has been shown. But what he has seen he expresses with such power that people are compelled to look, some with such hungry eyes that they cannot do anything but hold themselves before Christ's slowly unfolding beauty, others walking away in baffled incomprehension. The reader, of course, also hears these words of witness, and if they are slightly less puzzling to us because of John's Prologue, there is still much that is unexplained, deliberately so. We, too, are being called to draw close, to come and see. We, too, are being called to store things up to make use of later.

The Baptist, 1:19-34

The Baptist delivers his testimony over the course of three days. On the first day, a group of priests and Levites, sent from Jerusalem, confronts him and asks the point of his unusual, attention-getting actions. Scholars note that the ritual washing of baptism was used to signify a new way of life and was reserved for Gentiles converting to Judaism.[1] Who was John claiming to be by demanding such actions from his fellow countrymen? John's answers are entirely self-effacing, as if to make the point that they are looking at the wrong thing. "I am not the Christ" (1:20), he replies, understanding that such a claim was probably what they had been sent to investigate. (*Christ* is the Greek translation of the Hebrew *Messiah* or "anointed one," a term used for Israel's long-awaited, Davidic figure who, after being anointed king, was expected to lead Israel back to a position of power and glory. "I will raise up your descendant after you, who will come forth from you, and I will establish his kingdom," God had told David. "He shall build a house for My name, and I will establish the throne of his kingdom forever" [2 Sam 7:12-13].) I am not claiming to be that great figure, John tells his suspicious questioners. Nor is he Elijah, whose return had been predicted by the prophet Malachi "before the coming of the great and terrible day of the Lord" (Mal 4:5) or "the Prophet" like Moses that Moses himself had anticipated rising up to direct his people (Deut 18:15). But surely, they insist, John must be claiming something of that magnitude, in so deliberately turning conventions upside down. Who are you then? they ask.

The Baptist continues to point away from himself. I am merely a voice, he says: "a voice of one crying in the wilderness, 'Make straight the way of the Lord'" (1:23). Those questioning him would have recalled the words of the prophet Isaiah, charged with delivering the good news that God had declared an end to Israel's long exile in Babylon. Get ready, Isaiah had said, God was about to lead his people home. Even now, if they listened, a voice could be heard calling for that path home to be prepared:

> Clear the way for the Lord in the wilderness;
> Make smooth in the desert a highway for our God.
> Let every valley be lifted up,
> And every mountain and hill be made low;
>
> . . . . .
>
> Then the glory of the Lord will be revealed,
> And all flesh will see it together;
> For the mouth of the Lord has spoken. (Isa 40:3, 5)

I am that voice, John tells the delegation from Jerusalem: the voice Isaiah heard in the wilderness, all those years before—a truly startling statement. Who is he? He is the voice Isaiah heard crying "Make straight the way of the Lord." His actions, there in the wilderness, are announcing the fact that, in some unexpected way, Israel's captivity is about to end.

The delegation ignores these words, our first example of the world's failure to "comprehend" what would seem to be right in front of its eyes. John has pointed them to the "glory of the Lord," but they want something with which to pin him down: "Why then are you baptizing, if you are not the Christ, nor Elijah, nor the Prophet?" (1:25). He does not answer, at least not directly. Instead, he points beyond himself again:

I baptize in water, but among you stands One whom you do not know. It is He who comes after Me, the thong of whose sandal I am not worthy to untie. (1:26-27)

He has just declared that the glory of the Lord is about to be revealed; now he insists that that glory is standing among them, in the form of a person far greater than he. You cannot make his glory out, John says, but I can. I can see it. One can imagine them turning and looking blankly at the faces of those crowding about them. Who is he talking about?

The next day, Jesus himself walks by, and the Baptist answers the delegation's question, though it is unclear if they are even there to hear his answer:

The next day he saw Jesus coming to him, and said, "Behold, the Lamb of God who takes away the sin of the world! This is He on behalf of whom I said, 'After me comes a Man who has a higher rank than I, for He existed before me.' And I did not recognize Him, but in order that He might be manifested to Israel, I came baptizing in water." (1:29-31)

Look, he says—this is the one I was describing yesterday. John has already quoted these words of testimony in the Prologue, as if to suggest that this identification is where we have to begin, if we hope to make sense of things. Why is John baptizing? In calling people to live new lives and picturing that renewal with the cleansing waters of baptism, he is pointing to a truer, deeper baptism, one performed by a figure of immeasurably higher rank than he: "the Lamb of God who takes away the sin of the world."

This is an extraordinary thing to say. John's questioners would not have expected it, focused as they were on the high and significant titles of prophet or king. And the reader does not expect it. The Prologue had described Jesus as God's Word—life spoken to all those who would embrace him. Its description of Jesus as a manifestation of God's glory had been echoed by the Baptist's declaration that God's glory was about to be revealed. But this is new information—that Jesus speaks life to the world by cleansing it and taking away its sins, and that he does so as God's sacrificial Lamb. This is not only the Baptist's central insight, it is the central insight of the entire Gospel. It bursts out here, its significance having been recorded by the narrator in the Prologue, and then is quietly tucked away until much later, when the reader is ready to take it. In a sense, the Baptist has seen something that no one else is prepared to accept, and it is characteristic of the way the narrator works that he records the statement, allowing it to begin working on us even before we are able to give it our full attention.

We are not told how the Baptist came to see Jesus as the Lamb of God. Most commentators note two possible sources for the image. The first is the unblemished Passover lamb whose blood was shed and put on the doorposts and lintels of Israel's houses the night the angel of death "passed over" them and slew the firstborn of the households of the Egyptians (Exod 12). The second is Isaiah's vision of God's "Suffering Servant," "pierced through for our transgressions, / . . . crushed for our iniquities," quietly taking on "the iniquity of us all / . . . Like a lamb that is led to slaughter" (Isa 53:5, 7). The narrator will, in time, borrow from both these sources as he develops his description of who Jesus was and what his life, death, and resurrection meant, but for now we are simply shown the insight, not the steps leading up to it.

All the Baptist tells us is that God has called him to notice and testify to certain things. For example, God gave him a sign by which he was to recognize the one through whom God was about to pour out the cleansing waters of his Spirit:

> And John bore witness saying, "I have beheld the Spirit descending as a dove out of heaven, and He remained upon Him. And I did not recognize Him, but He who sent me to baptize in water said to me, 'He upon whom you see the Spirit descending and remaining upon Him, this is the one who baptizes in the Holy Spirit.' And I have seen, and have borne witness that this is the Son of God." (1:32-34)

We do not see the Spirit descend. It happened some time before, and what we have before us is the Baptist's account of the event. The narrator seems to have veiled certain things in order to put us in the position of those who first heard these words. We glimpse glory through the words of witnesses, this suggests, through the words of a text, through trying to listen. "I am not the Christ," John had said the day before, but this person walking by now is: "This is the Son of God" (1:34). "Son of God" is another term for God's anointed Messiah (see Ps 2:1-7), and those who heard the Baptist speak would clearly have taken it that way and rejoiced, or scoffed. But the reader, listening hard and trying to make out these words, might also remember the Prologue's description of Jesus as God's "only begotten" (1:14), sensing the true reason for John's self-effacement before this figure whose sandal he is unworthy to untie.[2] That, it seems to me, is the power of his words.

Denise Levertov, "Agnus Dei"

In "Agnus Dei" (Lamb of God), the final poem in a six-part "agnostic Mass" entitled "Mass for the Day of St. Thomas Didymus" published in 1982, Denise Levertov powerfully walks us through the experience of holding ourselves before John's baffling words.[3] Intending to use the various sections of the Mass as a musical framework to think about "the threatened world"—crying for mercy (Kyrie), praising the earth (Gloria), working out what she believes (Credo)—Levertov actually captures, in the course of the sequence, the moment when belief in something much more specific began to stir in her.[4] She writes that she began the sequence as a "personal, secular meditation"[5] on what she called "the unknown God," the spirit expressing itself through the world's "flow and change, night and / the pulse of day" (Gloria), whose name is "written / in woodgrain, windripple, crystal" (Benedictus), but that in the course of writing the sequence, "the unknown began to be revealed to me as God, and further, God revealed in the Incarnation."[6] The fifth section of the sequence records the moment when an awareness of the world's vulnerability—its movements and beauties so easily undone by the "gross / cacophony of malevolence" or the annihilating "downspin of time"—suddenly opened her eyes to the Incarnation and God's inexplicable entry into the world of flesh: "The word / chose to become / flesh. In the blur of flesh / we bow, baffled."

In the sixth and final section of the poem, "Agnus Dei," having "discovered myself to be in a different relation to the material and to the liturgical form from that in which I had begun," Levertov turns to John's words, recorded in the Mass, as if they had been addressed to her in her expectant confusion.[7] What we hear, through her words, is the terrible and utterly unexpected vision of vulnerability captured in the Baptist's words:

> Given that lambs
> are infant sheep, that sheep
> are afraid and foolish, and lack
> the means of self-protection, having
> neither rage nor claws,
> venom nor cunning,
> what then
> is this 'Lamb of God'?
>
> This pretty creature, vigorous
> to nuzzle at milky dugs,
> woolbearer, bleater,
> leaper in air for delight of being, who finds in astonishment
> four legs to land on, the grass
> all it knows of the world?
>   With whom we would like to play,
> whom we'd lead with ribbons, but may not bring
> into our houses because
> it would soil the floor with its droppings?

What terror lies concealed
in strangest words, *O lamb*
of God that taketh away
the Sins of the World: an innocence
                    smelling of ignorance,
                    born in bloody snowdrifts,
                    licked by forbearing
dogs more intelligent than its entire flock put together?

                              God then,
                    encompassing all things, is
                    defenseless? Omnipotence
                    has been tossed away, reduced
                    to a wisp of damp wool?

                              And we
                    frightened, bored, wanting
only to sleep till catastrophe
has raged, clashed, seethed and gone by without us,
                    wanting then
to awaken in quietude without remembrance of agony,

                    we who in shamefaced private hope
                    had looked to be plucked from fire and given
                    a bliss we deserved for having imagined it,

                    is it implied that *we*
                    must protect this perversely weak
                    animal, whose muzzle's nudgings
                    suppose there is milk to be found in us?
                    Must hold to our icy hearts
                    a shivering God?

So be it.
          Come, rag of pungent
          quiverings,
                    dim star.
                              Let's try
                    if something human still
                    can shield you,
                              spark
          of remote light.[8]

Levertov leads us back to these words before they became familiar. In choosing to become flesh, God chose to become vulnerable; vulnerability, then, must be part of his nature, making manifest some part of him unseen in her meditation on the "deep, remote unknown" in the early sections of the sequence. But what are we to make of that vulnerability—God having come to earth as a lamb, a creature "having / neither rage nor claws, / venom nor cunning," a creature "with whom we would like to play," holding himself before us with "an innocence / smelling of ignorance, / born in bloody snowdrifts, / licked by forbearing / dogs more intelligent than its entire flock put together?"

It makes no sense, she says in the second half of the poem, struggling with the picture: "God then, / encompassing all things, is / defenseless? Omnipotence / has been tossed away, reduced / to a wisp of damp wool?" This is so different from what we would choose, so alien from our human nature. Look at our record, she says. Given danger or catastrophe, human beings choose to "sleep," letting the clash go "by without us, / wanting then / to awaken in quietude without remembrance of agony." Catching a glimpse of the world's brokenness, we turn away, clinging to some "shamefaced private hope" of being "plucked from fire and given / a bliss that we deserved for having imagined it." How could God be so different? How could he turn to the broken world *in* brokenness? How could faith embrace that difference? What we hear is the poet taking these words in as if for the first time, allowing them to challenge and unsettle and stir her to respond: "Must [we] hold to our icy hearts / a shivering God," terrified as he is led to the slaughter? What is fascinating about this poem is that we witness the moment that she first recognizes herself as being addressed by these words, her "icy heart" stirred and warmed by the vulnerability of God expressed in Jesus. Without being able to say why God speaks himself forth in such a form, with no real theology yet to explain what the Baptist had seen, she turns to the image itself, embracing, in the lamb's pungent fragility, the very form in which the God of light had chosen to come near:

> So be it.
>   Come, rag of pungent
>   quiverings,
>   dim star.
>   Let's try
>   if something human still
>   can shield you,
>   spark
>   of remote light.

Seven years later, in 1989, Levertov returned to this moment in a poem with the similar title "St. Thomas Didymus."[9] Taking Thomas as her "twin,"

Levertov writes in his voice, imagining that, as seems to have been the case with her, the problem of innocent suffering must have tormented him. She links Thomas with the father in Mark 9:20-29 whose child is wracked with convulsions caused by an unclean spirit. At the sight of "this child [who] lost his childhood in suffering, / . . . cruelly punished / who has done nothing except be born?" both Thomas and the father cry out "Lord, I believe, help thou / mine unbelief." Without an answer to that problem, Levertov's Thomas refuses to believe—until the moment that the risen Christ draws Thomas' hand into his wounded side, into the very vulnerability that had stirred Levertov those seven years before. What she sees now, through Thomas, is that in Christ God deliberately gave up his omnipotence for a defenseless vulnerability in order to bring about a world in which "all things," even the most inexplicable moments of suffering, were somehow understood and made whole. God became vulnerable in order to redeem or rescue those who could not rescue themselves:

> But when my hand
>   led by His hand's firm clasp
> entered the unhealed wound,
>   my fingers encountering
> rib-bone and pulsing heat,
>   what I felt was not
> scalding pain, shame for my
>   obstinate need,
> but light, light streaming
>   into me, over me, filling the room
> as if I had lived till then
>   in a cold cave, and now
> coming forth for the first time,
>   the knot that bound me unraveling,
> I witnessed
>   all things quicken to color, to form,
> my question
>   not answered but given
>   its part
> in a vast unfolding design lit
>   by a risen sun.

In the Lamb's suffering, then, Levertov sees light—the light of God "quicken[ing]" all things "to color, to form." In embracing rather than "shielding" this vulnerability, the poet arrives at a vision of a world made whole by the Lamb's sacrifice, in which her deepest questions are "not answered but given / [their] part / in a vast unfolding design." But this is seven years in the future. What we see in "Agnus Dei" is the moment before any such explanation has taken hold. This is the moment we find ourselves in as readers as well, hearing John's words and asking whether this vision of God is enough in itself to stir the heart to life, watching as the "nudgings" of a "shivering God" bring those who can hear out of the heart's "cold cave," blinking in the light.

Disciples' Call, 1:35-51

The call to come and see is continued on the third day by Jesus himself. He walks by a second time and John again identifies him as the Lamb of God. Two of John's disciples leave him and begin trailing behind Jesus. "What do you seek?" he says, and it is obvious that they do not really know. They have heard John's testimony, but it is no more clear to them than it is to anyone else. "Rabbi, where are you staying?" they guardedly ask. "Come, and you will see" (1:39), he responds, understanding that they are interested in him and not where he lives.[10] He invites them to spend time with him, and a day later they emerge with the news that "We have found the Messiah" (1:41). Once again, the narrator keeps us back at a certain distance. We do not know what Jesus says to them, only that a day in his presence convinces them of John's Messianic claim that "this is the Son of God." They seek out Andrew's brother Simon with the news, and again we learn nothing of their interaction other than the remarkable fact that Jesus not only already knows who he is, but also who he will become, looking at him and saying, "You are Simon the son John; you shall be called Cephas" or Peter (1:42).

The next day they go to Galilee, and the same pattern is repeated. Jesus finds Philip and invites him to spend time with him. "Follow Me" (1:43), he says. Philip does, a screen is drawn, and when we next see Philip he too is declaring that they have found the Messiah, "Him of Whom Moses in the law, and also the Prophets wrote, Jesus of Nazareth, the son of Joseph" (1:45). Philip tells Nathaniel, and Nathaniel comes to see, although with some resistance. Exactly as he had with Simon, Jesus greets Nathaniel as someone who, although they have not met, he already knows: "Behold, an Israelite indeed, in whom there is no guile" (1:47). Nathaniel sputters, "How do You know me?" And Jesus replies, "Before Philip called you, when you were under the fig tree, I saw you" (1:48). Nathaniel is convinced by this, taking it for a sign and agreeing that this must indeed be the Messiah: "Rabbi, You are the Son of God; You are the King of Israel" (1:49).[11]

Jesus has something deeper in mind, however. He accepts their use of the title Messiah, but he wants them to open the term up—he is more than that, or more than they understood by that, and the startling fact that he knows them (the only part of these conversations the reader has been privy to) seems to be a key to what, in time, he will show them:

> Because I said to you that I saw you under the fig tree, do you believe? You shall see greater things than these. . . . Truly, truly, I say to you, you shall see the heavens opened, and the angels of God ascending and descending on the Son of Man. (1:50-51)

Jesus is calling their attention to Jacob's vision in Genesis 28. There, fleeing from his family because of his older brother's anger at having been tricked out of his birthright, Jacob sleeps out in the open one night with a rock for a pillow, utterly alone:

> And he had a dream, and behold, a ladder was set on the earth with its top reaching heaven; and behold, the angels of God were ascending and descending on it. And behold, the Lord stood above it and said, "I am the Lord, the God of your father Abraham and the God of Isaac; the land on which you lie, I will give to you and your descendants. Your descendants shall also be like the dust of the earth, . . . and in you and in your descendants shall all the families of the earth be blessed." (Gen 28:12-14)

I have not abandoned you, God says to Jacob. I know you and am bound to you. I have great plans for you and your descendants, for all of the earth, in fact, through you. Despite the way it seemed to Jacob in his isolation, heaven and earth were not separated but were joined by an unseen ladder upon which the angels of God continually ascended and descended, ministering to the world. What Jesus tells Nathaniel and the others is that *he* is the ladder Jacob saw. Come and spend time with me, he says. In time you will see that I am the unseen ladder, now suddenly visible, through which God will join heaven and earth. He knows you, through me. You have not been abandoned. This is too much, of course, to take in at this point, but Jesus' welcome is not. He knows them, and his invitation to come and see what God is doing is completely clear.

With his reference to himself as "the Son of Man," Jesus introduces another term, which, like Lamb of God and Messiah, the reader and those who first heard his words take note of but do not fully comprehend. For the moment, we hold them in suspension, unresolved. Scholars note that the simplest meaning of the term is "human being," the son of a man. Certainly most of those who heard Jesus use that term to identify himself would have taken it that way. But, as N. T. Wright and others point out, Jesus seems to be making a deeper point as well. Perhaps the tone of his voice—"Truly, truly, I say to you"—might have alerted them to this. In Daniel 7, the prophet had a vision of "one like a Son of Man," that is to say, a human being, being presented to the "Ancient of Days" and being given dominion over an everlasting, universal kingdom:[12]

> And to Him was given dominion,
> Glory and a kingdom,
> That all the peoples, nations, and men of every language
> Might serve Him.
> His dominion is an everlasting dominion
> Which will not pass away,
> And His kingdom is one
> Which will not be destroyed. (Dan 7:14)

What Jesus is suggesting is that he is this victorious king, and that through the establishment of his kingship, heaven and earth will be joined, for their benefit. This is more than Nathaniel or the reader can puzzle out yet, but we are being called to open our eyes, to ready ourselves to take in more and more.

3

LIFE (JOHN 2:1–4:54)

After the Prologue and these opening acts of giving witness, John puts together a three-chapter arc (chapters 2–4) in which Jesus begins to describe himself and the life God is offering the world through him.[1] Moving with his disciples from a wedding in Cana up to Jerusalem and then back to Cana, Jesus is confronted with various needs. He responds, and as he does so, he transforms the situations into pictures of the new life he is offering. "Come and see," he had said to the curious. Now he offers them ways to see. Think of it this way, he says—giving the reader something to handle and work with as well, asking if we can make out what he is saying, asking if we are willing to trust him.

Wedding in Cana, 2:1-11

Jesus first dramatizes the life he has come to offer almost casually, in passing. Three days pass from the conversation with Nathaniel, and Jesus and his disciples are at a wedding in Cana of Galilee, in the northern part of Israel, away from Jerusalem and the center of power. The mother of Jesus is there as well, and when she notices that the wine has run out, creating a serious problem for the host, she turns to her son and tells him. His reply has puzzled commentators: "Woman, what do I have to do with you? My hour has not yet come" (2:4). One can see why this is troubling. "Woman," as Jesus uses the term, while not insulting (as it is to our ears), is certainly not intimate.[2] It establishes a distance between mother and son that had not been present before. D. A. Carson points out that the idiom he uses, "What do I have to do with you," means "What do you and I have in common," which helps us see what is going on. The life that they had held in common is now at an end.[3] But Jesus' words also point forward, toward another life that will be initiated when his "hour" comes. That life *will* be held in common. The hour is not yet identified, but as the reader will discover, Jesus is using the term to point toward his crucifixion and resurrection—the hour in which his glory will be fully visible and the work he was sent to accomplish will be completed. His words to his mother locate us; we are in a space before his hour has come. As a number of commentators point out, we will be reminded of this exchange at the close of the Gospel, when Jesus speaks to Mary from the cross and uses exactly this term, "Woman." There, his hour fully come, Jesus will reach out and embed her within another family.[4] The cross from which he speaks is what they will have in common.

Not yet understanding this, Mary nonetheless accepts the change in their relationship. Assuming, however, that events along the way might play a part in the unfolding of that hour, she again calls attention to the need at hand, trusting her son to make something out of the situation. "Whatever He says to you, do it," she tells the servants. And Jesus acts, responding to the bridegroom's need with what John calls the first of his "signs" (2:11)—a dramatic manifestation of his identity. (John will describe seven of these signs as the Gospel moves on: this one; healing the royal official's son [4:46-54]; healing the man who could not walk [5:1-15]; feeding the 5,000 [6:5-13]; walking on the sea [6:16-21]; giving sight to the blind man [9:1-7]; raising Lazarus from the dead [11:1-44].) For the first time, the reader is drawn into the circle of those who are able to see. Out of sight of the headwaiter and the bridegroom, but in sight of the disciples, Jesus has the servants fill six stone water pots, "set there for the Jewish custom of purification, containing twenty or thirty gallons each" (2:6). The servants do so, to the brim, and Jesus directs them to draw some and take it to the headwaiter. He tastes the "water which had become wine" and, without knowing its source, pronounces it the best wine served on the occasion, kept inexplicably until the end. The disciples see all of this and "believe in Him" (2:11).

What do they believe? They do not have the whole story yet, for his hour has not yet come. They are certainly confirmed in their earlier identification of Jesus as the long-promised Messiah. More than that they probably cannot articulate, but it seems fair to say that they "believed," without being able to spell it out, that they had witnessed a remarkable truth about the man they are following. The narrator understands a good bit more. As the Prologue has made clear, he is writing from a position after Jesus' glory had been fully manifested. What he sees, looking back, is that, in changing the water into something rich and remarkable and abundant, Jesus was not only solving the wedding party's problem, he was picturing the life he was about to offer. That is why John calls this event a "sign." He understands that Jesus is about to transform the way one comes to God—replacing the old "custom of purification" with the overflowing presence of God himself. The disciples, on some level, believe this. The reader takes it all in, not yet understanding what it means, but having been given an image to ponder and return to and unfold: "This beginning of His signs Jesus did in Cana of Galilee, and manifested His glory, and His disciples believed in Him" (2:11).

Richard Wilbur, "A Wedding Toast"

It is difficult, in reading the Gospel, not to get ahead of ourselves. We would prefer to join the narrator in his confident understanding of what this sign means, but there is also something to be said for slowing down and letting the image do its work at its own speed. Richard Wilbur's "A Wedding Toast," published in 1976, lets us do exactly that. Focusing on the extravagance of the sign, Wilbur's toast invites us to join him as he puzzles out and attempts to articulate its significance:

> St. John tells how, at Cana's wedding-feast,
> The water-pots poured wine in such amount
> That by his sober count
> There were a hundred gallons at the least.
>
> It made no earthly sense, unless to show
> How whatsoever love elects to bless
> Brims to a sweet excess
> That can without depletion overflow.
>
> Which is to say that what love sees is true;
> That the world's fullness is not made but found.
> Life hungers to abound
> And pour its plenty out for such as you.
>
> Now, if your loves will lend an ear to mine,
> I toast you both, good son and dear new daughter.
> May you not lack for water,
> And may that water smack of Cana's wine.[5]

In the course of his toast, as we will see, Wilbur is drawn deeper and deeper into the implications of the sign, finding in the wedding of his son and the emotions it unlocks a way to enter the image on its own terms.

The poem begins by focusing on the fullness of the gesture—Jesus not only produced wine when the feast was about to founder, but he produced it extravagantly, a fact John stresses by taking the time to count the six stone water pots and remind us, "soberly," that each held at least twenty gallons. Wilbur comments, colloquially, in the second stanza, that such an outpouring "made no earthly sense." We use that phrase all the time to suggest amazement—such an abundance seemed crazy; it made no earthly sense, a hundred gallons being much more than was needed to save the host from embarrassment. "Unless," he continues, Jesus was making a point, blessing the wedding by demonstrating how love works—that "whatsoever" it touches it transforms. One can imagine the faces of his son and daughter-in-law confirming the thought. The beloved, under the lover's touch, "brims to a sweet excess" that "can without depletion overflow," never reaching an end, always offering more of herself or himself to know and love and treasure.

That, Wilbur continues in the third stanza, is what the miracle meant, in an "earthly sense." And it is true, he says, caught up in the day and all of its promises. What "love" saw in blessing the marriage in Cana is what all of us see today, he says—that there is a "fullness" to life not created through effort and toil but "found." The lover's sense that he has found in the beloved a fullness that has always been there, waiting to be noticed and drawn out, is true not just about lovers but about the world as a whole. The world is "hunger[ing] to abound / and pour its plenty out for such as you," Wilbur assures the happy couple and all within earshot. Believe that, he says, raising a glass. Lean into its promises as you lean into each other.

Wilbur's toast, then, in the last stanza, is that their lives not be lacking in water. May all good things flow to you, he says. But more than that, he adds: "may that water smack of Cana's wine." Might your lives together overflow with the fullness love sees in its beloved—and not just on a day like this, but always and so deeply that there is not bottom. "Smack" is a perfect word, for it lets us hear, as all of those gathered drink to the lovers, an audible chorus of assent. Yes, our lips say in chorus, we all agree.

But there is something else here as well, what we might call the "spiritual sense" that has been running alongside the earthly one throughout the poem. What the father also looks forward to is the two young lovers living lives "smacking" of the wine poured out at Calvary—what John would call the wine of God's very presence, pictured in Cana's "sweet excess." "Of his fullness we have all received," John wrote in his Prologue. What Wilbur quietly points to is a second sort of fullness also present in the world: "Life" itself, true life, "hunger[ing] to abound," eager to "pour its plenty out for such as you." Such a fullness is "not made but found," by anyone with eyes to see. Wilbur has been working his way toward this thought since the phrase "no earthly sense," marking the fact that there was a spiritual sense to the sign, but refusing to unpack it until after he had articulated the earthly sense of abundance, poured out before the lovers and noted by their glowing father. That picture established and alive within, it takes but the turn of a phrase for the speaker to bring what it points to into play. So, I would argue, with all of John's signs—the more we allow them to unfold within us, the more they "smack of Cana's wine."

Temple of His Body, 2:13-25

In the next scene John records, after a brief interlude in Capernaum, we are given a second way of picturing the new life offered believers. Jesus and his disciples go up to Jerusalem for the first of the three Passovers recorded in the Gospel. They enter the temple, the central focus of Jewish life. The temple is where God's presence dwells, where people draw near and worship, but what Jesus and the disciples discover is a great hubbub of buying and selling, intimacy with God having been replaced by the loud seductions of trade. What Jesus does is take the temple back, insisting, in a flurry of overturned tables and driven-out animals, that it be used as God intended, for people to come into his presence. "Stop making My Father's house a house of merchandise" (2:16) he says, cleansing it and re-establishing its proper function. His disciples are amazed at the intensity of his response, and a passage of Scripture comes to mind to describe the way he is acting: "His disciples remembered that it was written 'Zeal for Thy house will consume me'" (2:17). What they remember is Psalm 69, where David was similarly overcome by the intensity of his identification with the house of God:

> Because for Thy sake I have borne reproach;
> Dishonor has covered my face.
> I have become estranged from my brothers,
> And an alien to my mother's sons.
> For zeal for Thy house has consumed me,
> And the reproaches of those who reproach Thee have fallen on me.
> (Ps 69:7-9)

Not surprisingly, since they have been thinking of him as the Davidic Messiah, Jesus, in his zeal, seems to his disciples a kind of David, consumed by his love for the place where God dwells.

It does not take long for the reproaches once directed toward David to come raining down on Jesus. The Jewish leaders "answer" (2:18) his actions by demanding a sign demonstrating his right to act in such away, much as the delegation sent to John the Baptist had. They do not expect such a sign to be produced, of course. They see only a person out of control, whirling around, destroying things. But Jesus gives them what they want, focusing their eyes even more intensely on himself: "Destroy this temple, and in three days I will raise it up" (2:19). The leaders scoff, unable to make sense of the riddle: "It took forty-six years to build this temple, and You will raise it up in three days?" (2:20). The leaders shrug off his words as if they had no weight at all, which makes the narrator's intervention all the more powerful: "But He was speaking of the temple of His body" (2:21). Speaking from a position after Christ's hour had come, John understands how charged this statement is and calls the reader to pause and take notice.

What did John understand? First of all, that Jesus had been speaking metaphorically.[6] He continues, "When therefore He was raised from the dead, His disciples remembered that He said this; and they believed the Scripture and the word which Jesus had spoken" (2:22). When Jesus was raised from the dead, his disciples remembered his claim to be able to raise the temple and understood that he had been talking about his own body. They believed Scripture—that David's zealous defense of the temple, metaphorically lead-ing to his body being consumed, had literally been enacted in the life and death of Jesus—and they believed his word, that he had predicted that he would die and be raised again to life. Richard Bauckham remarks that in passages like this "John is putting his readers in a better position than are any of the characters in the story for understanding a major theme in the words of Jesus"—that is, "his coming death and resurrection."[7] This is certainly true. One of the ways John encourages the reader to make the story his or her own is by giving us glimpses of where he is heading, continually reminding us that these things have deeper resonances than are first apparent and urg-ing us to pay attention.

But John wants us to notice something else when he brings this story to a halt with the word *But*. When he spoke of his body as the temple, Jesus was doing more than simply anticipating his death and resurrection through a striking metaphor. He was claiming to *be* the temple where God's presence now dwelt. When his body was destroyed, what had kept people from being able to come into God's presence would be tossed out and overturned; and when his body was raised, God's presence would once again be accessible. In cleansing the temple and making it possible for people to enter into God's presence, Jesus was picturing the new life his death would bring about, just as he had when he transformed the water set aside for purification into the wine of abundance. Imagine the boldness behind this. It is as if Jesus understood the temple as having been put into place in order to point to him. This, once again, is more than those who heard Jesus understood at the time, and it is more, perhaps, than the reader understands at this stage of the story, but John is preparing us to think in a new way. With the pause created by the word *But*, he is putting us on notice that everything Jesus touches or attends to is poised to speak out about his grandeur. John is writing out of the experience of having this insight gradually dawn on him, and he is putting his readers into a position where we can begin to experience the tug of its unfolding.

Emily Dickinson, 962 (A Light exists in Spring)

Emily Dickinson's poem on the light of early March lets us hear what it is like to muse over this striking prediction. "I know that He exists," she writes in one poem, but then continues, "Somewhere—in Silence— / He has hid his rare life / From our gross eyes."[8] Because of this, God's presence was something in which she could never be confident, and was often something she doubted. And yet the promise of this passage, intimacy restored in the raising up of a new temple, must have spoken to her deeply, perhaps nowhere more poignantly than in the play of light across a landscape, with everything it touches being brought to life by its presence:

A Light exists in Spring
Not present on the Year
At any other period—
When March is scarcely here
A Color stands abroad
On Solitary Fields
That Science cannot overtake
But Human Nature feels.

It waits opon the Lawn,
It shows the furthest Tree
Opon the furthest Slope you know
It almost speaks to you.

Then as Horizons step
Or Noons report away
Without the Formula of sound
It passes and we stay—

A quality of loss
Affecting our Content
As Trade had suddenly encroached
Opon a Sacrament—[9]

This is a poem about natural light, but a light that is experienced with such intensity that one can sense John's Prologue somewhere behind it as the light takes on flesh and almost speaks to her. All will be restored, it says—or almost says. The ending of the poem, returning to but reversing the promise of the temple scene, is profoundly and sadly shaken in its confidence.

In the first two stanzas of the poem, the poet is caught up in a sense of wonder. There is something precious and fleeting about this early March light, she writes, locating it in time while also whispering it "exists," it is "present." Touching distant fields and turning them to "Color," the light seems to take on flesh, "stand[ing] abroad" and drawing all eyes to it. It cannot be understood by "Science," she insists. It cannot be tracked down and analyzed. It speaks, rather, to the heart, to our "Human Nature," and one takes it in by "feel[ing]." Much as John suggested in his Prologue, to "comprehend" such a light, one must "receive" it, allowing it to touch and draw to the surface one's inner world. Almost like a person, the light "waits upon the Lawn" for you and then races out to show you "the furthest Tree / Opon the furthest Slope." It lights up the world, fanning its wonders out like bolts of cloth, all for your benefit. No wonder she insists, as we do when a thing touches us deeply, that "It almost speaks to you." It seems fully present, calling us to itself.

But it only "almost speaks." The phrase goes another way as well, acknowledging what the speaker desperately wants but cannot quite have. It almost speaks—this intimate presence, standing before her as early March light or whispering to her from the pages of John's Gospel—and then "It passes." The passing is inexplicable. "Horizons" that had been miraculously brought near simply "step" away. "Noon," in all its overwhelming glory, suddenly echoes away into nothingness—soundless echoes from a soundless gun, leaving no "Formula of sound" to mark or explain its sudden passing. One can sense how bewildering this would be. "It passes and *we* stay—" (emphasis mine). We join her in realizing that we have been abandoned into time, perhaps even becoming a part of that "we" because of that sober realization.

What we share, what we experience in reading the poem, is the "quality" or intensity of the "loss / Affecting our Content" when the light is removed. Having understood what it would be like to sense grace almost speaking to us, we then are left with nothing. Seriously entertaining these words of

Jesus is no simple thing. Imagine, says Dickinson, the temple cleansed and the "furthest Tree / opon the furthest Slope" almost speaking to you and then having it all "step" away again. It would be as if "Trade had suddenly encroached / Opon a Sacrament," the steady roar of buying and selling filling the space again where God had almost been. What Dickinson lets us hear is how much is at stake in taking these words seriously, how much one risks in letting them unfold.

Born from Above (I), 3:1-8

With that in mind, still in Jerusalem, probably still at Passover after the cleansing of the temple, we turn to a third illustration of the life God is offering the world through Jesus. Drink in God's fullness, Jesus has said. Come into his presence. Respond deeply, he now adds—allow your heart to be changed. In this famous scene in which Nicodemus visits by night, John slows the narrative and allows Jesus to unfold this image, and the idea behind it, at some length.

As a leading figure in the religious establishment, Nicodemus approaches Jesus from a position of strength, greeting him as a fellow teacher: "Rabbi, we know that You have come from God as a teacher; for no one can do these signs that You do unless God is with him" (3:2). He means to signal respect. Those of us charged with sorting such things out acknowledge that you have "come from God," and we are curious about your teaching. This seems harmless enough, but Jesus understands that although Nicodemus has seen the signs, he has not understood what they point to. He does not believe, and Jesus pushes back hard to get his attention: "Truly, truly, I say to you, unless one is born again, he cannot see the kingdom of God" (3:3). The "kingdom of God" is the world over which God reigns—his long-awaited rule over a rebellious earth, the gathering of his own into a single family. This is what Jesus is inviting people to enter—a world in which heaven and earth are joined again and God is known in his fullness. Nicodemus, the "teacher of Israel," would have assumed that he was uniquely positioned to enter such a realm, and so this rebuke comes as a slap to the face. It is as if Jesus had said, "You need to start all over again. None of your learning will get you into the kingdom of God. You need to be utterly changed." That change, Jesus adds, can only come from "above"—"born from above" being another way "born again" can be translated.[10] On his own, Nicodemus is powerless to bring it about. He is dead to that realm, and a dead man cannot bring himself to life.

It is no surprise that Nicodemus does not understand the implied offer. How is he dead? What does he not understand? This is absurd, he sputters, literalizing what Jesus has just said in an attempt to make the claim that there is no real life in him look ridiculous: "How can a man be born when he is old? He cannot enter a second time into his mother's womb and be born, can he?" (3:4). Jesus does not rise to the bait. Instead, he calmly repeats the idea, sensing that underneath the bluster Nicodemus somehow wants to understand: "Truly, truly, I say to you, unless one is born of water and the Spirit, he cannot enter into the kingdom of God" (3:5). How does this help? In order to enter the kingdom or see the kingdom—in order to know God—one must be "born from above" or "born of water and the Spirit." The additional phrase seems, if anything, simply to intensify the riddle.

But perhaps not. The phrase "water and the spirit" has a scriptural resonance that Nicodemus would have recognized. As a number of commentators point out, Jesus seems to be recalling another prophecy about the return of Israel from exile—in this case one drawn from the book of Ezekiel.[11] There, God looks forward to the time in which he would draw the remnants of scattered, disgraced Israel together again:

> For I will take you from the nations, gather you from all the lands, and bring you into your own land. Then I will sprinkle clean *water* on you, and you will be clean; and I will cleanse you from all your filthiness and from all your idols. Moreover, I will give you a new heart and put a new *spirit* within you; and I will remove the heart of stone from your flesh and give you a heart of flesh. And I will put My *Spirit* within you, and cause you to walk in My statutes, and you will be careful to observe My ordinances. And you will live in the land that I gave to your forefathers; so you will be My people and I will be your God. (Ezek 36:24-28)

God here tells Israel that he is in the process of re-establishing his kingdom, bringing its scattered members home from exile. And he will do two things with those he calls back. He will sprinkle them with "clean water," cleansing them from the filthiness they have absorbed in turning for life to things other than him—"idols." And he will change their hearts, replacing their lifeless and unresponsive "hearts of stone" with "hearts of flesh" alive and alert to his presence. Cleansed, they will be able to enter again into God's presence; inwardly alive, they will be able to respond and draw near, living with him forever.

Nicodemus, according to Jesus, is in exile. He is scattered and filthy; his heart is like a stone. But Jesus is offering to bring him back to life—to wash away his failures and to give him a beating heart. But he cannot do this on

his own, which is why Jesus describes it as a birth "from above." For Nicodemus to enter into God's presence, the new temple, God himself must act,
giving him a "new heart" and putting a "new spirit" within him. Nicodemus
cannot do it: "That which is born of the flesh is flesh, and that which is born
of the Spirit is spirit" (3:6). Anything Nicodemus creates is still flesh, dead
to the things of the spirit. Only the Spirit can produce spiritual life. Drink,
Jesus has said. Come near, he has whispered. Be born again, he now adds:
let that old, clenched heart be flooded anew with the life it thought it would
never know.

This again is a lot to take in, which Jesus acknowledges when he turns to
Nicodemus and says, "Do not marvel that I said to you, 'You must be born
again'" (3:7). Of course he marvels; Jesus has just turned upside down most
of what he has always understood, using the most ordinary of terms. Jesus
continues, "The wind blows where it wishes and you hear the sound of it, but
do not know where it comes from and where it is going; so is everyone who is
born of the Spirit" (3:8). Jesus is playing with the Greek word *pneuma* here,
which means both wind and spirit. Look around you, he says. The wind is
invisible, but you can see the way it makes branches and trees lash and bend.
So too with the Spirit. Because you cannot see it or control it or predict its
movements, you have been living as if it did not exist, falling back on effort
or position or knowledge in order to make some sort of life for yourself.
But that is not life, he tells Nicodemus. Without that wind moving through
you, you are not alive. You do not know God—you can have no part of
his kingdom. I'm reminded of a comment the Austrian philosopher Ludwig
Wittgenstein made to his sister Hermine when she was puzzled by a series
of radical changes he had made to his life. Perhaps with this passage in John
in mind, he said to her, "You remind me of somebody who is looking out
through a closed window and cannot explain to himself the strange movements of a passer-by. He cannot tell what sort of storm is raging out there or
that this person might only be managing with difficulty to stay on his feet."[12]
You have lived too long inside, Jesus is saying to Nicodemus; of course you
do not understand what I am talking about. Come out where the Spirit blows
and let it change your heart.

Charles Wright, from "A Journal of the Year of the Ox"

Jesus' image here—the moving, uncontrollable wind of the Spirit, invisible save in its effects—is one that Charles Wright has repeatedly turned to.
Something in the image calls out to him, and in a number of poems he

measures himself against it. I mean this quite literally. In a June 12 entry from a year-long poetic journal kept in 1985, watching the wind move invisibly through his trees, Wright considers the notion that, as another poem puts it, "we live in two landscapes, as Augustine might have said, / One that's eternal and divine, and one that's just the backyard, / Dead leaves and dead grass in November, purple in the spring."[13] Hearing Jesus' words to Nicodemus, Wright asks what he is to make of those moments when the two landscapes are laid across each other, when, as Jesus said, the wind of the Spirit touches the world of the flesh. Not much, he finally concludes, stepping back from the offer to Nicodemus but, in his bemused and wistful way, still testifying to the certain existence of what he cannot reach:

—Horn music starts up and stutters uncertainly
                              out of the brown house
    Across the street: a solo,
    A duet, then three of them all at once, then silence,
    Then up and back down the scale.
    Sunday, the ninth of June, the morning
    Still dull-eyed in its green kimono,
                        the loose, blown sleeves
    Moving complacently in the wind.
    Now there are two, then all three again
                            weaving a blurred, harmonic line
    Through the oak trees and the dogwood
    As the wind blows and the sheer nightgown of daylight glints.

    Where was it I heard before
    Those same runs and half-riffs
                            turned through a summer morning
    Come from one of the pastel buildings
    Outside the window I sat in front of looking down
    As I tried to practice my own scales
                            of invisible music
    I thought I heard for hours on a yellow legal pad?
    Verona, I think, the stiff French horn
    Each weekend echoing my own false notes
                            and scrambled lines
    I tried to use as decoys to coax the real things down
    Out of the air they hid in and out of the pencils they hid in . . .

    Silence again. For good, now,
    I suspect, until next week,
                        arduous harmony,
    Unalterable music our lives are measured by.

What will become of us, the Italian French horn player,
These players, me, all of us
                    trying to imitate
What we can't see and what we can't hear?
Nothing spectacular, I would guess, a life
Scored more or less by others,
                    smorzando here, *andante* there:
Only the music will stay untouched,
Moving as certainly as the wind moves,
                    invisible in the trees.
                    —12 June 1985[14]

As the poem begins, the poet hears the starts and stops of horn music from a trio practicing across the street on a sleepy Sunday morning—one, then two, then three of them at once, uncertain stutters "up and back down a scale." Almost casually, he introduces the image of the invisible wind of the Spirit, noting the way the "loose, blown sleeves" of the trees, morning's "green kimono," move "complacently in the wind." The poet seems at first barely awake, but something soon begins to stir; the musicians begin to work in earnest and a "blurred harmonic line" weaves its way through the "oak leaves and the dogwood" while the "wind blows and the sheer nightgown of daylight glints."

What the stuttering horns stir is Wright's memory, taking him back in time to a similar conjunction of forces. "Where was it I heard before / Those same riffs and half riffs / turned through a summer morning," he asks, beginning the poem's second section. Verona, he remembers. A "stiff French horn / Each weekend echo[ed] my own false notes / and scrambled lines" as he sat writing and staring out a window. This would be the Verona of his early years as a poet, when he was practicing his "own scales / of invisible music" and trying with his broken notes to "coax the real things down / Out of the air they hid in." "Invisible music" is a phrase borrowed from Dickinson, itself another take on Jesus' image:

This World is not Conclusion,
A Species stands beyond—
Invisible, as Music—
But positive, as Sound—
It beckons, and it baffles—
Philosophy—don't know—
And through a Riddle, at the last—
Sagacity, must go—[15]

Invisible but positive, beckoning but baffling, this music can never be known directly—as Philosophy and the flummoxed Nicodemus would attest—but it might be approached as a "Riddle." That is how Wright understands those Verona mornings. He was using his words to "coax the real [words]" out of the air, never successfully but always deeply engaged. In both scenes, then, Verona and his Charlottesville yard, the "false notes and scrambled lines" of the poet and the musicians move alongside a third force, invisible but clearly present—the blowing wind of Virginia, and the "invisible music / I thought I heard" of Italy.

In the third section, Wright returns to his backyard. In the interval in which he had remembered and thought about Verona, the trio had finished its work for the week and "Silence" had returned. What he realizes, in that silence, is that the "real things" would be forever out of reach—an "arduous harmony, / Unalterable music our lives are measured by." What they had all been doing, "these players, me, all of us," is "trying to imitate / What we can't see and we can't hear." The players' "blurred" lines moving across the unseen wind in the first section and the poet's "scrambled" lines held up against an invisible music he only "thought [he] heard" in the second both come up short. They cannot touch what they cannot fully take in. "That which is born of the flesh is flesh," Jesus told Nicodemus, "and that which is born of the Spirit is spirit" (3:6). This is the same thought, transposed to the world of composition.

When Wright "measures" himself against that wind, holding himself up against these words of Jesus, what he sees in himself is "Nothing spectacular." His will be a life "Scored more or less by others," guided, dominated, even made sense of by those he rubs shoulders with. This is the world of trade or the flesh. What Wright says back to the Gospel is that for him the "real things" are out of reach—he cannot touch them. And yet, they exist. Even as his own lines break and stumble—we see this in their arrangement on the page—they reach toward and are moved by a music that "will stay untouched, / Moving as certainly as the wind moves, / invisible in the trees." He is not certain about his own position, anything but, but the wind he points to is—moving always as it wills.

Born from Above (II), 3:9-21

After Jesus tells Nicodemus that unless God acts to bring him to life he will never enter his kingdom, the teacher is truly puzzled. "How can these things be?" (3:9), he asks, less resigned to his position than Wright's speaker. Or as others have translated the phrase, "How can this happen?"[16] How could such a birth come about? All of his initial confidence is gone. The "we" who had figuratively been behind him backing him up (3:2) vanish, and he stands there, alone and needy. Look at me, Jesus says:

> Are you the teacher of Israel, and do not understand these things? Truly, truly, I say to you, we speak that which we know, and bear witness of that which we have seen; and you do not receive our witness. If I told you earthly things and you do not believe, how shall you believe if I tell you heavenly things? (3:10-12)

Jesus takes Nicodemus' opening bluster about what "we know" and transforms it. Jesus is the one who is actually speaking with authority: "we speak that which we know, and bear witness of that which we have seen." (This seems to be a sort of "royal we," though one can also imagine Jesus linking himself and the Spirit whose invisible presence he has just described.) What has Jesus seen? What is he asking Nicodemus to believe? He is asking him to believe that God is offering him life through Jesus, "life" being the "earthly" term Jesus has been using to picture the restored relationship with God he has been sent to establish.

Jesus quotes a passage of Scripture in order to demonstrate his authority: "And no one has ascended into heaven, but He who descended from heaven, even the Son of Man" (3:13). This sounds like another riddle, but Nicodemus would have recognized the quotation. In Proverbs 30, Agur forcefully confesses how little he understands about God and his ways. Nicodemus, Jesus is suggesting, would do well to make a similar confession: "Surely I am more stupid than any man, / And I do not have the understanding of a man. / Neither have I learned wisdom, / Nor do I have the knowledge of the Holy One" (Prov 30:2-3). Agur goes on, posing a series of rhetorical questions that make the point that no one, in fact, knows the Holy One. No one has ascended into God's realms and reported back:

> Who has ascended into heaven and descended?
> Who has gathered the wind in His fists?
> Who has wrapped the waters in His garment?
> Who has established all the ends of the earth?
> What is His name or His son's name?
> Surely you know!
>
> (Prov 30:4)

There is no such person. No one was there when God gathered the winds and wrapped the oceans around the earth. His ways are hidden and unknowable.

But that is no longer the case, Jesus is saying. Who has this knowledge? Who speaks as if he had "ascended into heaven and descended?" He does—the very one who once "wrapped the waters in His garment" has now descended from heaven and is standing before Nicodemus and speaking to him about the things of God. One can imagine Nicodemus staring and trying to take this in.

What did he descend from heaven to say? Simply this—that God was offering life to those who were dead, and he was doing it through his Son:

> And as Moses lifted up the serpent in the wilderness, even so must the Son of Man be lifted up; that whoever believes may in Him have eternal life. (3:14-15)

Jesus continues his tutorial, taking Nicodemus back to the book of Numbers where the children of Israel, having spoken against God and doubted his care for them, were punished with fiery serpents. Many die. They turn to Moses for help, and under God's direction, he creates a bronze representation of a serpent and puts it on a pole. Lifting the serpent up, Moses commands those who are about to die to turn and look at it, and live (Num 21). Just so, Jesus is inviting Nicodemus to look at him in faith and live. As Richard Bauckham points out, the Son of Man being "lifted up" is a charged image combining two ideas whose significance will be unfolded as the Gospel moves forward.[17] First, of course, Jesus will be quite literally lifted up when he is put to death. As the children of Israel had looked up at the death they deserved and lived, so hearts of stone, equally mired in death, will be invited to look to the cross and live. And second, the "lifting up" of Jesus will in time be seen as an exaltation or enthroning—the cross becoming the throne upon which the Son of Man will take possession of the kingdom he has died to establish. How, then, can these things happen? How can an unresponsive heart become a heart alive to the things of God? How can Nicodemus enter that kingdom and live? By "receiv[ing] our witness" (3:11) and taking in these words.

Much of this, of course, is still in the future. That death has not happened yet. Nor can Nicodemus see from here how it could be a source of life. But he surely understands that in charging him to look not to himself but to the Son of Man for life, Jesus has presented him with an utterly new way of thinking—one that he must have turned over in his mind in the days that followed. We do not know how Nicodemus responds to these words because John, as he often does, turns elsewhere, opening space for the reader to wrestle with these issues, but we do know that Nicodemus turns up two more times in the Gospel. Once, he argues with the other Pharisees that they are not treating Jesus fairly (7:45-52). A second time, after Jesus has been crucified, Nicodemus is one of the two men who carry his body away from the cross, bind it in linen and spices, and lay it in a new tomb (19:38-42). In both cases, Nicodemus does indeed seem to be looking away from himself and his own interests and toward another source of life.

Many commentators argue that at this point John breaks away from Jesus' encounter with Nicodemus and speaks directly to the reader.[18] If this is the case, verses 16-21 become John's meditation on verses 14 and 15. The word *For*, in verses 16 and 17, helps us follow his thinking. God lifted up his Son out of love, John writes: "*For* God so loved the world that He gave His only begotten Son, that whoever believes in Him should not perish, but have eternal life" (3:16). He was acting to save the world, not judge it, doing something the world could not do for itself: "*For* God did not send the Son into the world to judge the world, but that the world should be saved through Him" (3:17). Judgment, John adds, comes into play only in this sense: that people judge themselves, in turning away from life and choosing death:

> And this is the judgment, that the light is come into the world, and men loved the darkness rather than the light; for their deeds were evil. For everyone who does evil hates the light, and does not come to the light, lest his deeds should be exposed. But he who practices the truth comes to the light, that his deeds may be manifested as having been wrought in God. (3:19-21)

In offering life, the light exposes the fact that those who stand before it are in darkness. This is the peculiar tension animating the words of Jesus. He is speaking out of love, offering life, but that life appears as a gift only to those who know they need it. To everyone else, it is an insult or a threat or an unwelcomed judgment. Think again about Nicodemus, coming to Jesus "by night" (3:2). As he wrestles with these words, is he turning away from the light, refusing to have his deeds exposed? Or is he "practic[ing] the truth" (3:21), allowing his heart to be transformed by the light, "wrought [into life] in God"? We do not know how Nicodemus responds, which seems quite deliberate on John's part, a way of inviting his readers to imagine both responses, moving with his heart as it begins to stir, or turning away as it stiffens and comes to a halt.

Henry Vaughan, "The Night"

In his meditation on this passage, published in 1655, Henry Vaughan takes up the invitation I have just described and imagines a Nicodemus who eagerly responded to Christ's invitation to come to the light. What's interesting is that Vaughan finds his way to this response through the image of Nicodemus coming by night. Instead of assuming, as many have, that he came at night out of self-protection, thus keeping one foot in the world of darkness and its blinded opposition to the light, Vaughan imagines a Nicodemus who loved the light and came to know God through it. What to do with the darkness by which he came to the light then? To make sense of this image, Vaughan imagines a different sort of darkness, one that draws a person near to God rather than one that blinds him. In doing so, he is led deeper into himself and his own blinded busyness. Recognizing this, seeing his world for what it is, Vaughan's speaker is powerfully drawn to the words through which he now hears the Gospel addressing him. "Come to me at night" the passage says to him. "O for that night!" he responds, hungry with yearning:

> Through that pure Virgin-shrine
> That sacred vail drawn oe'r thy glorious noon
> That men might look and live, as Glo-worms shine,
>   And face the Moon,
>   Wise Nicodemus saw such light
>   As made him know his God by night.
>
>   Most blest believer he!
> Who in that land of darkness and blinde eyes
> Thy long expected healing wings could see,
>   When Thou didst rise,
>   And, what can never more be done,
>   Did at mid-night speak with the Sun!
>
>   O who will tell me, where
> He found thee at that dead and silent hour?
> What hallow'd solitary ground did bear
>   So rare a flower,
>   Within whose sacred leafs did lie
>   The fullness of the Deity.
>
>   No mercy-seat of gold,
> No dead and dusty Cherub, nor carv'd stone,
> But his own living works did my Lord hold
>   And lodge alone;
>   Where trees and herbs did watch and peep
>   And wonder, while the Jews did sleep.
>
>   Dear night! this world's defeat;
> The stop to busie fools; care's check and curb;
> The day of Spirits; my soul's calm retreat
>   Which none disturb!
>   Christs progress, and His prayer time;
>   The hours to which high Heaven doth chime.

God's silent, searching flight;
When my Lord's head is fill'd with dew, and all
His locks are wet with the clear drops of night;
    His still, soft call;
His knocking time; The soul's dumb watch,
When Spirits their fair kindred catch.

    Were all my loud, evil days
Calm and unhaunted as is thy dark Tent,
Whose peace but by some Angel's wing or voice
    Is seldom rent,
Then I in Heaven all the long year
Would keep, and never wander here.

    But living where the Sun
Doth all things wake, and where all mix and tyre
Themselves and others, I consent and run
    To ev'ry myre,
And by this world's ill-guiding light,
Erre more than I can do by night.

    There is in God (some say),
A deep, but dazzling darkness; as men here
Say it is late and dusky, because they
    See not all clear;
O for that night! where I in him
Might live invisible and dim![19]

In the first three stanzas, Vaughan's speaker addresses Christ directly. He begins by noting that, while still in the darkness, Nicodemus was nonetheless able to recognize and respond to "thy glorious noon." Vaughan has John's Prologue in mind, recalling both the notion of Christ as "light shining in the darkness" (1:5) and the idea of him manifesting his Father's "glory" (1:14). In the dark, Vaughan writes, Nicodemus saw the glory of Christ radiating from the "pure Virgin-shrine" of his fleshly body. Like a "Glo-worm" shining in the moon's reflected light, Nicodemus came alive in response to Christ's noon, covered though it was by the "sacred vail" of flesh drawn about him so that "men might look [on him] and live." Vaughan's Nicodemus saw the light of God's glory and was not consumed. He came to God by night, and lived.

Nicodemus looked to Christ with the eyes of a "believer," the second stanza asserts. In a "land of darkness and blinde eyes," he saw, in Christ, the rising of the "long expected" sun predicted by the prophet Malachi: "the sun of righteousness ris[ing] with healing in his wings" (Mal 4:2). He saw Malachi's "Sun" rise, Vaughan says to Christ—there in your flesh, but also there in what his faith looked forward to, your being lifted up, both on the cross and at your resurrection. And most extraordinary, that night, "at midnight," he actually "[spoke] to the Sun." Where was that place, Vaughan asks in the third stanza, "where / He found thee at that dead and silent hour?" "Who will tell me?" he asks, yearning for that intimate encounter he has now unfolded in the Gospel. What ground bears such a flower, in whose form "the fullness of the Deity" (a quotation from Col 1:19 and John 1:16), like the fullness of the sun, rested and drew people to himself? How can I find the place that flower grows? How can I speak with the sun?

Vaughan hesitates for a moment as he moves into the fourth stanza, dropping his direct address to Christ in order to think in an extended way about his own failure to respond to the light and speak to the sun. He hears himself being addressed by the words and approaches them through what they open up inside him. Perhaps place is not the issue, he suddenly says. What Christ made clear was that God was no longer confined to the temple or to the ark of the covenant with its "mercy-seat of gold," "dusty Cherub," and "carv'd stone" containing the law. No, as Nicodemus must have realized upon coming at night, Christ resided in and was made visible by "His own living works"—the initial signs Nicodemus had noted and those works yet to be performed, culminating in his crucifixion and resurrection. The works were "living" because they had life in them; they were able to bring to life what had no life in itself. It was in those living actions that Christ resided, while Jerusalem slept all about him.

That notion of Jerusalem sleeping prompts a second thought. Not only has he not been looking for God in the right place, but he has not come at night. He has been asleep, or to put it another way, he has not found a "night" in which to search. Stanzas five through eight work this out. By "night," Vaughan writes in the fifth stanza, he means the time in which the "world's" busy demands have been defeated and put aside and its "cares" "check[ed] and curb[ed]." Night, the putting aside of worldly concerns, would be the "day of Spirits" then, the time in which spirits stir up life. Night would be the "calm" into which the soul could "retreat" and find itself again. Vaughan's point, and it seems a very modern one, is that there is no such night for him. The busy world beats all around him.

So he moves even deeper inside himself, trying to imagine Nicodemus' night. Night is when Christ rose and prayed. It is when he moved (or "progress[ed]") toward God. It is when Christ—here Vaughan borrows from the Song of Solomon—comes as the soul's lover. In the Song of Solomon, the lover comes into the garden of his beloved, knocking at her door and crying out, "Open to me, my sister, my darling, / My dove, my perfect one! / For my head is drenched with dew, / My locks with the damp of the night" (Song 5:2), and Vaughan imagines his Lord's head "fill'd with dew," his locks "wet with the clear drops of night" as he comes to him—"His still, soft call; / His knocking time." One can hear the deep yearning in these lines as the poet boldly joins the "soul's dumb watch" as its lover comes to him.

This yearning, then, at the turn to stanza seven, seems to prompt the speaker to turn and speak directly to his lover. Newly filled with all he has lost, Vaughan's speaker sees his Lord more clearly:

> Were all my loud, evil days
> Calm and unhaunted as is thy dark Tent,
> Whose peace but by some Angel's wing or voice
>   Is seldom rent,
>   Then I in Heaven all the long year
>   Would keep, and never wander here.

Oh that he could have such days, he sighs—days that were "nights." If he did, he would never "wander" as he does now. It would be as if he were in heaven "all the long year," in "thy dark Tent" or tabernacle, dwelling with God in peace. Instead, he confesses in stanza eight, he is in the "Sun" where "all things wake" and make their demands. He is never still, never pure. He constantly "consent[s] and run[s] / To ev'ry mire." The light of this world is opposed to the true light; it is an "ill-guiding" one, leading him away from stillness and the Spirit's embrace, leading him, by its very clarity, deeper and deeper into "err[or]."

Vaughan's speaker sees himself as busy, learned, filled with the world, and lost. He is blinded by his own drive to know and follow after every new thing. Like the Nicodemus of our reading, Vaughan's speaker acknowledges that he is blind and does not know. He admits that it is not more of the world's light he needs.[20] What he desires is what the Nicodemus he imagined coming by night had—the care-silencing night of God's presence itself. And so, seemingly stirred by the Spirit as he speaks, the poet turns to that presence, that sweet, inviting darkness. Like the Israelites to the serpent lifted up in the wilderness, he turns, with his need fully awakened, to life:

> There is in God (some say)
> A deep, but dazzling darkness; as men here
> Say it is late and dusky, because they
>   See not all clear;
>   O for that night! where I in him
>   Might live invisible and dim!

God's darkness is "deep" because it overwhelms every attempt to know and control, but it is also "dazzling," since it contains the sun of God's glory. The speaker is so humbled by the failures of his own busy mind that he can only attribute such a description of God to others who have told him so—"some say" this. But he has in fact imagined such a darkness in the course of the poem. It would be like a "dusky" twilight in which cares and demands would no longer be clear. It would be a night in which he would grow "invisible" in God's presence and, because of God's nearness, he would "live," eternally. It would be his own version of the night in which Nicodemus knew his Lord, the night in which God came near. "O for that night!" Vaughan concludes, reaching out toward it even as it reaches out to him.

I Must Decrease, 3:22-36

Three times Jesus has described the gift God is offering the world through him, and three times John has linked those descriptions to the issue of belief. Now, following the encounter with Nicodemus and the conclusion of Passover, Jesus and his disciples leave Jerusalem for the Judean countryside. The narrator's attention passes back one last time to John the Baptist, and the call to believe is even more forcefully foregrounded.

Away from Jerusalem, Jesus spends time with his disciples and begins baptizing, which stirs up a potential clash with John the Baptist, who is doing the same. Someone from Jerusalem, a "Jew," raises the issue of "purification" (3:25) with John's disciples, apparently contrasting his symbolic cleansing with Jesus' claim to baptize in God's own Spirit (1:33), an approach now drawing great crowds.[21] Exaggerating to get their concern across, John's disciples pass on this information: "Rabbi, He who was with you beyond the Jordan, to whom you have borne witness, behold He is baptizing, and *all* are coming to Him" (3:26). The Baptist's reply is masterful. He has said all along that he had been sent in advance of God's anointed one (3:28). Since the "all" who are flocking to Jesus have "been given him from heaven" (3:27), this would mean that "all" the world has been given to him. Hearing this is like the best man hearing the bridegroom's shout at the consummation of his marriage, says John. It is exactly what he has been waiting for. Christ is the groom, and "all" the world is his bride: "He who has the bride is the bridegroom; but the friend of the bridegroom, who stands and hears him, rejoices greatly because of the bridegroom's voice. And so this joy of mine has been made full. He must increase, but I must decrease" (3:29-30). John understands what God is doing and rejoices. He had said that God was about to accomplish a great work through Jesus, and this confirms it. He glorifies God by making Jesus large and himself small. Like Vaughan's Nicodemus, he rejoices at finding himself dim or invisible in the powerful, world-changing light of Christ.

A number of commentators suggest that, as with 3:16-21, in verses 31-36 we again hear the narrator commenting on these remarks. If so, John is agreeing with the Baptist that Jesus "comes from above" and is "above all" (3:31). The Father has given the world to Jesus as his bride, lavishing his attention on it: "For He whom God has sent speaks the words of God; for He gives the Spirit without measure. The Father loves the Son, and has given all things into His hand" (3:34-35). Jesus has spoken to the world God's intention to save it, pouring out the very life of his "Spirit" in each of the scenes we have examined.[22] But that word and life need to be received, and with that thought it becomes clear that the narrator is addressing the reader. He says, of Jesus, "What He has seen and heard, of that He bears witness; and no man receives His witness. He who has received His witness has set his seal to this, that God is true" (3:32-33). John the Baptist set his seal to the fact that what Jesus said about God was true, and now so does the narrator. To receive and rejoice in these words is to believe and be filled with a life "from above." In much the same terms he used in his comments at 3:16, the narrator turns to the reader and speaks directly to us. You have seen these pictures, he says. "He who believes in the Son has eternal life; but he who does not obey the Son shall not see life, but the wrath of God abides on him" (3:36). To rejoice with John the Baptist is to see and receive the Son as the bridegroom, as life itself. It is to enter the kingdom of God.

Samaritan Woman, 4:4-42

After this, Jesus and his disciples begin to move again, passing through Samaria on the way to Galilee, and as they do so, Jesus encounters a Samaritan woman who has come to fill a water pot during the heat of the day. This is another well-known story. Jesus draws her into conversation, offering the most fully developed account we have seen yet of the new life that has come into the world, inviting her to drink deeply of the "living water" of God's presence. What we see here, as Jesus opens himself up to her and something inside begins to stir, is what belief looks like. To this point, John has told us about belief—that the disciples believed after seeing the water transformed into wine; or that, in time, they believed his words about the temple. Now, he allows us to come alongside as the woman works out what Jesus is saying to her and receives it. Much as we have done with the poets we have examined, we watch the way she takes his words in—which is to say, we watch her drink.

Passing through Samaria, Jesus and the disciples come to Jacob's well. It is noon ("about the sixth hour") and Jesus rests at the well while his disciples go into the town of Sychar to buy food. A Samaritan woman comes out to draw water. She is alone and is surprised when he speaks to her, saying, "Give Me a drink" (4:7). She understands how strange this is, a Jewish man ignoring the gulf between them and reaching out to her in a way that exposes both vulnerability and need. In a sense, Jesus is reenacting the incarnation, taking on flesh and its insistent demands in order to draw her near. Acutely aware of the step he has just taken, her first response is to draw attention to it: "How is it that You, being a Jew, ask me for a drink since I am a Samaritan woman?" (4:9). She does not draw away, however, and seeing this, Jesus offers her more. He says, "If you knew the gift of God and who it is who says to you, 'Give Me a drink,' you would have asked Him, and He would have given you living water" (4:10). If you knew who I was, you would have asked *me* for a drink, giving her something to focus on—"living water," some sort of gift from God. She does not understand, but the reader does, having seen versions of this gift already.

Living water is running water, drawn from a moving source. She senses that he is talking about something more than the water of the well, however, and begins, with his encouragement, to explore that thought: "Sir, you have nothing to draw with and the well is deep; where then do You get that living water?" (4:11). If not this well, where else would he draw from? Is there another well? A greater one? "You are not greater than our father Jacob, are You, who gave us the well, and drank of it himself, and his sons, and his cattle?" There is some skepticism in her tone, I think, but she is taking him seriously, trying to work out what he means. So Jesus unfolds even more. You are right, he says. I *am* talking about something more than this well and this water, and I *am* claiming to be greater than Jacob: "Everyone who drinks of this water shall thirst again; but whoever drinks of the water that I shall give him shall never thirst; but the water that I shall give him shall become in him a well of water springing up to eternal life" (4:13, 14). A good teacher, he opens up the metaphor for her: living water—life itself bubbling up from deep inside.

Having seen versions of this in the previous chapters, the reader understands that he is offering her God's presence, welling up inside like a spring. The reader perhaps even recognizes that Jesus has drawn the image from Jeremiah 2:13, where God describes himself as "the fountain of living waters," forsaken by his people: "For My people have committed two evils: / They have forsaken Me, the fountain of living waters, / To hew for themselves cisterns, / Broken cisterns / That can hold no water." This is more than the woman can yet take in, but, standing in the presence of Jesus, she senses that something she had once forsaken has now been returned to her. Lifting her eyes from the broken cisterns of her life, she responds with the only words she trusts, the language of physical things: "Sir, give me this water, so I will not be thirsty, nor come all the way here to draw" (4:15).

And now something interesting happens. Jesus steps into her framing of the encounter—we are talking about physical things, safe to say yes to—and changes the subject. "Go, call your husband," he says. "I have no husband," she replies. And then, utterly at ease in her presence, he replies, "You have well said, 'I have no husband'; for you have had five husbands, and the one you have now is not your husband; this you have said truly'" (4:17-18). Think how this must strike her. Not only does he know her checkered past, he has known it all along. When he first spoke to her, he knew it, and he knows it now. Understanding everything about her, he nevertheless drew near to her, responding in a way that gave her the very thing she most desired—that sense that someone could look at her and know her and love her; that she might no longer be seen as defiled.

She takes this in but then abruptly shifts the conversation away from the connection being established between them: "Sir, I perceive that You are a prophet. Our fathers worshipped in this mountain, and you people say that in Jerusalem is the place where men ought to worship" (4:19-20). But perhaps she is doing more than steering the conversation away from her sexual history. Perhaps she is really asking where God dwells and where he could be worshipped. What would have triggered that question, at this moment? Not the difference between Jewish and Samaritan views on worship—that would have been an assumed fact throughout their conversation; there is no reason for it to suddenly arise now. No, what caused her to ask about worship was Jesus standing before her, his presence stirring in her the desire to come near to God, to drink him in and worship. In acting so improbably—knowing her and not turning away—Jesus has displayed, in her presence, God's deepest nature, a glory "full of grace and truth" (1:14). Being in the presence of that glory, she wants to worship. Walking with her through the process, we begin to understand how the invisible wind of the Spirit does its work.

Jesus responds to her question about worship by pushing her to make yet another leap. Just as he has led her from water to living water, now he takes her from worship to "true worship":

> Woman, believe Me, an hour is coming when neither in this mountain, nor in Jerusalem, shall you worship the Father. You worship that which you do not know; we worship that which we know, for salvation is from the Jews.

But an hour is coming, and now is, when true worshippers shall worship
the Father in spirit and truth; for such people the Father seeks to be His
worshippers. God is spirit, and those who worship Him must worship in
spirit and truth. (4:21-24)

You were an outsider, he begins. You worshipped what you did not know. But
now that does not matter. What matters is that an hour is coming in which
all outsiders will be able to worship in "spirit and truth." God's Spirit welling
up inside her has made her alive to the things of the God. She is responding,
"in spirit," to the fullness of his glory—his "truth." This is the worship God
desires, Christ says—drinking in the living water of his presence.

What does she make of this? She uses the term *Messiah* to acknowledge the authority of his words: "When that One comes, He will declare all
things to us" (4:25). And Jesus responds in just the way she had hoped: "I
who speak to you am He" (4:26). (Literally, "I who speak to you am," a first
brushing contact with Jesus' eventual identification of himself as "I am,"
God himself.)[23] I am the Messiah—the one who approached you first, speaking to you as if you mattered, giving myself to you while knowing exactly
who you were. Take your place in the new kingdom, he says. Through me,
the living water of God's presence will well up inside of you, changing you
into someone free to worship "in spirit and in truth."

Interestingly, the disciples sweep back into view at this point and obscure
a verbal declaration of belief on the woman's part. This would seem to be
no accident. Much as when the disciples encountered Jesus in chapter 1 or
when Nicodemus spoke with him in the previous chapter, we find a screen
drawn and are forced to imagine for ourselves the way her heart responds.
And surely it does respond, for, just as we have been able to experience the
unfolding of belief in the woman's pausing and leaping, testing and pulling back, we see now the effect on her of the presence of Jesus. We see a
new woman, driven by the invisible wind of his love for her. She abandons
her water pot and returns to the city, an inner confidence that she is both
known and loved welling up inside of her. Now, instead of pulling away from
people because of her history and her anticipation of how they must view her,
she approaches them with the fact that Jesus told her "all the things that
[she had] done" (4:29). She is no longer ashamed of those "things." Jesus has
called them to the surface and then transformed them into testimony—glis-
tening markers of how much she is loved. Come and see, she says, echoing
earlier words in the Gospel, "This is not the Christ, is it?" Her eyes are alive
to his glory, a response drawn out of her "from above"—from the one who
"descended" to speak with her. And the people of the city come, hearing his

words themselves, many of them believing, feeling their own needs welling up and their own broken selves made whole. What they drink in is the good news of life coming not just to Jerusalem but to all the "world" (3:16). "It is no longer because of what you said that we believe," they tell her, "for we have heard for ourselves and know that this One is indeed the Savior of the world" (4:42).

And what about the disciples? As we watch them struggle to catch up we are reminded how demanding this new way of understanding God actually is. They return, marvel that Jesus is talking to a woman, but say nothing. Instead, they turn to the physical task at hand and say, "Rabbi, eat." And as is his way, Jesus takes the term "eat" and turns it into another figure of speech. Do not just think of food, he says, think of real food: "I have food that you do not know about." Not food he has kept for himself to eat in secret: "My food is to do the will of Him who sent Me, and to accomplish His work" (4:32, 34). And what does that mean? He answers their unspoken question—again, as is his way—by bringing the metaphor to life. You know what a harvest is, he says. Well, think about a real harvest. Look out on those spring fields: "Do you not say, 'There are yet four months, and then comes the harvest?' Behold, I say to you, lift up your eyes, and look on the fields, that they are white for harvest"? (4:35) They look up, and they are. As with the temple and the true temple, or wine and true wine, he re-directs their eyes to something unseen but actually there—in this case, the springtime fields full of people streaming out from the city, eager to hear and be gathered in: the true harvest. As the metaphor is unfolded, one realizes it is no metaphor at all. As with all the metaphors we have traced, it is a vision of a new world, enacted and made flesh in him.

Robert Frost, "Directive"

Jesus draws the Samaritan woman toward the living water by letting her experience her own neediness, a deep desire to be known and loved, and then, in the way he responds to her, offering her just what she is thirsty for. In his late poem "Directive," published in 1947, Robert Frost considers this invitation to drink deeply of the living water and responds, "Yes, I think I understand this. It's what poetry says as well—come, lose yourself, drink." In describing the journey poems offer to take us on, Frost also works out what the Gospel has in mind. He offers another window on belief:

> Back out of all this now too much for us,
> Back in a time made simple by the loss

Of detail, burned, dissolved, and broken off
Like graveyard marble sculpture in the weather,
There is a house that is no more a house
Upon a farm that is no more a farm
And in a town that is no more a town.
The road there, if you'll let a guide direct you
Who only has at heart your getting lost,
May seem as if it should have been a quarry—
Great monolithic knees the former town
Long since gave up pretense of keeping covered.
And there's a story in a book about it:
Besides the wear of iron wagon wheels
The ledges show lines ruled southeast northwest,
The chisel work of an enormous Glacier
That braced his feet against the Arctic Pole.
You must not mind a certain coolness from him
Still said to haunt this side of Panther Mountain.
Nor need you mind the serial ordeal
Of being watched from forty cellar holes
As if by eye pairs out of forty firkins.
As for the woods' excitement over you
That sends light rustle rushes to their leaves,
Charge that to upstart inexperience.
Where were they all not twenty years ago?
They think too much of having shaded out
A few old pecker-fretted apple trees.
Make yourself up a cheering song of how
Someone's road home from work this once was,
Who may be just ahead of you on foot
Or creaking with a buggy load of grain.
The height of the adventure is the height
Of country where two village cultures faded
Into each other. Both of them are lost.
And if you're lost enough to find yourself
By now, pull in the ladder road behind you
And put up a sign CLOSED to all but me.
Then make yourself at home. The only field
Now left's no bigger than a harness gall.
First there's the children's house of make believe,
Some shattered dishes underneath a pine,
The playthings in the playhouse of the children.
Weep for what little things could make them glad.
Then for the house that is no more a house,

But only a belilaced cellar hole,
Now slowly closing like a dent in dough.
This was no playhouse but a house in earnest.
Your destination and your destiny's
A brook that was the water of the house,
Cold as a spring as yet so near its source,
Too lofty and original to rage.
(We know the valley streams that when aroused
Will leave their tatters hung on barb and thorn.)
I have kept hidden in the instep arch
Of an old cedar at the waterside
A broken drinking goblet like the Grail
Under a spell so the wrong ones can't find it,
So can't get saved, as Saint Mark says they mustn't.
(I stole the goblet from the children's playhouse.)
Here are your waters and your watering place.
Drink and be whole again beyond confusion.[24]

In "The Figure a Poem Makes," Frost describes a poem's movement as a kind of a journey: "It begins in delight, it inclines to the impulse, it assumes direction with the first line laid down, it runs a course of lucky events, and ends in a clarification of life—not necessarily a great clarification, such as sects and cults are founded on, but a momentary stay against confusion."[25] The poem's journey, and the momentary stay it arrives at, takes place, for Frost, against a dark background in which nothing stays whole for long. As he once put it in a letter, "The background is hugeness and confusion shading away from where we stand into black and utter chaos; and against the background any small man-made figure of order and concentration. What pleasanter than this should be so?"[26] It is not pleasant at all, of course, as anyone knows who has seen a home, an idea, or a political ideal tatter and dissolve, but the half-smile tone of voice able to say such a thing is important to Frost. In speaking this way, he calls attention to himself making the best of the "momentary stay against confusion" he has arrived at. As Frost puts it in another essay, such a tone of voice is "at home in . . . metaphor" and its momentary take on things. It is fully aware that the "small man-made figure" it has constructed is a fragile thing. But it is "safe" because it knows "how far you may expect to ride it and when it may break down with you."[27]

It is interesting, then, that in "Directive," Frost uses John's image of "living water" (4:10) to describe the momentary stay against confusion that a poem leads its readers toward. "Here are your waters and your watering place," he concludes: "Drink and be whole again beyond confusion."

By pointing to the Gospel and Christ's claim to satisfy our longings to be known and loved and made whole, Frost asks us to think of poetry as engaging the same desires, but on a human and more fleeting level. Recognizing that John's "living water" flows underneath the poem's playful tone lets us appreciate just how seriously Frost means what he says about his art, but it also lets us hear the playful, inner boldness that Jesus is calling out of those considering his claims.

Frost's poem is a "Directive" in the sense that a guide speaks to us and leads us on the path that most poems follow—through the loss of one way of making sense of the world and into the presence of a new one. This, of course, is also the path of the Gospel. The words of "Directive" are those that most poems whisper, underneath their immediate details: come in, get lost, find yourself anew, drink and be whole. The speaker begins by inviting us to follow him "Back out of all this now too much for us"—back out of a world we can no longer handle, where our old ways of coping have broken down. Jesus' tone of voice said much the same thing to the Samaritan woman. Frost's speaker urges us to follow him to back "in . . . time" to a place where a house and a farm and a town once stood but now no longer do. They have crumbled and decayed and collapsed. People have moved out, farms have been abandoned, trees have begun taking over the fields again. Back there, at that "house that is no more a house / Upon a farm that is no more a farm," all is "made simple by the loss / Of detail." Frost gives us enough of the literal world to imagine this house and the long road back into the country we must take to reach its ruins, but his point is a larger and more metaphoric one: that this is where all poems would take us—through the remains of the old, into the possibility of something new.

The poem gives us an imagined New England. Urging us forward on our journey back, our guide directs us up a road passing between great outcroppings of rock: "monolithic knees the former town / Long since gave up pretense of keeping covered." We follow a trail worn by "iron wagon wheels," and we pass ledges "ruled" with lines chiseled long ago by "an enormous Glacier" whose "coolness [is] . . . / Still said to haunt this side of Panther Mountain." What our guide is doing, he says, is "getting [us] lost." He carries us along, as all poems do, by giving us enough details to draw us into the drama with him. Soon, to confirm that we have followed him into this lost world, he offers us imaginative work to do. Do not "mind the serial ordeal" of being watched by what seem to be forty sets of eyes peering out at you, one after another, from the "cellar holes" of forty abandoned houses, he says. And we count them out as we pass them by, crumbled house after crumbled house. Do not think twice about "the woods' excitement over you" when a "light rustle rushes to their leaves" as you pass by. That is nothing. It is merely "upstart experience." Those second-growth trees, filling in abandoned fields, are too full of themselves. They think they are something, but all they have done is "shaded out / A few old pecker-fretted apples trees" that no one now lives to tend. These last images—the trees and the eyes—are comic, of course, but what the speaker is doing is making us engage the images along with him, drawing us deeper and deeper into this world where all has been worn away and lost. This is just what we have seen Jesus do with images he uses to describe himself.

As we near the end of the journey, the work the poem asks us to do becomes more and more explicit. "Make yourself up a song" about this road that someone once took home from work, our guide says. Climb the height where two "village cultures" once met and joined each other. Realize that "Both of them are lost." And then, if you are "lost enough to find yourself," pull the road up "behind you / And put up a sign CLOSED to all but me." "Make yourself at home" in this place where only traces remain of a life that is now lost, our guide says, his words a version of Frost's remark that poetry teaches us (or guides us) to be "at home in metaphor"—at home in its fragile, momentary stays against confusion. As many commentators have noted, Frost is adapting biblical language in this notion of being lost enough to find yourself. Mark 8:35 is often mentioned: "For whoever wishes to save his life shall lose it; but whoever loses his life for My sake and the gospel's shall save it." We also find similar language in John 12:25: "He who loves his life loses it; and he who hates his life in this world shall keep it to life eternal." Just as in the Gospels one is called to turn from a life that is no life at all ("lose" it in Mark, "hate" it in John) and receive a new one offered as a gift, so, in poetry, one must experience the loss of old ways of seeing and organizing the world in order to discover, in their loss, a new way to move forward. The Samaritan woman takes just this journey as Jesus leads her deeper and deeper into herself. The difference, of course, and Frost calls attention to this, is that poetry's new world, its deep spring of living water, is a made thing, something temporary. But the road there follows a Gospel trajectory.

Having led us to this place where field and farm have been absorbed, Frost's speaker points out a child's playhouse and shattered playthings, and then the "belilaced cellar hole" where the house itself once stood. "Make yourself at home" in their loss, he says. His closing words are much celebrated and much debated:

Your destination and your destiny's
A brook that was the water of the house,

Cold as a spring as yet so near its source,
Too lofty and original to rage.
(We know the valley streams that when aroused
Will leave their tatters hung on barb and thorn.)
I have kept hidden in the instep arch
Of an old cedar at the waterside
A broken drinking goblet like the Grail
Under a spell so the wrong ones can't find it,
So can't get saved, as Saint Mark says they mustn't.
(I stole the goblet from the children's playhouse.)
Here are your waters and your watering place.
Drink and be whole again beyond confusion.

What he has led us to—what all poems desire to lead us to, he suggests—is
the brook that was once the water of the house. The brook, being "near its
source," is "Too lofty and original to rage." We are high up on the mountain,
and the spring that the brook flows from, its origin, is nearby. This close to its
source, the brook is too small to threaten its banks. But the narrator means
more than this, of course. He has led us to a secular version of John's "living
water," bubbling up from our "source" and "origins." Drinking it will make
us momentarily "whole again beyond [the] confusion" of that world "now
too much for us" with which we began. To reach it, we have had to make our
selves at home in the fragility and limits of our old ways of thinking, for it is
only in becoming "lost" to their claims that we can open ourselves to a new
way of ordering the world.

Poetry's insight, its living water, is not available to everyone. As with
the Samaritan woman, it is reserved for those whose eyes have been opened.
Frost is quite explicit about this, linking the way one comes to understand the
landscape a poem guides its readers through to the way one comes to understand Jesus' parables. As Jesus says in Mark 4, he speaks in parables so that
those who are "outside" the kingdom (Mark 4:11) and have not yet grappled
with the failure of their own claims to be alive will find his words resistant to
sense. Poetry works in much the same way. The playhouse "goblet" set aside
for us to drink from is hidden in the arch of a cedar, "Under a spell so the
wrong ones can't find it." Only those who know what it is like to be needy
and thirsty can find their way to the inner landscape it offers to guide us
through, and only those able to do what it calls us to there can lose ourselves
deeply enough to draw near and taste its waters. Belief works in the same way.
What Frost found in the account of the Samaritan woman was an image for
the momentary wholeness poems attempt to lead us toward and a description
of the way in which one is prepared and made ready to receive it. What he

responds back with is his own account of how personal and uncertain—how playful and even dreamlike—such a movement inevitably must be. In doing so, he has allowed us to feel the inner texture of belief, making visible a play of mind and heart normally walled off as "CLOSED to all but me."

Return to Cana, 4:43-54

We end the Cana to Cana arc with an elegant coda, returning to the place where we saw the first "sign." In each scene along the way, Jesus has described himself and called for those around to believe what he has said through the images of new wine, new temple, and new heart—that through him, God is offering the "living water" of his presence. In this final scene, as Jesus restores a dying child, we are offered a "second sign" (4:54) that summarizes the point of the entire sequence: that in believing in Jesus one is brought from death to life. And what is that life? It is knowing God, drinking him in, gazing at his glory, worshipping in his presence.

This story is introduced with a note of tension. Jesus comes to Galilee but, as the narrator notes, unlike in Samaria, in both Galilee and Judea he is less readily received: "Jesus himself testified that a prophet has no honor in his own country" (4:44). He is received in Galilee, but only because of the miracles he has performed. The story begins with an official from Capernaum coming to Cana in order to seek Jesus out, having heard of his return. His son is sick and he is desperate. He asks Jesus to "come down and heal his son; for he was at the point of death" (4:47). Jesus is quite abrupt with him, charging both the man and those who gather around them with only being interested in displays of power. They are focused on healing, not belief, having noticed the signs but not what the signs have been pointing to. Like all of us, they have their sick and dying, and what they think about is relief: "Unless you people see signs and wonders, you simply will not believe" (4:48).

It might seem as if Jesus has dismissed the man, but the man shakes this off, so focused is he on his need: "Sir, come down before my child dies" (4:49). So Jesus enters the situation, not to reward the man for persistence but to make it possible for him, and the reader, to see what is actually at stake. He says, "Go your way, your son lives," and the narrator remarks, "The man believed the word that Jesus spoke to him, and he started off" (4:50). Returning home without Jesus at his side means that the man has trusted him, believing that he has the power to heal his son, even without being physically present.

As the official goes down to Capernaum, he meets his slaves who have come to tell him that his son lives, and something important happens. Instead of simply celebrating and hurrying home, the official asks when his son began to get better. He is interested in Jesus, not simply in his son. He is curious about Jesus himself, not simply his ability to give him what he desperately needs. When he is told that his son got better at the very hour Jesus declared "Your son lives," the man believes in Jesus himself, not just in his power to change things: "he himself believed, and his whole household" (4:53). With the entire Cana to Cana sequence in mind, we might say that he understood that he himself was dying, not just his son. And he must have communicated this to his entire household, for they all turn to Jesus for life. Like the father pausing on the road to inquire at what hour his son was saved, their eyes are drawn up from the burden of their physical needs toward something extraordinary—life itself reaching down toward them.

4

BLINDED (JOHN 5:1–10:42)

In chapters 2–4 of the Gospel, the Cana to Cana arc, Jesus has pictured the life he is offering the world in a number of striking ways, each linked to the other. It is abundant (the wedding wine) because it is lived out in God's presence (the restored temple), that presence embraced by a newly responsive heart (born from above) or welling up inside (living water). All people need to do is to believe that this is so and receive the gift. There is little opposition in these chapters, although his words are often not fully understood. Instead, we focus on what characters do to take these words in, how they wrestle with them. The poets we have examined—coming at night, getting lost enough to be found, being driven by the Spirit's wind—unfold this journey toward belief in strikingly different ways.

In chapters 5–10, however, something quite different occurs. Jesus continues to describe himself and the life he offers, illustrating his claims with miraculous signs, but now, as he does so, people pull back and resist, unable to see, refusing to hear. Jesus does not avoid this opposition, nor does he, for the most part, defend himself. Instead, he focuses on their resistance, treating opposition as itself a sign, as much a source of insight as any of his miracles. Five confrontations dominate these chapters. In each of them, Jesus describes himself and calls people to believe—to rest in him, take him in, see God at work; to recognize God's voice in him. And in each encounter, opposition arises, often from the religious establishment but sometimes from within the ranks of his followers. Although the arguments are about different issues, Jesus consistently makes a single point—that people cannot make out what he is saying because they do not know God. Because they do not trust God or rely on him or have a place in their lives for him, when he speaks, they cannot take in his words. Jesus is a foreign language to them, utterly unreadable as long as they are bound to their flesh-centered ways of making sense of things and feeling alive. Jesus focuses on this point because it is precisely the problem he has come to address. They are dead to the things of God. To those who understand the dilemma they are caught in, Jesus quietly replies, "Come to me—come and live, rest and see."

Healing on the Sabbath, 5:1-47

This sequence begins with Jesus and his disciples back in Jerusalem for an unnamed feast. At the pool of Bethesda, where a great crowd of the "sick, blind, lame, and withered" wait for a cure, Jesus approaches a man, sick for thirty-eight years and unable to walk, and asks him, "Do you wish to get well?" (5:6) or, as it could also be translated, "Do you wish to be whole?" The man's reply is revealing. He complains that, because he cannot walk, he cannot get to the healing waters of the pool fast enough: someone always steps in before him. He offers an excuse, having understood the question as an implied accusation, along the lines of "Have you really tried?" to which he essentially replies, "You don't know how hard I have tried." But Jesus is not making an accusation, and he is not interested in the man's excuses. He is interested in making the man whole, so he overrides his faulty thinking and says, "Arise, take up your pallet and walk" (5:8). And the man does. He hears what Jesus says and responds, walking away whole and transformed—a living picture of the life Jesus has come to offer.

John does not seem concerned with what the man believed at the moment he arose. Instead, he immediately turns to the conflict arising out of the event. "Now it was the Sabbath on that day," he begins, an edge to his voice. When the Jewish leaders see the man carrying his pallet, they stop him and confront him with having broken the Sabbath by "working." The man offers another excuse: "He who made me well was the one who said to me, 'Take up your pallet and walk'" (5:11). Tucked into his excuse is the fact that a miracle has occurred, but the leaders are not interested in that. "Who is the man" who told you to do such a thing? they ask. Standards have been broken, and they intend to get at the one responsible. They are part of the same world as the man who cannot walk—a world of requirements not to be ignored. The man has been crushed by that world, and they have been elevated by it, but it is the same world. The man replies that he cannot tell them who told him to pick up his pallet because he does not know. (Afterward, Jesus finds him and tells him to sin no more, making the point that he is in the grips of a much deeper problem, yet to be dealt with, a problem only pictured by his physical brokenness.) Still working the angles, the man passes on Jesus' name to the authorities and drops out of the story.

With that, a chess match begins between Jesus and the authorities, one that will continue for many chapters. It gets very serious very quickly, so much so that within a few verses we learn that the authorities are seeking to kill him (5:18). Why is that? It has to do with the Sabbath, and we immediately find ourselves in the middle of a scene in which the authorities confront Jesus—the word is actually "persecute"—for healing on the Sabbath. Their focus has shifted from the man carrying a pallet to Jesus healing, which they see as an even greater breach of Sabbath rules, despite its miraculous nature. What right did he have to do such a thing? Jesus responds by claiming to be working alongside his Father: "My Father is working until now, and I Myself am working" (5:17). The authorities are enraged, "because He not only was breaking the Sabbath, but also was calling God His own Father, making Himself equal with God" (5:18). As a number of writers have pointed out, the focus of their rage seems to be on "making himself."[1] He seems to be attempting to make himself God's equal. That must be a lie, they say. By no amount of effort could a man make himself God's equal.

We need to think for a moment about the issue of the Sabbath, for it is no accident that Jesus healed the man on that day. The Sabbath is the Jewish day of rest, established in the Ten Commandments to remember God's creation of the heavens and earth and the way he rested on the seventh day and looked back over his completed work (Exod 20:8-11). The Sabbath is also linked with the day God brought Israel out of slavery in Egypt, redeeming it from oppression (Deut 5:14-15). In both cases, resting on the Sabbath is a declaration that God has done the true work of creating the world and redeeming his people. Israel is to rest in the fact that God is at work on her behalf. Much as he used the temple to point to himself as the true temple, then, Jesus is using the Sabbath to point to himself as Israel's true rest. By making the man whole on the Sabbath, Jesus is looking ahead to his re-creation and redemption of the world. He is calling those who hear him to rest in his power to accomplish such a task—to believe he can make them whole. And that, of course, is what the authorities cannot accept—Jesus claiming to do work that only God could do.

I am indeed making that claim, Jesus says, focusing on the heart of their objection. He is following his Father's lead: "Truly, truly, I say to you, the Son can do nothing of Himself, unless it is something He sees the Father doing" (5:19). And what is that work? Bringing the dead to life:

> For just as the Father raises the dead and gives them life, even so the Son also gives life to whom He wishes. For not even the Father judges anyone, but He has given all judgment to the Son, in order that all may honor the Son, even as they honor the Father. He who does not honor the Son does not honor the Father who sent Him. Truly, truly I say to you, he who hears My word and believes Him who sent Me, has eternal life, and does not come into judgment, but has passed out of death into life. (5:21-24)

God has sent the Son, Jesus says, so that those who believe in him would not "come into judgment" and be separated from God forever, but would be spared that fate—passing "out of death into life." To "hear" that offer, to rest in it and believe it, is to "honor" both the Son and the Father whose work he is doing. It is to honor the Sabbath and keep it holy.

He is doing that work right now, Jesus continues: "Truly, truly, I say to you, an hour is coming and now is, when the dead shall hear the voice of the Son of God; and those who hear shall live" (5:25). By "the dead," Jesus means the spiritually dead, those who are alive "now" at this "hour" but have no ability to respond to God on their own. Some of them will "hear" his voice and draw near—the Samaritan woman is a good example. And some will not "hear" his voice—making the "judgment," as we saw in 3:19, that they have no need of such an offer. The authorities standing before him are the obvious examples. You can almost sense them stirring, incredulous. And then Jesus steps it up a notch. At the end of time, at "an hour [which] is coming" (5:28), everyone, living and dead, will hear his voice, and what will be made clear then is whose deeds were "wrought in God" (3:21) and whose were wrought in "darkness" (3:19): "all who are in the tombs shall hear His voice, and shall come forth; those who did the good deeds to a resurrection of life, and those who committed the evil deeds to a resurrection of judgment" (5:28-29). Jesus is about to create a world in which all who are estranged might draw near to God and be made whole, resting in him, but not everyone sees himself as estranged. It is as if Jesus says, "Do you wish to get well?" and none of the leaders realize that he is talking to them.

Why can they not hear? Jesus lists the evidence they seem to be willfully ignoring: his own words (5:31), the testimony of John the Baptist (5:33-35), the miraculous signs (5:36), and his Father's words in Scripture (5:37-39). This last failure seems particularly striking: "You search the Scriptures, because you think that in them you have eternal life; and it is these that bear witness of Me; and you are unwilling to come to Me, that you may have life." Why? His answer is very simple: "you do not have the love of God in yourselves" (5:42). They cannot make sense of Jesus because they do not love God. Because they have no real feel for life in his presence, they have no real feel for its absence. No one needs to drag them down to the pool when the water is stirred up, they think. They are already whole. No one needs to remake the world, as if from scratch: "How can you believe, when you receive glory from one another, and you do not seek the glory that is from the one and only God?" (5:44). As long as glory, or life, can be found in others, there is no reason to seek it in God, and certainly no need to accept it as a gift. For all their words otherwise, their failure to understand the Sabbath makes it plain that they do not understand God. They cannot make sense of the thought that a life exists that can only be had as a gift. That failure to comprehend is the very deadness Jesus seeks to wake them from.

Wendell Berry, "The Sabbath Poems 1979, II"

In 1979, Wendell Berry began a series of poems composed on the Sabbath or on Sabbath-like moments, "in silence, in solitude, mainly out of doors," "when heart and mind are open and aware."[2] He eventually collected 145 of these poems in *A Timbered Choir: The Sabbath Poems 1979–1997*. The second poem of the first series puts into play a number of the crucial ideas Berry would return to over the course of two decades and powerfully engages Jesus' account of himself as God's Sabbath rest. If those Jesus spoke to could not understand him because they could not understand the Sabbath and what it said about God, Berry unfolds the other side of the story—allowing the Sabbath to lead him back to life rather than away from it:

> Another Sunday morning comes
> And I resume the standing Sabbath
> Of the woods, where the finest blooms
> Of time return, and where no path
>
> Is worn but wears its makers out
> At last, and disappears in leaves
> Of fallen seasons. The tracked rut
> Fills and levels; here nothing grieves
>
> In the risen season. Past life
> Lives in the living. Resurrection
> Is in the way each maple leaf
> Commemorates its kind, by connection
>
> Outreaching understanding. What rises
> Rises into comprehension
> And beyond. Even falling raises
> In praise of light. What is begun

Is unfinished. And so the mind
That comes to rest among the bluebells
Comes to rest in motion, refined
By alteration. The bud swells,

Opens, makes seed, falls, is well,
Being becoming what it is:
Miracle and parable
Exceeding thought, because it is

Immeasurable; the understander
Encloses understanding, thus
Darkens the light. We can stand under
No ray that is not dimmed by us.

The mind that comes to rest is tended
In ways that it cannot intend:
Is borne, preserved, and comprehended
By what it cannot comprehend.

Your Sabbath, Lord, thus keeps us by
Your will, not ours. And it is fit
Our only choice should be to die
Into that rest, or out of it.[3]

The poem begins with a bit of wit about the poet celebrating the Sabbath not in church but in the woods. He "resume[s] the standing Sabbath / Of the woods," where not the faithful but "the finest blooms / Of time return" and where "path[s]" are "worn" rather than one's Sunday best. It is a "standing Sabbath" because, as the poet walks and pauses, he silently takes his place in the company of the standing trees. It is a standing Sabbath as well because it is a permanent one, its offer of rest available each time the poet enters the woods.

Berry's reference to the returning "blooms of time" in the first stanza leads him to describe the woods, in the next several stanzas, as a place where time continually rolls on. Paths are "worn" that, in time, "wear [their] makers out," and when their makers disappear, the paths do as well, "in leaves / Of fallen seasons," their ruts "fill[ing] and level[ing]" again. But this is not an end; what was past "Lives [again] in the living" as all things rise and fall and rot and rise again. The "resurrection" celebrated in the woods is visible in the way "each maple leaf / Commemorates its kind," repeating a pattern by means of a "connection" that "Outreach[es] understanding." Turning to the woods, Berry finds a world complete without him, whole without any intervention on his part.

With the mention of "understanding" in the fourth stanza, a new train of thought begins, and the conflict between Jesus and those who would control the Sabbath begins to come into play. The poet works his way to this idea gradually. "What rises," he says, "Rises into comprehension / And beyond." He is thinking of the way leaves, trees, and flowering things reach up and comprehend or take in the sunlight, but then he acknowledges that that they are doing more than that, something "beyond" comprehension. Perhaps we could call that something more "praise," he continues: "Even falling raises / In praise of light." Even the falling leaves of the forest, opening up spaces for the eye, seem to be raising a chorus in praise of the light.

In this blooming, dying world, where "What is begun" is always "unfinished," the Sabbath mind, as it "comes to rest among the bluebells / Comes to rest in motion." So the poet writes in the fifth stanza. Pausing, he finds himself called to take his rest in a world continually "swell[ing]" and "fall[ing]." All around him, "Being" is taking on shape and "becoming what it is." Such a world is a "Miracle and parable / exceeding thought." As with the parables of Jesus, it can be entered and engaged with, but it is, in its deepest rhythms, "Immeasurable." To rest in such a power would be to love it rather than seek to control it, precisely the idea the authorities in John stumbled over. Berry's celebration of this "miracle . . . exceeding thought" lets us hear what was at stake in Jesus' Sabbath healing. "My Father is working until now, and I am working" (5:17), he said. Can you rest in that? Are you willing to embrace its deep satisfactions?

What is it that cannot "come to rest in motion," in such a world? It is the "understander" in us, Berry writes in the seventh stanza, that which seeks to "enclose" and control those things that, as the upraised trees demonstrate, are more properly greeted with praise. Understanding does not lift itself up toward the light; it "Darkens" it, boxing it in.[4] Berry is playing with the word *understanding* here: if in understanding we "stand under" the light, what we are actually doing is casting our own long shadow over everything, blocking the light. There is "No ray that is not dimmed by us." So too with the Jewish leaders and the Sabbath. In trying to "enclose" and control what they should have "loved," they were dimming the light suddenly pouring down on them in Jesus. They loved "understanding" more than they loved God.

But look at what they were missing, writes Berry in the last two stanzas. What happens if we trade understanding for rest? Rather than losing the world in our rush to figure things out and "receive glory from one another" (5:44), we gain it back, as a gift: "The mind that comes to rest is tended / In ways that it cannot intend," "comprehended / By what it cannot comprehend." "Coming to rest in [a] motion" out of our control, we find ourselves at home in a fullness not created by human hands, one that bears and preserves and comprehends us more fully than we can ourselves.

To welcome the Sabbath, then, is to rest in the thought that we do not bear the responsibility of saving ourselves; it is to see something true about our place in the world. To not welcome the day but rather to control it and wield it as a club, is to darken and obscure that same world. What Berry has found on his Sabbath walk is the same home in the swelling and rising world that Jesus had offered on that earlier Sabbath in Jerusalem. To not be able to rest is to not be able to accept God's love; it is to find in the words of Jesus not an invitation but threats and confusion:

> Your Sabbath, Lord, thus keeps us by
> Your will, not ours. And it is fit
> Our only choice should be to die
> Into that rest, or out of it.

"Your will," he says to God, not our own; what sustains us is a moving, immeasurable will that, though it cannot be contained or mastered, opens itself on a Sunday morning and says "Come, and be at peace." Much depends on understanding what is being offered. Just as Jesus said to those he spoke with, "Our only choice," the only "judgment" we make, is whether we would "die / Into that rest"—into its rhythms, its promises of life and continuity—"or out of it," alone. In unfolding that invitation, Berry's poem makes very clear the dramatic shift in thinking Jesus was calling for in healing on the Sabbath. As Berry puts it in another poem in this series, what Jesus is offering is nothing less than an eternal rest "Bewildered in our timely dwelling place, / Where we arrive by work, we stay by grace."[5]

Bread of Life (I), 6:1-40

Some amount of time passes and we find ourselves outside of Jerusalem, on the "other side" of the Sea of Galilee. A great crowd has followed Jesus "because they were seeing the signs which He was performing on those who were sick" (6:2). Jesus withdraws up a mountain and sits with his disciples. The second of the Gospel's three Passovers is at hand. Jesus turns his eyes upon the great multitude coming toward him and says to Philip, "Where are we to buy bread, that these may eat?" (6:5). The answer would be nowhere—there is nowhere to buy bread sufficient for this crowd. Or the answer would be "from God," if Philip happened to remember Isaiah 55: "Ho! Everyone who thirsts, come to the waters; / And you who have no money come, buy and eat. / . . . Why do you spend money for what is not bread, / And your wages for what does not satisfy?" John writes that Jesus "knew what He was intending to do" (6:6) and was testing the disciples to see where they would turn in their need. Andrew produces a boy with five barley loaves and two fish, clearly not sufficient, and Jesus takes the loaves, gives thanks, and distributes them, miraculously multiplied, to the entire crowd, numbering over 5,000. He does the same with the fish. We are reminded of the abundant wine spilling forth at Cana. Jesus is picturing God giving life to a hungry world—freely, fully, and unexpectedly. When everyone is filled, Jesus has the disciples "gather up the leftover fragments that nothing may be lost" (6:12), twelve baskets in total, refusing to allow any of it to be lost or discarded, underlining the value of all that has been created.

The people, as might be expected, get excited, declaring that Jesus is, "of a truth the Prophet [spoken of by Moses] who is to come into the world." Moses, of course, is much on their minds at Passover. Jesus, however, understands that they have not understood the sign he had just performed and, "perceiving that they were intending to come and take Him by force to make Him king, withdrew again to the mountain by Himself alone" (6:15). They see him as the Messiah, Israel's long-awaited king, but a king they can make use of, a tool to return them to a place of power in the world they rightfully should possess. He is someone they can use to gain what counts for them as life—someone they can "take" and "make" into what they think they need and deserve. It is no wonder Jesus withdraws to the mountain, alone. They do not understand what he has done.

A second act follows. Jesus stays on the mountain while the disciples, in full view of the crowd, get into a boat and start to cross the Sea of Galilee to Capernaum. It is evening, then dark. The wind blows, the waves pick up, and after rowing for 3 to 4 miles, the disciples see Jesus "walking on the sea and drawing near" (6:19). They are frightened. It is dark, and they have never seen anyone do such a thing before. He draws near and then says to the frightened disciples, "It is I [or more literally, "I am"]; do not be afraid" (6:20). The disciples respond by "receiv[ing] Him into the boat" (6:21). This seems important. Unlike the previous scene, there is now no thought of "taking" or "making" him into anything. Jesus simply displays his glory and calms them down so that they can receive him. They do, and immediately the boat is safely at the shore.

The third act occurs the next day. The crowd arises. They cannot find Jesus, but they know that he had not entered into the boat—the only boat there— along with his disciples. The situation does not make sense. Other boats arrive, and the crowd gets into them, crossing over to Capernaum in search of Jesus. They are anxious, confused, intent on getting their hands on him again, awhirl with activity. When they find him, they try to work out when and how he got there, but Jesus quiets them, talking to them instead about what their frantic pursuit shows about the orientation of their hearts:

> Truly, truly, I say to you, you seek Me, not because you saw signs, but because you ate of the loaves and were filled. Do not work for the food which perishes, but for the food which endures to eternal life, which the Son of Man shall give to you, for on Him the Father, even God, has set His seal. (6:26-27)

You are starving, he says, but the food you are pursuing is no food at all. Look at the way you are rushing around. You have misunderstood what you saw yesterday. The sign was pointing to another sort of food, one that would give you "eternal life"—life with God forever. In their frantic trip across the Sea and in their aggressive plans the night before, they had been "working" for the wrong thing. Are they hungry for God, Jesus asks them now. At least partially understanding, they reply, "What shall we do, that we may work the works of God?" (6:28). And Jesus responds, echoing the call he made in the previous scene to come to him and rest: "This is the work of God, that you believe in Him whom He has sent" (6:29). Believe that in Jesus God is offering them true food that will not perish. Rest in that, he says; take that "into their boat."

This, of course, is what they cannot do, and John focuses on their resistance, much as he had after the healing at Bethesda. Being literal-minded people, they ask for something tangible before they will believe—perhaps the sign Jesus performed the day before, but increased manyfold: "What then do You do for a sign, that we may see, and believe You? What work do You perform? Our fathers ate the manna in the wilderness; as it is written, 'He gave them bread out of heaven to eat'" (6:30-31). Moses miraculously fed his people in the wilderness for forty years, and they want to see something as impressive as that before believing. Jesus deftly corrects them, and as he does so, he spotlights the real issue. God was the one who gave them manna in the wilderness, and in doing so he was not simply sustaining them day by day, he was pointing them toward the true food he would eventually provide in Jesus: "Truly, truly, I say to you, it is not Moses who has given you the bread out of heaven, but it is My Father who gives you the true bread out of heaven. For the bread of God is that which comes down out of heaven and gives life to the world" (6:32-33). Jesus is the true bread the manna pointed toward. The work *he* performs "gives life to the world" forever. Half understanding, they blurt out, like the Samaritan woman, "Lord, evermore give us this bread" (6:34).

So Jesus spells it out: "I am the bread of life; he who comes to Me shall not hunger, and he who believes in Me shall never thirst" (6:35). As most critics who write about the Gospel point out, Jesus' "I am" formulation here initiates a series of similar claims, reaching its moment of highest intensity in 8:58 when he identifies himself as "I am" itself—God himself in all his majesty and glory.[6] But they are far from taking this in—as Jesus says, they "have seen Me, and yet do not believe" (6:36). What is interesting, though, is that he does not press for a response, he simply adds what he also knows to be true. Despite their resistance, he assures them, God is still in charge. All the Father has given him *will* come to him in time, and when they come, they will be welcomed in and held on to forever. Remember the leftover fragments of food? None of them were lost. So too those who come to him—none of them will be lost; every fragment touched by God will be raised up on the last day:

> But I said to you, that you have seen Me, and yet do not believe. All that the Father gives Me shall come to Me, and the one who comes to Me I will certainly not cast out. For I have come down from heaven, not to do My own will, but the will of Him who sent Me. And this is the will of Him who sent Me, that of all that He has given Me I lose nothing, but raise it up on the last day. For this is the will of My Father, that everyone who beholds the Son and believes in Him, may have eternal life; and I Myself will raise him up on the last day. (6:36-40)

One can hear how attractive this is—how valuable they are to God. Although they do not yet respond, Jesus has turned their resistance into another opportunity to call them to himself.

Elizabeth Bishop, "A Miracle for Breakfast"

Elizabeth Bishop's sestina "A Miracle for Breakfast," written in 1937 after living in New York City and pondering its Depression-era soup lines,[7] approaches this scene from a more skeptical position. There are no miracles in her world, she responds—or if there are, they occur somewhere else, on what she calls "the wrong balcony." And yet, she suggests, in working out the sign's collapse—walking us through her disappointment in it—she has found her way to another sort of miracle, still possible in her hungry world. Bishop's imagination is stirred to life by the Gospel story, and even though belief seems not to be an option, she lets us feel the continuing power—the attractiveness—of its vision of a world made new.

> At six o'clock we were waiting for coffee,
> waiting for coffee and the charitable crumb
> that was going to be served from a certain balcony,

—like kings of old, or like a miracle.
It was still dark. One foot of the sun
steadied itself on a long ripple in the river.

The first ferry of the day had just crossed the river.
It was so cold we hoped that the coffee
would be very hot, seeing that the sun
was not going to warm us; and that the crumb
would be a loaf each, buttered, by a miracle.
At seven a man stepped out on the balcony.

He stood for a minute alone on the balcony
looking over our heads toward the river.
A servant handed him the makings of a miracle,
consisting of one lone cup of coffee
and one roll, which he proceeded to crumb,
his head, so to speak, in the clouds—along with the sun.

Was the man crazy? What under the sun
was he trying to do, up there on his balcony!
Each man received one rather hard crumb,
which some flicked scornfully into the river,
and, in a cup, one drop of the coffee.
Some of us stood around, waiting for the miracle.

I can tell what I saw next; it was not a miracle.
A beautiful villa stood in the sun
and from its doors came the smell of hot coffee.
In front, a baroque white plaster balcony
added by birds, who nest along the river,
—I saw it with one eye close to the crumb—

and galleries and marble chambers. My crumb
my mansion, made for me by a miracle,
through ages, by insects, birds, and the river
working the stone. Every day, in the sun,
at breakfast time I sit on my balcony
with my feet up, and drink gallons of coffee.

We licked up the crumb and swallowed the coffee.
A window across the river caught the sun
as if the miracle were working, on the wrong balcony.[8]

The poem begins in a fairly straightforward way, establishing the six
end words it will work and rework in various orders and emphases. It is early
morning, and a group of people are waiting, perhaps in line, "for coffee and

the charitable crumb." "Crumb," in its first use seems to be a metaphor for the little bit with which charity is willing to part. The food is to be served from a "balcony," an unexpected detail that begins to push the poem toward fable or dream, since that is not how one imagines food being distributed, unless it is by some "king of old" or a "miracle." The sun just touches the river behind the crowd. A cold hour passes, the second stanza tells us. A ferry crosses the river, and the restless crowd begins hoping the coffee "would be very hot" and the charitable crumb "would be a loaf each, buttered, by a miracle." Finally a man steps out on the balcony.

In the third stanza, we begin to hear echoes of the feeding of the 5,000. Like Christ on the mountain, the man on the balcony seems at first not to be focused on the crowd below. He is "looking over [their] heads toward the river," and even when a servant "handed him the makings of a miracle, / consisting of one lone cup of coffee / and one roll," the boy's lunch in John having become a rich man's breakfast, his head seems to remain "so to speak, in the clouds." He is not particularly concerned about the crowd, and no miracle occurs. Instead, the man breaks the roll and distributes "one rather hard crumb" and "one drop of coffee" to each of the hungry. Some walk away; some stand around, "waiting for the miracle," which never occurs. To this point, Bishop has used John's miracle ironically: the crowd, cold, patient, hungry, hoping for their bellies to be filled, expecting a miracle, receives nothing of the sort. It is that sort of world.

But then, with the fifth stanza, the poem makes a fascinating turn. No miracle occurs. Neither divine intervention nor its social equivalent, a stirring of human generosity, seems possible in Bishop's world. And yet, "with one eye close to the crumb," the poet sees something. The crumb, under the pressure of her yearning imagination, becomes a "beautiful villa." The smell of coffee issues forth from its doors, and a "white plaster balcony" on the outside draws the eye in to its carved out "galleries and marble chambers." The crumb, by the sixth stanza, becomes a "mansion" where she can sit in the sun and, "feet up" on the balcony, "drink gallons of coffee." Bonnie Costello suggests that the crumb is a version of nature itself, and the "miracle" is the way even the very small portion we have each been granted has been transformed "through ages, by insects, birds, and the river / working the stone."[9] It is not that the world is without miracles, this reading suggests, but that they are the ordinary ones, common to all of us, of life on this planet.

But I hear something else here as well. In its demonstration of the hungry speaker's imagination being stirred to receive the world as a gift, the poem takes quite seriously the Gospel's call. "Come to me and eat," Jesus says. "Do not work for the food which perishes, but for the food which endures to eternal life" (6:27). And how are they do that work, to "work the works of God"? By "believ[ing] in Him whom He has sent" (6:29). Putting miracles aside, Bishop continues to respond to the Gospel's declaration that there is more to the world than eating and being filled (6:26). Imagination, for her, takes the place of belief, with the poet's response to the crumb—drawing close, coming to see, giving oneself over, and being filled—clearly echoing the Gospel's language. Jesus has the people sit down, feeds them, and then directs their eyes to eternal life. Bishop's speaker, in quite similar terms, imagines a mansion where, "Every day, in the sun, / at breakfast time I sit on my balcony / with my feet up, and drink gallons of coffee." "Eternal life" becomes "Every day," and the multiplied loaves become "gallons of coffee," but the parallel is clear. Although the poem turns to a different source of life, in the manner in which it comes "close to the crumb," it powerfully reproduces the movements of belief, helping us see the response for which Jesus is calling. The poem concludes with a "window across the river [catching] the sun" and the suggestion that whatever miracle is to be found in this hungry world would have to occur over there, "on the wrong balcony," but it also insists, along with the Gospel, that coming to see is, in itself, part of the miracle, one that opens wide the doors of previously unlooked-for mansions.

Bread of Life (II), 6:41-71

In the first part of the discussion that follows the feeding of the 5,000, Jesus claims that he is the "bread of life," sent by God to "give life to the world" (6:33)—true food, producing a life that will not perish. Not unlike Bishop's speaker, those gathered around him cannot accept this. They have seen the miracle, but they cannot take it in. In the second part of the discussion, as their grumbling rises, Jesus explains why they cannot understand. They are turning to each other, rather than God, for help. Until God draws them in and teaches them, they will draw a blank. What Jesus is claiming is so radical that it cannot be understood from the outside. One must be drawn to it.

John mentions two complaints. First, a party that he calls "the Jews," presumably the Jewish authorities, begins to grumble about Jesus calling himself "bread that came down out of heaven" (6:41). How could someone whose mother and father are known say of himself that he has come down from heaven? Jesus does not answer the criticism in the way they expect, with an argument about parentage. He says, rather, that in "grumbl[ing] among [them]selves" (6:43) they have missed the point, and will always miss it, "unless the Father who sent Me draws [them]" (6:44). He reminds them of Isaiah's account of a great day of restoration when God will draw near and pour out his heart and make himself known. Even now, says Jesus, that opening up of God's heart has begun: "It is written in the prophets 'And they shall all be taught of God.' Everyone who has heard and learned from the Father, comes to Me" (6:45, Isa 54:13). But they are still looking to each other and not to God. They are not coming to him. Why? What is it they have missed? Jesus stirs them to find out. His description of himself as "the bread which comes down from heaven" is no casual metaphor, he explains. Bread gives life through being eaten, and Jesus challenges those who hear him to respond by eating him: "the bread also which I shall give for the life of the world is My flesh" (6:51). Clearly he intends to shock them. Unless God was teaching them and drawing them in, this would have simply sounded repulsive. His flesh, his death—how could they find "life" in such a notion?

Most of them cannot, and, as before, they begin "to argue with one another" (6:52). "How can this man give us His flesh to eat?" (6:52), they ask. Jesus responds by making his language even more explicit and even more difficult to take in: "Truly, truly, I say to you, unless you eat the flesh of the Son of Man and drink His blood, you have no life in yourselves" (6:53). What could he be driving at? He gives them one clue. His flesh and blood are "true food" and "true drink" because the one who eats and drinks them "abides in Me, and I in him" (6:56). And through that connection to him, they will gain a connection to his Father, to life itself: "As the living Father sent Me, and I live because of the Father, so he who eats Me, he also shall live because of Me" (6:57). These are extraordinary words, and, as Jesus says, until God makes them clear, they will remain just that—words, difficult and troubling. Even His "disciples," by which John means not the Twelve but the larger group following Him, draw back, saying, "This is a difficult statement, who can listen to it?" (6:60). "As a result of this," John adds, "many of His disciples withdrew, and were not walking with Him anymore" (6:66).

But Jesus does not back away from the difficulty of his words. What they are stumbling over accurately describes the path he is on. What will they do when they are in fact confronted with actual flesh and blood, broken on the cross as he is lifted up to God? "What then if you should behold the Son of Man ascending where He was before?" (6:62). Will they then believe? Will they be able to take that in? God is about to pour his Spirit out on them and give them life, but it is life is bound up in his death. What would they have to understand about themselves in order to take that in? At the very least, it seems, they would need to see that their own attempts to make sense of their lives had come to nothing: "It is the Spirit who gives life; the flesh profits nothing; the words that I have spoken to you are spirit and are life" (6:63).

Clearly, this is not something they can do on their own: "For this reason I have said to you, that no one can come to Me, unless it has been granted him from the Father" (6:65).

There are two ways of responding. Many walk away, offended and bewildered. They have heard talk about life and been drawn in, but now his words have turned dark and offensive. Jesus turns to the Twelve and says, "You do not want to go away also, do you?" (6:67). And to that, Peter replies, as if they were once again receiving Jesus into their storm-tossed boat, "Lord, to whom shall we go? You have the words of eternal life" (6:68). They do not understand those words yet, but they sense life in them. Something is tugging at them, something they want to understand, something they need to understand. The reader, of course, knows more than any of the parties involved here. We have been told that Jesus will die and be raised (2:22). We have heard him described as Lamb of God (1:29). But even so, we are left in much the same position as those in the scene, uncertain as to how to take some of its most basic terms. What will we do with that uncertainty?

Emily Dickinson, 1715 (A word made Flesh is seldom)

In poem 1715, partially discussed in the "Introduction," Emily Dickinson listens in as the Jewish leaders quarrel with each other about "How . . . this man [can] give us his flesh to eat" (6:52) and then offers her own experience in reply:

> A word made Flesh is seldom
> And tremblingly partook
> Nor then perhaps reported
> But have I not mistook
> Each one of us has tasted
> With ecstasies of stealth
> The very food debated
> To our specific strength—
>
> A word that breathes distinctly
> Has not the power to die
> Cohesive as the Spirit
> It may expire if He—
>
> "Made Flesh and dwelt among us"
> Could condescension be
> Like this consent of Language
> This loved Philology[10]

Her initial response in the first stanza is fairly direct. Though the experience may be "seldom" and "trembling" and "[un]reported," each of us *has* taken the Word in and "partaken" of his flesh. Quietly, in private, "Each of us has tasted / With ecstasies of stealth / The very food debated" in this section of John. Dickinson leaves open the question of whether she is speaking about "A word," perhaps another writer's powerful phrase, or "the Word," but in either case, she has partaken of its life, just as Jesus had claimed. Dickinson understands, along with D. A. Carson, that what Jesus meant by "eating" his flesh was "believing" in its power to create life.[11] Yes, she replies, despite evidence to the contrary, each of us, at some level, *has* responded to this call to eat his flesh and turn to him for life. The real issue, she suggests, is the "specific strength" of each response. Christ is a strong taste—we see this in these middle chapters of John—and it comes down to how much of what he says we have the "specific strength" to handle. Jesus made exactly this point when he pushed the call to eat his flesh and drink his blood far past what anyone listening to him could reasonably stomach or comprehend. But, says Dickinson, each of us who hears these words *does* respond to them, however guarded or uncomprehending that response might be.

With the second and third stanzas though, Dickinson does a fascinating thing. She offers an account of what, according to her own "specific strength," *she* has taken from these startling words. In a sense, we have seen this in each of the poets we have examined—the Gospel calls out to them, and they each work out, for themselves, what coming to Jesus at night or resting in him might mean. What I have seen of the "word made Flesh," she writes, is that its power rests in its "power to die." Through death, words create life. Through its death, the Word was consumed, absorbed, and built upon. The Word became flesh so that it could die, and it died so that it could give life.

She has seen this in her own writing. What she has learned is that, as attractive as it might be to remain pure and untouched, to "breathe distinctly" outside of the give and take of words, to do so would be to give up the "power to die" and thus the power to nourish and give life. There is power in taking on the risky, undefended flesh of language. She has experienced this for herself. God saw this and willingly shattered his "Cohesive[ness]" in order to "expire," deliberately putting aside his glory and "condescen[ding]" to take on flesh, a gesture that she has willingly repeated in order to make herself available to be absorbed. "How can this man give us his flesh to eat?" the religious leaders asked. He could do it because he knew what sort of life that would follow, Dickinson responds, drawing on her own experience as a writer.

Through her own "consent of Language," her willingness to speak and be heard, no matter the cost, in order to give life to others, Dickinson understood what Jesus was talking about. Writing, for her, embraces language—embraces its costs and complications, its brokenness and its life. It is a "loved Philology"—literally a love, *phileō*, of the Word, or *logos*. She seems to me quite serious in teasing this out of the word *philology*, for in loving language, in writing, she has in fact discovered a love for the Word, John's Logos. She has eaten the very food debated, as she has entered into language, to her specific strength.

Tabernacles, 7:1–8:59

Six months later, we arrive at the Feast of Booths or Tabernacles, where the people commemorate God's faithfulness to them during the wilderness wandering by returning to Jerusalem and living in temporary structures made of branches, remembering how, with no permanent home, they once lived in the sustaining presence of God himself. Water-drawing and lamp-lighting ceremonies are part of the celebration, recalling the water God miraculously provided for his people in the wilderness and the pillars of cloud and fire leading them through the desert.[12] As he did with the feeding of the 5,000 and the healing of the man who could not walk, Jesus uses the ceremonies to illustrate the life he is offering, once again forcing the people to confront the question of whether what he says about God is true or not.

The sequence begins with Jesus in Galilee, unwilling to go to Judea and Jerusalem because the Jews there "were seeking to kill Him" (7:1) and his "time had not yet fully come" (7:8). His unbelieving brothers urge him to follow the crowds there in order to "show" himself, but Jesus tells them that he is bound by God's timing and not the world's: "My time is not yet at hand, but your time is always opportune. The world cannot hate you; but it hates Me because I testify of it, that its deeds are evil. Go up to the feast yourselves" (7:6-8). What the world hates is the testimony that it is dead in its sins, starving for God, incomplete without him. Jesus stays behind, then goes up on his own, later and in secret, following his own sense of timing.

When he arrives, he hears much talk and grumbling. The leaders "seek" but cannot find him, and the crowd is arguing about who he is and what his intentions are (7:11, 12). No one can pin him down. Suddenly, Jesus enters the temple and begins to preach. His understanding of Scripture is so powerful and compelling that the Jewish leaders marvel and ask, "How has this man become learned, having never been educated?" (7:15). They know that he can claim no rabbi or school or tradition as the source of his authority, and yet the power of his words is obvious. Jesus responds that the authority of his words rests on the one who has given them to him: "My teaching is not Mine, but His who sent Me" (7:16). All they would have to do to test this out would be to take God at his word and turn to him: "If any man is willing to do His will, he shall know of the teaching, whether it is of God, or whether I speak from Myself" (7:17). If his teaching were not of God, he points out, if it were not true, there would be no life and power in it, a fact that would become immediately obvious.

Their refusal to consider his words is, for Jesus, a powerful illustration of the very problem he has come to address. He repeats the fact that his words are not his own: "He who speaks from himself seeks his own glory; but He who is seeking the glory of the One who sent Him, He is true, and there is no unrighteousness in Him" (7:18). Righteousness is conformity to God's will. Jesus claims to be speaking rightly, in absolute agreement with the one who sent him. Those who are seeking to kill him, on the other hand, are "judg[ing] according to appearance" and not with "righteous judgment" (7:24). This should be obvious, he says: claiming to support Moses in their defense of the Sabbath, they have in fact turned their back on Moses and God's revealed will by seeking to destroy an innocent man. They are judging wrongly, missing the truth.

The crowd has the same problem. Seeing that their rulers have not prevented Jesus from speaking, they assume that they must have identified him as the Messiah. How could that be, they say to one another. Is there not a tradition that says the Messiah will come from an unknown place? We know where this man is from. Jesus overhears them, and swings around to them. They too are judging by appearances and have missed the truth: "You both know Me and know where I am from [i.e., Nazareth]; and I have not come of Myself, but He who sent Me is true, whom you do not know" (7:28). They do not know him, and they do not know God. They cannot make out the truth, even when it takes on flesh and dwells in their midst. The scene rapidly disintegrates. Some in the crowd believe, others turn away. The chief priests and Pharisees hear of this and send officers to seize him. They come back empty-handed, reporting that "Never did a man speak the way this man speaks" (7:46). And through it all, Jesus continues to call people to himself, making it clear that his invitation holds only for a little while, for "then I go to Him who sent Me," and when that happens, the truth will utterly slip out of their hands: "You shall seek Me, and shall not find Me; and where I am, you cannot come" (7:33-34).

All of this establishes the context for what Jesus does on the last day of the feast. As water is poured out on the altar, reminding people of God's promise to pour out his Spirit on them, Jesus cries out to all who can hear him, opponents and the curious alike:[13] "If any man is thirsty, let him come to Me and drink. He who believes in Me, as the Scripture said, 'From his innermost being shall flow rivers of living water'" (7:37-38). This is the truth he has come to speak. As the narrator explains, "But this He spoke of the Spirit, whom those who believed in Him were to receive, for the Spirit was not yet given, because Jesus was not yet glorified" (7:39). Through me, Jesus says, God will pour out his Spirit on you. He will enter your life, change your heart, and, as the prophet Isaiah wrote, "You will be like a watered garden, / And like a spring of water whose waters do not fail" (Isa 58:11). But they need to come to him. They need to recognize that on their own they are scorched and dry and lifeless, wandering forever in an ancient wilderness.

We seem to be in the same scene, the Feast of Tabernacles, when we jump ahead to 8:12, reading Jesus' words there as a response to the ceremony's lamps. (Here, I am following the suggestion of most scholars who see 7:53–8:11 as added later.) Jesus has just identified himself with the water poured out on the altar. Now he points to the lamps and says, "I am the light of the world; he who follows Me shall not walk in the darkness, but shall have the light of life" (8:12). Here again is the truth. Through him, the light of God's presence has broken into a world that had turned away from him, estranged and in rebellion—all of which Jesus means by "darkness." What he offers is "light"—light that leads out of darkness and back to life, another common idea in the prophets:

> Arise, shine; for your light has come,
> And the glory of the Lord has risen upon you.
> For behold, darkness will cover the earth,
> And deep darkness the peoples;
> But the Lord will rise upon you,
> And His glory will appear upon you.
>
> (Isa 60:1-2)

The shock behind his words, of course, is that Jesus is not claiming to be a prophet and announcing or pointing to the light of God's presence, he is claiming to be that light and asking them to follow him, believing that this is so.

Once again, the Jewish authorities refuse to accept his words, and John takes us through an analysis of their blindness. The exchange is long and heated, but it comes to a familiar conclusion. "If I speak the truth," Jesus says, "why do you not believe Me?" And he answers the question himself:

"He who is of God hears the words of God; for this reason you do not hear them, because you are not of God" (8:46-47). Not being of God is the problem he seeks to overcome. To get there, those he speaks to will have to be convinced this is so.

The Pharisees begin this exchange by responding, "Your witness is not true" (8:13). He is not the light of the world or living water, despite what the events surrounding him seem to suggest. Jesus replies that they have just proved his point; only someone caught up in the dark and unable to see could ignore the support for his claim: "Even in your law it has been written, that the testimony of two men is true. I am He who bears witness of Myself, and the Father who sent Me bears witness of Me" (8:17-18), by the testimony of his miracles. To claim that he is lying is to be swaddled in the very darkness that Jesus has come to address: "You know neither Me, nor My Father; if you knew Me, you would know My Father also" (8:19).

The question is: "Why?" What holds them back and keeps them in the dark? Jesus' answer is sin—by which he means being bound by or drawn to some other source of life than God himself. He says to the uncomprehending leaders: "I go away, and you shall seek Me, and shall die in your sin; where I am going, you cannot come" (8:21). They struggle with this, trying to make out where he is going, and he responds even more bluntly: "I said therefore to you, that you shall die in your sins; for unless you believe that I am [He], you shall die in your sins" (8:24). Sin binds them tight, holds them in the darkness of estrangement. Its hold can only be broken by belief, says Jesus, and when they press him as to who he is, that they should believe, he points to the cross:

> When you lift up the Son of Man, then you will know that I am [He], and I do nothing on My own initiative, but I speak these things as the Father taught Me. (8:28)

The "I am [He]" formulation, seen twice here in verses 24 and 28, is, I think, deliberately open-ended, with the "He" being implied and not stated. They are being called to fill it in, but they cannot. Unless you believe that I am the Messiah, the One sent by God, the light that will lead you to God, the truth—any of these formulations would start them down the path that would lead them to belief. But another commitment has blinded them, kept them in the dark. When he is lifted up on the cross, Jesus says, then the light of God's presence, reaching out in utter disregard for himself, will fully pierce their darkness. Then, says Jesus, sin's hold will be broken and the truth will be seen. Come to him now, he pleads, in anticipation.

Many do come to him, John writes (8:30), but as Jesus presses them to fully take in what he is saying, they pull back in incomprehension. It does not take much to unsettle them, just the simple encouragement to hold on to the truth of what he has said about how God has reached out to them: "If you abide in My word, then you are truly disciples of Mine; and you shall know the truth, and the truth shall make you free" (8:31-32). These verses are so familiar that we might be taken aback by the stunned response of these "believers": "They answered him 'We are Abraham's offspring, and have never yet been enslaved to anyone; how is it that You say, "You shall become free"?'" (8:33). It is instructive to note their difficulty with this notion of "enslavement." They revert to a literal reading—as Abraham's children we have never been enslaved to another religion—in order to fend off the idea. But Jesus bores in. He is talking about enslavement to another source of life, which no one can break on his or her own: "Truly, truly, I say to you, everyone who commits sin is the slave of sin. And the slave does not remain in the house forever; the son does remain forever. If therefore the Son shall make you free, you shall be free indeed" (8:34-36). A slave's status is by definition not secure. Any assumption on their part that, as slaves, they are members of God's family is an assumption destined to be undone. He is offering to lift them out of slavery and into freedom and the full rights of the household, but as he does so, as this light draws near, the truth of their estrangement from God must also be acknowledged.

This explains, I think, why Jesus continues to push. Without their estrangement from God being brought to the light, they will never turn to him to make things right. He tosses Abraham back in their faces: "I know that you are Abraham's offspring; yet you seek to kill Me, because My word has no place in you" (8:37). Their real father is not Abraham at all, but the devil, the father of lies. That is why they find the truth to be so repellent: "If you are Abraham's children, do the deeds of Abraham. But as it is, you are seeking to kill Me, a man who has told you the truth, which I heard from God; this Abraham did not do. You are doing the deeds of your father" (8:39-41). Just as the devil hates the truth about God's mercy, so do they. They simply cannot accept it.

The struggle goes on. The Jewish leaders sputter and call him a Samaritan, insisting that some demon must be driving him to insult them in this way. Jesus repeats his offer, phrasing it this time in positive terms. Where before he had said that they would die in their sins unless they believed, now he says that if they trust in him they will never die: "Truly, truly, I say to you, if anyone keeps My word he shall never see death" (8:51). But this only heightens their incomprehension: "Now we know that You have a demon. . . .

Surely You are not greater than our father Abraham, who died? The prophets died too; whom do You make Yourself out to be?" (8:52-53). And so he tells them: "Truly, truly, I say to you, before Abraham was born, I am" (8:58). The novelist Reynolds Price describes this as a kind of incandescent flare—Jesus drawing all of his language about himself to a point and identifying himself with God's own name.[14] Who is he claiming to be? What is the truth they cannot take in? He is God himself, offering to free them from enslavement and draw them into his presence forever. That is why his words are so arresting and blinding.

Scholars agree that with this language Jesus is claiming divinity, although they differ as to whether he is alluding to Exodus 3, in which God identifies himself to Moses in the burning bush as "I am who I am," or to Isaiah 43:10, in which God tells Israel that he has called her "In order that you may know and believe Me, / And understand that I am He. / Before Me there was no God formed, / And there will be none after Me." In either case, the crowd understands, picking up stones in order to kill him for blasphemy. He has made himself out to be God and this cannot be borne, they say. It cannot be true. And John leaves it there, the words hanging in the air, the crowd wrapped in darkness and unable to comprehend, rising up against what God has shown them about themselves and about him.

John Donne, "Holy Sonnet XIV"

John Donne's "Holy Sonnet XIV," 1633, lets us hear what it would be like for the truth of Jesus' words about enslavement to suddenly break through. "Yes," Donne's speaker says back to this text, "I am enslaved. And that enslavement goes so deep that there is no way I can break its bonds on my own." Blunt, impassioned, violently self-rending, Donne's words, in the rush of their response, let us hear the force with which God would have to act to free him and, in doing so, they begin to turn our eyes toward the cross where that blow is actually delivered:

> Batter my heart, three person'd God; for, you
> As yet but knocke, breathe, shine, and seeke to mend;
> That I may rise, and stand, o'erthrow me, and bend
> Your force, to breake, blowe, burn and make me new.
> I, like an usurpt towne, to another due,
> Labor to admit you, but Oh, to no end,
> Reason your viceroy in mee, mee should defend,
> But is captiv'd, and proves weake or untrue,
> Yet dearely I love you, and would be lov'd faine,

But am betroth'd unto your enemie,
Divorce mee, untie, or breake that knot againe,
Take mee to you, imprison mee, for I
Except you enthrall mee, never shall be free,
Nor ever chast, except you ravish mee.[15]

In the first quatrain of this sonnet—or prayer—the poet calls on God, in his three persons, to "batter" or beat away at his closed, wayward heart. To use the language of the chapters we have been examining, he acknowledges that there is no love of God in his heart (5:42), no willingness to do his will (7:17), no place for God there (8:37). He feels this strongly. As of now, he complains, God seems merely to be "seek[ing] to mend" him. What he needs is something much more radical—he needs a new heart. "[M]ake me new," Donne's speaker cries, borrowing from Jesus' words to Nicodemus: bring me life "from above" (3:3). The force with which the poet acknowledges his estrangement from God is striking. So far, the speaker says, God has been "knock[ing]" at his door, "breath[ing]" and "shin[ing]" on him. (We see the Trinity in these verbs, God in his three persons.) But what the speaker needs, to be made new, is something much more powerful. He uses the language of paradox to get at this: for him to "rise and stand," he will have to be "o'erthrow[n]," his standing in the world completely torn down. Only God could accomplish this, the poet insists, having clearly seen the depths of his estrangement and separation. But God would have to act much more forcefully than he has so far. Donne throws himself into imagining this: the Father would have to "breake" down the door of his heart rather than knock; the Spirit would have to "blowe" through him rather than breathe; and the Son, the light of the world, would have to "burn" away the poet's excess in a holy flame rather than simply shine.

The second quatrain uses an extended metaphor to unfold Jesus' words about enslavement, turning them into a drama in order to fully acknowledge the truth behind them. I am like a town that has been conquered, he tells God—my loyalties seized or "usurpt" by a rival power. Although the speaker "labor[s]" to admit God into his heart, he cannot, because his heart is "to another due" and cannot on its own open its gates or tear down its defenses. "Reason," God's "viceroy" or deputy left behind to defend the city, has proved powerless. "Why do you not understand what I am saying?" (8:43), Jesus says to the leaders who can make no sense out of his offer to make them free. Because my reason has been taken captive, Donne replies, putting himself in their place. What should have defended his heart has proved "weake or untrue." It "judges according to appearance [and not] with righteous judgment" (8:24), and cannot do otherwise. The poet hears these charges and sadly agrees.

What is he to do then? The sestet, the last six lines of the poem, return to the opening plea. Although he is captive, "Yet dearely I love you, and would be lov'd faine," he says. Gladly, with pleasure ("faine"), would he be loved by God, but for that to happen, God must be the one to act. This is the truth that those who listened to Jesus in John 8 could not comprehend. Although the speaker loves God, he has become "betroth'd unto [God's] enemie," the father of lies, and there is no way out of that obligation short of God, in his superior power, stepping in to break it off—"divorc[ing]" the speaker from this agreement, "unty[ing]" the bond, "break[ing]" the knot. "Take me to you, imprison me," he pleads, his love language edged again with the desperation of the poem's opening lines. I am a captive, he bursts out, betrothed to someone I do not love. For me to be free to love again, you must act:

> for I,
> Except you enthrall mee, never shall be free,
> Nor ever chast, except you ravish mee.

The blunt, paradoxical language lets us see how complete an overturning of his world this would have to be. We can feel the poet straining to imagine this. He would have to be enslaved, "enthralled," in order to be made free. He would have to raped or carried away ("ravished") in order to be made chaste again. The language is violent, desperate, acknowledging by its intensity the strength of the bonds that hold him down.

And here, in the poem's turn to paradox, we touch on something not fully articulated in the Gospel until the cross: that God answered prayers such as this by breaking, unknotting, enslaving, and ravishing *himself*—not those who acknowledged in desperation the need for their own violent undoing but himself. "But He was pierced through for our transgressions, / He was crushed for our iniquities; / The chastening for our well-being fell upon Him, / And by His scourging we are healed" (Isa 53:5). This is the truth that will make Donne's speaker free, the light that will cut through his darkness. John will recall these words of Isaiah when he describes the crucifixion of Jesus, seeing Christ's undoing as his true "glory." He was pierced so that we could be made whole, scourged so that we could be healed. Donne's speaker, in being driven by his own desperation toward Isaiah's paradox—a scourging that healed, a ravishing that made one chaste—is slowly making his way toward such an idea.

Man Born Blind, 9:1-41

In these middle chapters, we have seen Jesus make a series of declarations about himself. He is the work God is performing in the world, the bread through which he feeds us, the truth by which he makes us free. Rest in that, Jesus says. Take it in. Trust it. But this is difficult to do unless your eyes are opened, an idea becoming more and more apparent to the reader. In the fourth scene of this sequence, Jesus turns directly to that issue. He heals a blind man and then invites those who are in the dark, far from God, to come to him for sight. Essentially, he is claiming to be the light through which we see God and find life. What he is about to do on the cross will open eyes and make God's glory plain, but it will only open the eyes of those who know they do not see. That, I think, is what the reader is now being called to consider.

We pick up the story in Jerusalem again. Jesus and his disciples pass "a man born blind," and the disciples ask, "Who sinned, this man or his parents, that he should be born blind?" (9:2). The issue is not who sinned, Jesus says. The issue is Jesus himself—what God is doing through him: "It was neither that this man sinned, nor his parents; but it was in order that the works of God might be displayed in him" (9:3). What works? God who is light is about to break into the darkness, giving the world the ability to see and draw near, and he will do this through his Son, who reminds his disciples that "While I am in the world, I am the light of the world" (9:5).

Jesus turns to the blind man, spits, makes clay, and applies it to the man's eyes. Then he tells him to wash it off in the pool of Siloam, which John translates for us as "Sent" (9:7). The man does so and comes back seeing, so changed by the gift that his neighbors are not sure if he is the same man who used to sit and beg. He insists that he is, and they begin to quiz him about how this has happened. He simply recapitulates the process: "The man who is called Jesus made clay, and anointed my eyes, and said to me, 'Go to Siloam and wash'; so I went away and washed, and I received sight" (9:11). When the neighbors ask him where Jesus is, he says he does not know. In fact, he has not yet seen him. At this point, the reader and the disciples understand a good deal more than the man does. We understand that this pictures what Jesus has come to accomplish; that in washing in the one whom God has "sent," believers can wash away what has separated them from God and blinded them to his true worth. They can be given eyes to see him.

The act, of course, draws opposition, and John settles down to study it. Light has come to darkness, and in the back and forth between the man born blind and the Pharisees, we see the two different responses to light John had described in his Prologue. The neighbors bring the man to the Pharisees, perhaps seeking an explanation or validation of the miracle. John notes that the healing occurred on a Sabbath, a fact that the leaders seem to know even before the man arrives, understanding it as another challenge to their authority. They ask the man "how he received his sight," and when he describes the way Jesus spat and anointed his eyes, some of them immediately declare that "This man is not from God because He does not keep the Sabbath" (9:16). A debate begins, with some arguing that he is obviously a sinner, and others that a sinner could not perform such signs. When the blind man himself is asked, he responds, "He is a prophet" (9:17). He has been listening carefully to their words, as a blind man would have learned to do, and he gleans from the debate about whether or not Jesus is "from God" a way to identify him—he is a prophet, someone sent from God. The blind man, we realize, is beginning to think on his own, the tension in the scene having prodded him to try and see for himself.

The leaders refuse to call him a prophet and begin to cast about for ways to prove that the man was not healed in the first place. Rather than look at the evidence before them, as the blind man had done, they try to free themselves from it. They shut their eyes. They call in the man's parents, trying to get them to confirm what they know must be true—that either this man is not their son, or if he is their son, he was not in fact born blind. Understanding that they are being asked to discredit something the Pharisees had already decided could not be true—knowing in fact that the Pharisees had "already agreed, that if anyone should confess Him to be Christ, he should be put out of the synagogue" (9:22)—the parents, out of fear, say only the minimum. Yes, he is their son, and yes, he was born blind. But as to "how he now sees," they have no idea. Their fear makes it obvious how hard the leaders are pushing to keep the world as they see it in place.

They call the formerly blind man back a second time and try to bully him, confronting him with the words, "Give glory to God; we know that this man is a sinner" (9:24). The man again turns their words over in his head. How do they know that? "Whether He is a sinner, I do not know; one thing I do know, that whereas I was blind, now I see" (9:25). He knows what he has experienced, and he will not budge. When they ask again "how" Jesus opened his eyes, perhaps looking for some conjuring trick, he reads the fear on their faces and understands what the real issue is: "I told you already, and you did not listen; why do you want to hear it again? You do not want to become His disciples too, do you?" (9:27). Jesus is not only healing, he is attracting followers. That is what their fear has let the blind man see. Enraged at both his cheekiness and his insight, the Pharisees "revile" the formerly blind man, seeking to discredit his position and firm up their own: "You are his disciple, but we are disciples of Moses. We know that God has spoken to Moses; but as for this man, we do not know where He is from" (9:28-29). Again the man listens to their words and thinks about what they reveal:

> Well, here is an amazing thing, that you do not know where He is from, and yet He opened my eyes. We know that God does not hear sinners; but if anyone is God-fearing and does His will, He hears him. Since the beginning of time it has never been heard that anyone opened the eyes of a person born blind. If this man were not from God, He could do nothing. (9:30-33)

They do not know where Jesus is from, and yet he opened the man's eyes, which would mean that he is no sinner, for clearly, God has heard him. It is simple logic, says the formerly blind man. Where is he from? He is "from God." It is that cut-and-dried.

They respond by expelling the man from the synagogue, attempting to silence him permanently. Jesus finds him and completes the miracle by opening his inner eyes. He finds the man and asks him, "Do you believe in the Son of Man?" (9:35). (The Son of Man, we remember, is both Jesus' name for himself and Daniel's term for the one he saw enthroned with the Ancient of Days to rule over all peoples and nations.) Cautious, but willing to be guided by this man whom he knows is from God, he replies, "And who is He, Lord [or "Sir"], that I may believe in Him?" (9:36). And then Jesus says an extraordinary thing, opening his eyes all the way: "You have both seen Him, and He is the one who is talking with you" (9:37). He is right before you. The man who opened your eyes, who you see now before you, is no prophet. He is the Son of Man, sharing in God's power and authority. With this, the man sees. Before him stands the center of his life. He responds, "'Lord, I believe.' And he worshipped Him" (9:38). That, it seems clear, is the work God "displayed in him" (9:3)—the creation of someone able to see God and stand in his presence and worship.

Jesus then explains what has just happened, drawing together both the man's unfolding illumination and the Pharisees' willful blindness: "For judgment, I came into this world, that those who do not see may see; and that those who see may become blind" (9:39). The Pharisees are nearby and overhear. The light of God's presence—his unfolding glory—has spurred some people to draw near and others to draw back. The judgment rendered is one they have rendered themselves. The Pharisees understand that he is speaking about them. "We are not blind too, are we?" they ask. In fact, they are not blind enough. They have not yet been forced to confront how little they know of God, how far away they are from any meaningful encounter with

him. Their positions have shielded them from this and given them a false
sense of security: "If you were blind, you would have no sin; but since you
say, 'We see,' your sin remains" (9:41). There is no life in them, the reader
understands, having seen their willful blindness, their insistence that they
could see perfectly well on their own.

Emily Dickinson, 336 (Before I got my eye put out—)

Emily Dickinson's response to this passage is a deeply mixed one. In poem
336, she hears Jesus say that he came into the world so that "those who do not
see may see;, and that those who see may become blind" (9:39) and responds
by holding her own experience up against his words. Yes, she agrees, true seeing must learn to accept its own blindness—that is what the Pharisees were
unable to understand—but, having done so, what assurance do we have that
those newly opened eyes will not simply be overwhelmed in their confrontation with the world's immensity? Poem 336 ponders these things in a sort of
charged, in-between space:

> Before I got my eye put out—
> I liked as well to see
> As other creatures, that have eyes—
> And know no other way—
>
> But were it told to me, Today,
> That I might have the Sky
> For mine, I tell you that my Heart
> Would split, for size of me—
>
> The Meadows—mine—
> The Mountains—mine—
> All Forests—Stintless stars—
> As much of noon, as I could take—
> Between my finite eyes—
>
> The Motions of the Dipping Birds—
> The Morning's Amber Road—
> For mine—to look at when I liked,
> The news would strike me dead—
>
> So safer—guess—with just my soul
> Opon the window pane
> Where other creatures put their eyes—
> Incautious—of the Sun—[16]

Dickinson begins by putting herself in the position of the Pharisees. Before I was blinded, she writes, before I had my "eye put out" by some unnamed crisis, I saw as they did, resting comfortably in my ability to see. I was like "other creatures," never realizing there was something else outside my range of vision. I saw what I expected, and I was blind to everything else—I knew "no other way." But then something happened, which she does not identify but invites the reader to imagine—the loss of a lover, the collapse of a stronghold, even the sudden sense of an unbridgeable distance from God. Now, she writes, having been forced to acknowledge her true blindness, she has had her eyes opened to another way of seeing.

The fifth stanza describes this "other way" as seeing with the soul—seeing inwardly and deeply, seeing truly. This would seem to be a great thing to gain, but as the second, third, and fourth stanzas suggest, there is something terrifying about the intensity of this new way of seeing. It is a charged, complicated gift, and Dickinson's poem forces us to consider the changed lives Jesus is calling for more slowly. She imagines it for us this way: what would happen if, having learned to "see" with her soul, she was then granted her "finite eyes" back? Perhaps she would be overwhelmed. If she could once again see the sky, she fears, her newly awakened soul would take in so much of it that her "Heart / Would split, for size of me—." The world would pour so deeply in that her heart would double, and then double again, splitting as it became too large for her body. If she could have it all back—meadows, mountains, forests, stars, the motion of birds, sunrise across a landscape—it would surely be too much. It would "strike [her] dead." "Noon" would simply be too much for "finite eyes" linked to a responsive soul, she reluctantly admits, even as everything inside her yearns for it to be otherwise, whispering "mine," "mine," "to look at when I liked."

What an unexpected response. Dickinson has turned her back on the Pharisees and their "seeing blindness." Something in her has been awakened, and there is no going back to the "other" life. And yet she is hesitant to fully embrace whatever stands before her. She cannot imagine surviving the encounter. It is as if the blind man had opened his eyes but then stepped back, surrounded by glory but too fearful to worship:

> So safer—guess—with just my soul
> Opon the window pane
> Where other creatures put their eyes—
> Incautious—of the Sun—

Dickinson's speaker hears the Gospel's invitation but pauses on this side of the windowpane, achingly aware of a beauty and terror just outside. There is, of course, nothing "safe" about this halfway position, as the stuttered "guess" in the first line I have quoted suggests. Her awakened soul is alive to a power that "other creatures," their eyes still intact, do not know enough about to be cautious of. She is deeply alive to its terrible beauty but is unable to imagine being fully in its presence. It is as if she had been shaken awake, but had not yet identified the one who broke into her blindness as the Son of Man—God himself coming near not to strike her dead but to touch her eyes and stroke her cheek. What would have to happen for her to be able to give herself to all that she yearns for and open her eyes? That is what still awaits us in the Gospel. Dickinson powerfully prepares us to hear it.

Good Shepherd, 10:1-42

In these central chapters, those opposed to Jesus have offered him a rich set of images with which to describe himself. Rest in me, he says to those who know they are not whole. Eat my flesh, he says to the hungry. Know the truth, he says to the enslaved. Let me open your eyes, he says to those who cannot see. Those opposed to Jesus do not see themselves this way. Not being "of God," they do not recognize his voice when he speaks to them in such a way. They do not understand what is becoming more and more clear to the reader—that in their willful refusal to see or be made whole they are in fact acting out the very names by which they are being called. Committed to a life elsewhere, they are blind to what is in front of them; they are hungry for what it offers but incapable of taking it in. In the last scene in this section, Jesus uses the irresponsibility of the leaders in putting the blind man out of the temple (9:34) to describe himself as the people's real leader, God's true shepherd. When that shepherd calls, he says, drawing together this entire sequence, he will call his sheep by name—hungry, thirsty, crippled, or enslaved—and his true sheep will recognize his voice and respond.

Jesus begins by asking those gathered around him to visualize a sheep-fold—an enclosure with walls to protect the sheep and a door, guarded by a doorkeeper, through which sheep can be led in and out:

> Truly, truly, I say to you, he who does not enter by the door into the fold of the sheep, but climbs up some other way, he is a thief and a robber. But he who enters by the door is a shepherd of the sheep. To him the doorkeeper opens, and the sheep hear his voice, and he calls his own sheep by name, and leads them out. When he puts forth all his own, he goes before them, and the sheep follow him because they know his voice. And a stranger they simply will not follow, but will flee from him, because they do not know the voice of strangers. (10:1-5)

As they have just demonstrated in their treatment of the blind man, the people's leaders are not acting as shepherds. They are acting like "thieves and robbers." Jesus is drawing from various Old Testament passages that compare Israel to a flock and its leaders to shepherds who, having been left in charge, ignore the needs of the sheep and think only of themselves. Ezekiel, for example, charges such leaders with feeding and enriching themselves at the expense of the flock: "Woe, shepherds of Israel who have been feeding themselves! Should not the shepherds feed the flock? You eat the fat and clothe yourselves with the wool, you slaughter the fat sheep without feeding the flock. Those who are sickly, you have not strengthened, the diseased you have not healed, the broken you have not bound up, the scattered you have not brought back, nor have you sought for the lost; but with force and with severity you have dominated them" (Ezek 34:2-4). Those who claim to lead you are merely thieves and robbers, Jesus calmly says. Ignore their voices.

When the people do not immediately understand this figure of speech, Jesus explains. In him, God has provided his flock with a door through which they can pass in to safety and out again to pasture. By ignoring that door—by deliberately turning their back on it and, metaphorically, clambering over the wall—their leaders have demonstrated that they are not interested in their sheep's well-being at all. They have revealed themselves to be not shepherds but thieves and robbers, strangers who should not be followed:

> Truly, truly, I say to you, I am the door of the sheep. All who came before Me are thieves and robbers, but the sheep did not hear them. I am the door; if anyone enters through Me, he shall be saved, and shall go in and out, and find pasture. The thief comes only to steal, and kill, and destroy; I came that they might have life, and might have it abundantly. (10:7-10)

By using this metaphor, Jesus reminds them that Israel has been in this situation before. What God had promised to do has now accomplished. Think, for example, of the passage from Ezekiel to which we have just referred. Because his appointed shepherds had shown themselves to be thieves and robbers, God promised that he himself would come and shepherd his people:

> "I will feed My flock and I will lead them to rest," declares the Lord God. "I will seek the lost, bring back the scattered, bind up the broken, and strengthen the sick; but the fat and the strong I will destroy. I will feed them with judgment." (Ezek 34:15-16)

Not only is Jesus the door, then, through which God will lead his people to life, he is also the shepherd—the good or true shepherd, taking on God's role and doing what Israel's leaders had failed to do. It is a breathtaking claim:

I am the good shepherd; the good shepherd lays down His life for the sheep. He who is a hireling, and not a shepherd, who is not the owner of the sheep, beholds the wolf coming, and leaves the sheep, and flees, and the wolf snatches them, and scatters them. He flees because he is a hireling and is not concerned about the sheep. I am the good shepherd; and I know My own, and My own know Me, even as the Father knows Me and I know the Father; and I lay down My life for the sheep. (10:11-15)

Unlike the failed or thieving shepherds, Jesus "know[s]" his own and his own "know" him. They know his voice and follow him, the blind man being the most recent example. Furthermore, because, like God, he owns the sheep and is no mere "hireling," he is willing to do all that is necessary to protect them and feed them and bring them home again. He is willing, in fact, to die for them—to "lay down his life for the sheep."

Laying down his life is no hyperbole, he continues. It is what God has called him to do for the sheep they both love. His death is how God will feed and bind up and bring back the scattered. Because he knows his Father and his Father knows him, Jesus can fulfill God's promise in Ezekiel to be their true shepherd: "For this reason the Father loves Me, because I lay down My life that I may take it again. No one has taken it away from Me, but I lay it down on My own initiative. I have authority to lay it down, and I have authority to take it up again. This commandment I received from My Father" (10:17-18). This is what those opposed to Jesus cannot accept. Not only has he accused them of being thieves and robbers, he has claimed a closeness to God that no man has ever claimed. What God desires, he desires, and he has been given the "authority" to bring it about. No wonder "division" arises again among those who hear these words.

Time passes, and John moves ahead to the Feast of Dedication. The same issues are on the table however, encouraging us to read the two scenes together. Jesus is in the temple again, walking in the portico of Solomon, and the Jewish leaders corner him and ask him to tell them plainly if he is the Messiah. They are looking for words to use against him, because Jesus has already made a number of clear claims as to who he is. He turns their question against them, saying that he has already told them, but they have refused to hear and accept his words—returning to his original figure of speech and identifying them as people who are not his sheep and do not recognize his voice:

I told you, and you do not believe; the works that I do in My Father's name, these bear witness of Me. But you do not believe, because you are not of My sheep. My sheep hear My voice, and I know them, and they follow Me;

and I give eternal life to them, and they shall never perish; and no one shall snatch them out of My hand. My Father, who has given them to Me, is greater than all; and no one is able to snatch them out of the Father's hand. I and the Father are one. (10:25-30)

Because he and the Father "are one," his voice is God's voice and the life he offers is the life God is offering them. That is the door they refuse to be coaxed through. Weak, scattered, broken, lost—nothing in them responds to such names. They cannot imagine God speaking to them in such a way, especially through the words of another man.

Their immediate response is to grab stones. For which of his "good works" are they seeking to stone him, Jesus asks. For blasphemy, they say, "because You, being a man, make Yourself out to be God" (10:33). Jesus' reply seems like a bit of sophisticated wordplay, taking the sting out his claim to be one with his Father: "Has it not been written in your Law, 'I said, You are gods'? If he called them gods, to whom the word of God came (and the Scripture cannot be broken), do you say of Him, whom the Father sanctified and sent into the world, 'You are blaspheming,' because I said, 'I am the Son of God'?" (10:34-36). But this is not evasive wordplay. Jesus is quoting Psalm 82 and the speaker's charge that Israel's rulers have grown corrupt and unjust. "How long will you judge unjustly, / And show partiality to the wicked?" Asaph asks. What God has called them to do is "Vindicate the weak and the fatherless; / Do justice to the afflicted and destitute," but these rulers have abandoned their charges, leaving them to "walk about in darkness," fragile and vulnerable. God has called his rulers to a high task, acting as gods ("elohim") in his place—"I said, 'You are gods, / And all of you are sons of the Most High.'"—but they have turned away from that task and failed to shepherd the flock. Asaph ends the psalm by calling on God to arise and "judge the earth" in the place of these false judges, "For it is Thou who dost possess all the nations" (Psalm 82:8).

And that is exactly what Jesus is now claiming to do. As "the Son of God" he is doing what these "sons of God" could not—what only God could do. He is doing the works of His Father (10:37)—shepherding, offering justice to the afflicted, defending the weak and powerless. "If I do not do the works of My Father, do not believe Me," he says. "But if I do them, though you do not believe Me, believe the works, that you may know and understand that the Father is in Me, and I in the Father" (10:37-38). But only those who see themselves as weak or lost or powerless can truly make sense of God reaching out this way to the downtrodden. And only those with such a notion of God can recognize his voice in the words of this magnetic, elusive man. Those who know God or are being drawn toward him hear his voice and, though perhaps from a great distance, recognize their names being called. Others find his words too much to take in, too difficult to hear, and, like the leaders, something that should be eliminated. What they cannot make out, they cannot abide coming near.

George Herbert, "The Collar" (1633)

In "The Collar," posthumously published in 1633, George Herbert dramatizes his shepherd calling his name, the effect on him being exactly as Jesus claims in the Gospel, but the story he tells about approaching that moment surprises us at every turn, suggesting that recognizing one's name in one's inner din is not always a straightforward process. Looking back on a moment of frustration in which he pounded on a table ("struck the board") and decided to free himself from what he saw as a dry, stunted life, Herbert's speaker gives such convincing voice to his reasons for taking action that we are shocked, along with him, when a different voice cuts through that clatter and calls him back. Exploring that hungry inner landscape along with the poet, we are being prepared, almost without our knowledge, to hear a different voice, gently offering to feed us:

> I struck the board and cry'd, No more.
> I will abroad!
> What? Shall I ever sigh and pine?
> My lines and life are free; free as the rode,
> Loose as the winde, as large as store.
> Shall I be still in suit?
> Have I no harvest but a thorn
> To let me bloud, and not restore
> What I have lost with cordiall fruit?
> Sure there was wine
> Before my sighs did drie it: there was corn
> Before my tears did drown it.
> Is the yeare onely lost to me?
> Have I no bayes to crown it,
> No flowers, no garlands gay? all blasted?
> All wasted?
> Not so, my heart; but there is fruit,
> And thou hast hands.
> Recover all thy sigh-blown age
> On double pleasures: leave thy cold dispute
> Of what is fit, and not. Forsake thy cage,

> Thy rope of sands,
> Which pettie thoughts have made, and made to thee
> Good cable, to enforce and draw,
> And be thy law,
> While thou didst wink and wouldst not see.
> Away; take heed:
> I will abroad.
> Call in thy deaths head there: tie up thy fears.
> He that forbears
> To suit and serve his need,
> Deserves his load.
> But as I rav'd and grew more fierce and wilde
> At every word,
> Me thoughts I heard one calling, *Child!*
> And I reply'd, *My Lord.*[17]

The majority of the poem is a past-tense recreation of what the speaker cried out, in his frustration. "No more," he shouts, to the wind or the dark, "I will abroad." He is convinced that the life he now lives is too confining. He has spent his time "sigh[ing] and pin[ing]" for what he deserves but seemingly can never have—"lines and life" as "free as the rode, / Loose as the winde, as large as store." There must be an "abroad" where those restrictions, that "Collar," would no longer hold him back. Here, it seems to him, God demands that he be always "in suit," always pleading for what he has lost. In such a world, the only "harvest" he anticipates is a "thorn" to draw more blood and reduce his inner store even further, in contrast to the overflowing bins and vats (the "cordiall fruit") he surely deserves. I'm not designed for such a life, he says: "No more."

Having said such a thing, he needs to justify himself. There once was wine, he argues, before his "sighs did drie it." There once was corn, before his "tears did drown it." He alone seems to have lost "the year," he laments, looking back over it and seeing it crowned with no "bayes," wreathed in no "garlands." All seems "blasted," "wasted," with no hope of a change. "Not so," he tells his heart. There still "is fruit" somewhere, and he still "hast hands." He needs to use them, busying himself about what he deserves, rather than wasting his time in endless debates about what is proper and what is not: "Recover all thy sigh-blown age / On double pleasures: leave thy cold dispute / Of what is fit, and what is not."

The speaker even adopts biblical language in talking with himself, making a version of the argument Jesus made to the "enslaved" Jews of chapter 9 who would not admit that they were not free. You are living in a "cage," he

tells himself. Break free of it; all it does is hold you back. It is made of nothing—its ropes are "sand," "petty thoughts" which have become "good cable,"
binding him tightly and "enforc[ing]" certain behaviors, "draw[ing]" him
into conformity with a "law" that is no law at all but only someone else's petty
standards. You are refusing to "see" he tells himself. You are "wink[ing]" at
something that seems blindingly obvious. Take your life back. Do not settle
for dust and dryness.

As if he has convinced himself of the wisdom of his initial outcry, the
speaker repeats it, this time in full confidence: "Away; take heed: / I will
abroad." That "deaths head" that had hung before him, reminding him that
this world was just a mist and judgment was inevitable? "Call [it] in." Those
"fears" that had set him endlessly disputing every little action? "Tie [them]
up." "*Thy* deaths head," "*thy* fears," he says: they are no longer his, just forces
lived so close to for so long that they had come to seem as inevitable as
breathing. But there is nothing inevitable about them, he tells himself. You
have a choice, and if you refuse to act, then you have chosen the load that
is weighing you down: "He that forbears / To suit and serve his need, /
Deserves his load." The genius of the poem lies in the convincing manner in
which Herbert renders this argument. Surely freedom is what we deserve—
an openness to life and not a cold clenched heart. And surely much of what
binds us is our own doing, some man-made law designed to hold the world's
frightening abundance in check. Did Jesus not say as much to those who
opposed him?

Having brought us to this point, Herbert suddenly pulls us up short.
"But as I rav'd and grew more fierce and wilde," he writes, and we are startled. That was raving? That was out of control? It did not sound like that, not
to the speaker and not, I think, to the reader. And that would be his point.
What let him recognize this as raving was another voice—the voice of the
one who knew his name:

> But as I rav'd and grew more fierce and wilde
> > At every word
> Me thoughts I heard one calling, *Child!*
> > And I reply'd, *My Lord.*

The voice did not pull him back and say "Watch yourself, you've gone too
far." It did not rein him in with stronger "cable." It simply said *"Child!"* And
in saying that, it offered him all he needed—home, security, a place where he
was known, standing in the world; all the things brought to the surface by
his outcry. By spilling out all that he thought he deserved, Herbert's speaker,
almost inadvertently, prepared himself to hear the voice of his Lord. That

quiet voice let him hear his own words by contrast—the hollow bravado of all that flashing rhetoric—and then calmly called him home.

How does a shepherd gather his sheep? He calls us by our true names—Needy, Broken, Enslaved, "*Child!*" Such a name, Herbert shows us, balances itself against all the pleasures we think we deserve—balances and comprehends them, refiguring a life as free as the road and as loose as the wind as a life with God forever. To turn away from that voice and hear in it only accusation, as we see in these central chapters of the Gospel, is to let the voices of the world take hold and draw one away from the very thing desired.

GLORY (JOHN 11:1–12:50)

After all the focus on not seeing, John 11 and 12 turn back to the inner circle of those who are willing to have their eyes opened, who wait expectantly even if all is not clear yet. The central focus here is the raising of Lazarus from the dead—the last sign. Raising Lazarus quite literally demonstrates what Jesus has come to accomplish. Life is dwelling with God, seeing him, taking him in, and resting—all of which the raising of Lazarus pictures. What is added to the discussion now is that Jesus will accomplish this—raise the dead to life with God—through his own death. All of the elements of this sequence point forward toward that. It is a difficult thing to see, difficult because we are blind to its necessity. But when its necessity dawns, as it does for the poets I turn to here, his death is seen as glory. Jesus is, in these chapters, laying out in advance this notion of glory, preparing us to see and understand, when it is finally revealed.

Lazarus, 11:1-53

John begins with the fact that Lazarus of Bethany, brother of Mary and Martha, is sick. Mary, he tells us, leaping ahead of himself, is the one "who anointed the Lord with ointment, and wiped His feet with her hair" (11:2), some days in the future. By referring to Jesus as "the Lord" and speaking to us as if we had already heard the story of Mary and appreciated its significance, John writes as if we were part of the inner circle of those who had been stirred and drawn toward the words of Jesus, rather than repelled or baffled by them. Whether that is true or not, it allows John to adopt a different tone, explaining, pointing forward, anticipating, inviting us to consider ourselves as among those who understood. The poets I consider in this chapter pick up on this tone of voice, responding to the Gospel as if from within its embrace.

The sisters of Lazarus send word to Jesus that "he whom You love is sick" (11:3). Jesus, who is some days' journey away, receives the news and tells his disciples, "This sickness is not unto death, but for the glory of God, that the Son of God may be glorified by it" (11:4). This is of course still quite mysterious, but it is exactly what the reader is about to see—God's glory unfolded as his Son overcomes the powers of death. Jesus "loved Martha, and her sister, and Lazarus," John continues, and then adds, "When therefore He heard that he was sick, He stayed then two days longer in the place where He was" (11:6). This gets our attention. Jesus stayed two more days before beginning his journey to Bethany—out of love. Letting those two days pass makes it clear that raising Lazarus is not an improvised response to an intervention gone bad but a deliberate sign, planned in advance and performed out of love. Loving Mary and Martha, Jesus waits two days, assuring their brother's death, in order to show them his glory, the greatest gift he can give them.

The days pass and Jesus tells his disciples that now it is time to travel to Bethany. Fearfully, they remind him that the Jewish leaders, clustered near Jerusalem, are seeking to kill him. He responds that as long as they walk in his light, their footing will be sure and they will not stumble. What he is about to do, he tells them, is something both very simple and almost impossible to comprehend: "Our friend Lazarus has fallen asleep; but I go, that I may awaken him out of sleep" (11:11). They at first take this literally, but Jesus of course means something much more radical: "Lazarus is dead, and I am glad for your sakes that I was not there, so that you may believe; but let us go to him" (11:14-15). This all along is what he has been calling them to believe—that he has the power to overcome death, leading them out of exile into the light of God's presence. This will be the culmination of all his signs and a turning point of the Gospel.

They arrive in Bethany and are informed that Lazarus has been in the tomb four days. A crowd from Jerusalem, only a few miles off, has gathered to console the sisters. Martha hears that Jesus is approaching and goes out to meet him, apparently without the crowd noticing. She says to him, "Lord, if You had been here, my brother would not have died. Even now I know that whatever You ask of God, God will give You" (11:21-22). This is a powerfully mixed set of statements. She knows he has power—he could have healed her brother—but she positions that power off to the side with the term "if"—if only he had been there, Lazarus would not have died. This is the sort of language we use when we try to make sense of a trauma: if only this had happened, the terrible thing would not have occurred. She is stunned and is casting about for words. And yet, not even knowing what to ask, she also knows that God hears him, and so she turns to him. Jesus responds, "Your brother shall rise again" (11:23). As many commentators have noted, Martha takes this as a comforting commonplace: the just will be raised again at the end of time. Yes, I know, she replies, "in the resurrection on the last day" (11:24).

But Jesus means more than this. He continues, "I am the resurrection and the life; he who believes in Me shall live even if he dies, and everyone who lives and believes in Me shall never die. Do you believe this?" (11:25-26). This is extraordinary. Resurrection and life are present here and now, he tells Martha. He has come not to point to these things in the future but to be these things now—bringing life to those spiritually dead, enabling them to live with him forever. "Do you believe this," he asks. I do, she says: "I have believed that You are the Christ, the Son of God, even He who comes into the world" (11:27). The tense is important here: I "have believed" that you are the Messiah, the one God sent to bring such blessings. She believes this, but she has not fully grasped that what she believes is about to come into play now.

For the moment, this offer stays suspended. Martha goes and tells Mary that Jesus has come and is "calling" for her. We remember him calling his sheep by name. Mary arises "quickly" and comes to him. The crowd sees her sudden movement and follows her, supposing she is going to the tomb to weep. Coming to Jesus, she falls at his feet—perhaps a more intense gesture than that of her sister—and greets Jesus exactly as her sister had: "Lord, if You had been here, my brother would not have died" (11:32). Again, this registers less as a complaint and more as a bewildered attempt to make sense of things. Where Martha was able to continue on and express her confidence that "even now" God was able to act through Jesus, Mary simply weeps. And Jesus responds to her as well, not with the statement about resurrection that he offered Martha but with his own tears:

> When Jesus therefore saw her weeping, and the Jews who came with her, also weeping, He was deeply moved in spirit, and was troubled, and said, "Where have you laid him?" They said to Him, "Lord, come and see." Jesus wept. (11:33-35)

Not yet at the tomb, Jesus is deeply moved and weeps. Carson explains that "deeply moved" means "outraged," which helps us see what is going on.[1] Seeing the tears of Mary and the Jewish crowd, Jesus is outraged at the hole death has torn in the very fabric of existence. He is outraged at what it signifies—that sin has opened a chasm between God and his creation. But he does not simply express outrage, he also weeps. If outrage occurs outside of a situation, weeping occurs inside. Weeping, he joins Mary in her grief. In doing so, he takes on the burden of her flesh and feels what she feels. He enters the human condition. "I am the resurrection and the life," he tells Martha. "I am here, in your pain," his tears tell Mary. The crowd does not understand, gawking and remarking "Behold how He loved him" (11:36)—which is true, of course, but not the point. Jesus is not weeping for his own loss—he knows he will see Lazarus again—but for the human situation, at how much we have all lost. That is what draws his tears.

When Jesus comes to the tomb, he is "deeply moved" again, but this time he is outraged from within their condition, within their tears. John's point is quite striking. Jesus has taken on flesh in order to strike back at the outrage of sin and death—coming not to announce resurrection but to accomplish it, here and now, in their flesh. Having come to the tomb, Jesus says "Remove the stone," and Martha, who we now discover is part of the crowd, replies, "Lord, by this time there will be a stench, for he has been dead four days" (11:39). "I am the resurrection and the life," Jesus had told her. "Do you believe?" Now, he returns to that suspended conversation: "Did I not say to you, if you believe, you will see the glory of God?" (11:40). You will see God's glory *now*, he says to those who believe, transforming death into life.

To make sure everyone understands that he and his Father are one in this extravagant act, Jesus prays, "Father, I thank Thee that Thou heardest Me. And I knew that Thou hearest Me always; but because of the people standing around I said it, that they may believe that Thou didst send Me" (11:41-42). "Lazarus, come forth" (11:43), he cries, and all becomes clear. Lazarus comes forth, bound hand and foot with grave wrappings, his face encircled with a cloth. Jesus has him unbound, his body having been won back from death and made whole again, a picture of the spiritual transformation Jesus will enter into death to accomplish. At this, many believe, but others return to Jerusalem and carry word to the authorities as to what he has done.

John chillingly completes the story by following the tale as it is carried back to Jerusalem. There, the chief priest and Pharisees convene a council in order to respond to these events. We are suddenly back in the world where no one can see. "If we let Him go on like this," they say, "all men will believe in Him, and the Romans will come and take away both our place and our nation" (11:48). This is how the surface looks. Belief, since it would be in somebody brilliantly "making himself" out to be someone he is not, would only lead to their being crushed by Rome's larger, also human, power. Their positions of authority would disappear, and the nation itself would be put at risk—all true, from their perspective. But Caiaphas, the high priest, tells them they are wrong to despair. They need to act: "You know nothing at all, nor do you take into account that it is expedient for you that one man should die for the people, and that the whole nation should not perish" (11:49, 50). To this, John quietly adds, from his own perspective outside of the story, anticipating the cross and the way the death of Jesus will in fact save many from perishing, that God was at work even in these unbelieving words: "Now this he did not say on his own initiative; but being high priest that year, he prophesied that Jesus was going to die for the nation, and not for the nation only, but that He might also gather together into one the children of God who are scattered abroad" (11:51-52). This is why Jesus took on flesh and wept with Mary—so that he could die in her place, becoming for her the resurrection and life, freeing her, and all those who believed, from the bonds of death.

Paul Mariani, "Pietà"

Paul Mariani's poem "Pietà" brilliantly gets at the glory Christ displays in raising Lazarus, focusing particularly on what we have just observed: his entrance into death—Mary's tears, the human condition—in order to bring about life. Retelling a story from a New Year's Eve party, Mariani, in this 2005 poem, finds in it a way to approach the Gospel:

> New Year's Eve, a party at my brother's.
> Hats, favors, the whole shebang, as we waited
> for one world to die into another.
>
> And still it took three martinis before
> she could bring herself to say it. How
> the body of her grown son lay alone there
>
> in the ward, just skin & bone, the nurses
> masked & huddled in the doorway, afraid
> to cross over into a world no one seemed
>
> to understand. This was a dozen years ago,
> you have to understand, before the thing
> her boy had had became a household word.
>
> Consider Martha. Consider Lazarus four days gone.
> *If only you'd been here*, she says, *if only
> you'd been here*. And no one now to comfort her,
>
> no one except this priest, she says, an old
> friend who'd stood beside them through the dark
> night of it all, a bull-like man, skin black

as the black he wore, the only one who seemed
willing to walk across death's threshold into
that room. And now, she says, when the death

was over, to see him lift her son, light as a baby
with the changes death had wrought, and cradle him
like that, then sing him on his way, a cross

between a lullaby & blues, *mmm, hmmm,* while
the nurses, still not understanding what they saw,
stayed outside and watched from the door.[2]

Mariani places us at a threshold of the year, waiting for "one world to die into another," and in that space, describes a woman's story about her son's death, presumably from AIDS. What she focuses on is his body, just after death, "alone there in the ward," even the nurses "masked & huddled in the doorway, afraid / to cross over into a world no one seemed / to understand." The empty ward is a version of death itself, the fearful space into which Lazarus and all of us cross over. No one "understands"—not the nurses, a dozen years ago when the disease was not yet "a household word," and not the reader, who, for all its familiarity, can do little more than peer in at death's isolating work.

"Consider Martha. Consider Lazarus four days gone," Mariani writes in the fourth stanza. There was something in the woman's lonely grief that called him back to the Gospel story. She was like Martha with Lazarus four days gone, desperately saying to Jesus, *"If only you'd been here"* and thinking not of his ability to change anything but only of her grief. An interesting thing happens here with the word "Consider," for as the poet does so, as he considers the Lazarus story through the light of her words, the poem shifts into the present tense. It is as if the Gospel had come alive for the poet in the mother's words. *"If only you'd been here,"* the woman "says," or words to that effect, describing her son's body and the empty ward, "no one now to comfort her." "She says," is repeated three times, insisting on the point. "Now" is repeated twice. Both stories are alive now as we wait "for one world to die into another."

There was no one there "except this priest, she says," an old friend who "stood beside them" through the terrible days. He was "the only one who seemed / willing to walk across death's threshold into / that room." "And now, she says," the moment happening before our eyes, "when the death / was over, to see him lift her son, light as a baby / with the changes death had wrought, and cradle him / like that, then sing him on his way." He cradled him like Mary did her own dead son—that famous, often-sculpted image—and sang a song of mourning and peace, lifting him "on his way."

Mariani sees Jesus in the priest. Or to put it another way, in the priest's "cross[ing] over into a world no one seemed / to understand," "walk[ing] across death's threshold" in order to embrace the woman's son, Mariani sees Jesus before the tomb of Lazarus. This is what it meant for Jesus to weep along with Mary—he was taking on the lonely horror of death for her, as no one else could. He was crossing over into the empty ward of death on her behalf, "walk[ing] across death's threshold" in order to bring healing and life. And what Jesus does here, he does even more explicitly on Calvary, Mariani quietly suggests, breaking one of his last lines to make the cross visible, speaking of the priest's song as "a cross / between a lullaby & blues." Jesus not only felt outrage at death's horror, he wept and took on its weight—took on the way it isolated Martha and cut her off from the one she loved; he entered its empty ward. What Mariani sees, as he considers the Gospel through the words of the mother, is that its words of comfort—offering to make a "lullaby & blues" out of our broken world—come at a terrible price. Unlike the rest of us who, along with the nurses, stand "outside" and watch, Jesus comes inside death, inside where Mary weeps. "If only you'd been there," we say, grieving over our private hurts and reaching out to anyone who will listen. And just there, Jesus crosses over. Do you "understand," the poet asks. Can you hear what I heard in her voice? Do you understand those tears?

Glory (I), 12:1-36

A series of scenes follow as Jesus and his disciples move to Jerusalem for the final Passover. All of them are linked to the raising of Lazarus, and each tells us more about the glory of God about to be revealed as Jesus enters the private ward of death on our behalf. In the first scene, we find ourselves in Bethany, just outside of Jerusalem. Jerusalem itself is crowded. Many there are expecting him, including the chief priests and Pharisees who are looking for a way to seize him and kill him. That tension hangs over a supper given in his honor in Bethany. Martha is serving, and Lazarus is reclining at the table with Jesus, but John's focus is on Mary. She does an extraordinary thing, taking a pound of very costly perfume and anointing Jesus with it, then wiping his feet with her unbound hair. Lowering, even humiliating herself in order to indicate how highly she exalts the one who has saved her brother, her act of adoration fills the house with its "fragrance" (12:3). Judas, who does not understand or share in the intensity of her feelings, criticizes the excess of her gesture, asking why the perfume had not been sold and the money given to the poor—a remark, John tells us, that covers over his heart's true concern. Jesus defends Mary with an enigmatic saying that many commentators have struggled with:

"Let her alone, in order that she may keep it for the day of My burial. For the poor you always have with you, but you do not always have Me" (12:7-8).

It is unlikely that Jesus means "Let her keep it for my burial," since she seems to have just poured it all out, at great expense and to powerful effect.[3] Perhaps what he is pointing out is that what she had kept for his burial she is using today, so great is her love for him. Let her alone, he says. It is a proper for her to value him in this way. But more than that, Jesus seems to be suggesting that in anointing him, she is actually preparing his body for death, as she had originally intended. She is using the perfume for the very purpose for which she had kept it. She does not understand this, of course. She is celebrating the one who raised her brother from the dead, but as she does so, Jesus suggests, she is looking forward to his death—the power through which he will bring life to the world. Looking back from the cross, John understands this and carefully links these scenes. The "glory of God" that Mary celebrates, the power through which Lazarus will truly be brought back to life, is that which he has seen fully and finally displayed in the Son's approaching, humiliating death.

The death of Jesus is anticipated once again in the celebration that accompanies his entrance into Jerusalem the next day. As Jesus moves toward the city, a great crowd comes out to meet him. Like Mary, they exalt him, waving palm branches and crying out "Hosanna! Blessed is He who comes in the name of the Lord, even the King of Israel" (12:13). Their words are drawn from Psalm 118—a celebration of a messianic figure sent by God to save his people:

> O Lord, do save, we beseech Thee;
> O Lord, we beseech Thee, do send prosperity!
> Blessed is the one who comes in the name of the Lord.
>
> (Ps 118:25-26)

"Hosanna" is the plea "Save us, we pray," taken from the first part of verse 25, but the identification of Jesus as the "King of Israel" is the crowd's own addition. "King of Israel," as we saw in Nathaniel's words in 1:49, is another term for Messiah, which tells us that they are celebrating him as Israel's promised king—the figure who will lead the nation back to prosperity and triumph. The palm branches they wave, scholars note, are also associated with national identity. Today, they believe, the king God has sent them, fresh from raising Lazarus from the dead and the possessor of great powers, has come to his national city to lead his people to victory.

Jesus confirms their identification of him as king by finding a young donkey to ride in to the city, deliberately echoing well-known words from the prophet Zechariah:

> Rejoice greatly, O daughter of Zion!
> Shout in triumph, O daughter of Jerusalem!
> Behold, your king is coming to you;
> He is just and endowed with salvation,
> Humble and mounted on a donkey,
> Even on a colt, the foal of a donkey.
>
> (Zech 9:9-10)

Those who remembered these words would have understood this as Jesus' claim to be their long-awaited king returning to his capital in victory. Riding on a donkey rather than a warhorse looks forward to the peace of the worldwide dominion that would follow. The multitude pouring out of the city joins the multitude following Jesus up from Bethany. No wonder the Pharisees complain to each other that their efforts to control and eliminate this threat to their power have come to nothing: "You see that you are not doing any good; look, the world has gone after Him" (12:19).

But, much as with Mary unknowingly celebrating the death of Jesus, John adds that there was something going on in Jesus' entrance into the city that was not understood until later, after the cross: "These things His disciples did not understand at the first; but when Jesus was glorified, then they remembered that these things were written of Him, and that they had done these things to Him" (12:16). Jesus' "glorification," we remember from 7:39, is his death and resurrection—being lifted up on the cross is understood, after the resurrection, to be a triumphant display of God's glory. John brings this up now in order to invite the reader to think twice. What did the disciples see on looking back from the perspective of the cross? First, they saw that these things, in the Psalms and Zechariah, "were written of Him," and second, that the verses alluded to had contexts that, although not taken into account then, were now seen as vitally important. If we return to Psalm 118, for example, we find that the conquering king celebrated in verse 26 ("Blessed is the one who comes in the name of the Lord") is a figure previously described in the psalm as broken, rejected, and "disciplined severely" (Ps 118:18). What the crowd was in fact celebrating, in the psalm and, unknowingly, on this day in Jerusalem, was God's use of this broken figure to save his people: "The stone which the builders rejected / Has become the chief corner stone. / This is the Lord's doing; / It is marvelous in our eyes" (Ps 118:22-23). What the disciples understood, after the cross, was that the crowd was celebrating not a figure of great might but a figure about to be broken and rejected.

So, too, the memory of Jesus coming to the city in "humility," on a colt, would have suggested a different sort of humility when looked back upon— not a conqueror's quiet assurance but a figure embracing his own humiliation and death. What the disciples saw was that the crowd, in its roaring support, was actually celebrating their king coming forward to be broken on their behalf—the Messiah, the King of Israel, but not the one they expected. John points us in this direction now, before the events of the final days, not to convince us but to prepare us to revise what we have understood in light of the cross. It is very deftly done.

Jesus makes much of this explicit in the next scene, after he and his disciples have entered the city. A group of Greeks, Gentile believers, there for the Passover, approach Philip and ask to see Jesus. The continual talk about him has drawn their interest. When this request reaches Jesus, he takes it as an indication that the "hour" to which he has been called has begun, and he explains what he means by the term "glorified": "The hour has come for the Son of Man to be glorified. Truly, truly, I say to you, unless a grain of wheat falls into the earth and dies, it remains by itself alone; but if it dies, it bears much fruit" (12:23-24). His death, in ways yet to be fully explained, will bear the fruit of many lives made new. The interest of Gentiles is an important signal because now what the Pharisees feared is coming true—the whole "world," both Jew and Gentile, is beginning to be drawn to him.

"Glorified" is a powerful, complex term. It means to be honored. When John uses the term, he is pointing to the honor that properly comes to Jesus as his innate glory is brought to light. So, in 2:11, Jesus "manifested his glory" in changing the water into wine. But deeper than this, John believes that the glory Jesus manifests is the very glory of God—he makes visible God's own nature. This was the core idea of the Prologue, where John testified that "the Word became flesh, and dwelt among us, and we beheld His glory, glory as of the only begotten from the Father, full of grace and truth" (1:14). It is what we just saw in the raising of Lazarus, where Jesus bringing him back from the dead made visible "the glory of God" (11:4, 40). To say, then, that when he is lifted up on the cross he will be "glorified" is to say that in his death, the grain of wheat falling to earth and dying, God's deepest nature will be made visible. What is most to be praised and honored about God will be made visible there, on the cross, in his humiliation. Richard Bauckham writes that

> [T]he revelation of who God is—to the world takes place in Jesus' death. . . . Here God is seen to be God in his radical self-giving, descending to the most abject human condition and, in that human obedience, humiliation, suffering and death, being no less truly God than he is in his cosmic rule and glory on the heavenly throne. It is not that God is manifest

in heavenly glory and hidden in the human degradation on the cross. The latter makes known who God is no less than the former does. . . . [On the cross] the glory of God whom no one has ever seen was revealed. In this act of self-giving God is most truly himself and defines himself for the world.[4]

The hour of his death—the hour in which God's deepest nature or glory will be revealed—is now here.

As the implications of this sink in, Jesus grows deeply troubled: "Now My soul has become troubled; and what shall I say, 'Father, save Me from this hour'?" (12:27). I take this to be a serious question. Feeling the horror of the hour approaching—his rejection and abandonment not simply by the crowds but by God himself—Jesus wonders for a moment if it might be otherwise. We might imagine a full, silent beat after this question, and then his resolute response: "But for this purpose I came to this hour." In that beat, we feel the weight of what he is about to enter. We understand that when he continues on and says "Father, glorify Thy name" (12:28), he is saying bring honor to yourself through the shattering I am willingly, consciously, about to undergo as an expression of your love. And God reassures him, in words meant for the ears of the crowd, "I have both glorified it, and will glorify it again" (12:28). God has glorified or brought honor to himself through the miracles and signs Jesus has already performed, and he reassures him that he will do so again in the events that are soon to follow.

His death, Jesus continues, will make God's power and love visible in a way never seen before. It will mark the defeat of the world's current order in which people, residing in darkness, are unable to love or even acknowledge the God who created them: "Now judgment is upon this world; now the ruler of this world shall be cast out" (12:31). And it will do so in such a powerful and visible way that people from all the earth will turn to the God of Israel: "And I, if I be lifted up from the earth, will draw all men to Myself" (12:32).

This is, of course, a lot to take in, and the crowd cannot make sense of the claim. How could he be the Messiah if he is to die or be taken away from them? The Messiah was to reign forever: "We have heard out of the Law that the Christ is to remain forever; and how can You say, 'The Son of Man must be lifted up'? Who is this Son of Man?" (12:34). There is really no way of answering this now, before his death and resurrection, so Jesus simply encourages them to cling to him and ponder what he has said. The reader is in much the same situation. We have seen him reaching out to the blind and the hungry and the lost, and now we see him reaching out to the crowd and offering to walk with them into the unimaginable end of the story. The light will not be with them much longer. Are they willing to trust him? "Walk while you have the light, that darkness may not overtake you; he who walks in the darkness does not know where he goes. While you have the light, believe in the light, in order that you may become sons of light" (12:35-36).

Gerard Manley Hopkins, "The Windhover"

The most powerful account I know of the glory expressed in Christ's brokenness can be found in Gerard Manley Hopkins' "The Windhover," a poem dedicated "To Christ our Lord," written in May 1877 but not published until after his death in 1918. What is most valuable about the poem is that it actually lets us experience the turn from one understanding of glory to another, exactly what Jesus was calling those who heard his words to in the Gospel. The poem acknowledges the conventional understanding of glory we all begin with and then, in a burst of insight, turns it on its head. Much like Robinson with her grandfather's tender curiosity alive in her head, Hopkins fills himself with the movements of a falcon, possessor of all the air, moving almost unconsciously in tandem with it, and then, when that flight is suddenly broken off, hears the words of Jesus. This is what it is like to be addressed by those words:

> I caught this morning morning's minion, king-
> dom of daylight's dauphin, dapple-dawn-drawn Falcon, in his riding
> Of the rolling level underneath him steady air, and striding
> High there, how he rung upon the rein of a wimpling wing
> In his ecstasy! then off, off forth on a swing,
> As a skate's heel sweeps smooth on a bow-bend: the hurl and gliding
> Rebuffed the big wind. My heart in hiding
> Stirred for a bird,—the achieve of, the mastery of the thing!
>
> Brute beauty and valour and act, oh, air, pride, plume, here
> Buckle! AND the fire that breaks from thee then, a billion
> Times told lovelier, more dangerous, O my chevalier!
>
> No wonder of it: sheer plod makes plough down sillion
> Shine, and blue-bleak embers, ah my dear,
> Fall, gall themselves, and gash gold-vermilion.[5]

The poem begins by slowly, ecstatically, describing a kestrel, a small falcon, that has caught the poet's eye as it rides the thermals. It is early morning, and the falcon is outlined by the dawn ("dapple-dawn-drawn"). In its grand, commanding position, it seems to be the "minion" or favorite of the morning, the "dauphin" or prince of its "kingdom," talking possession of all that is rightly his. The falcon is all strength and power as it commands the air, confidently responding as the air rolls, then grows steady, then rolls again. This is what glory looks like: the falcon "striding" across the sky, turning circles with such speed and force that its wing ripples or "wimples" at the pressure it takes on, turning circle after circle, then sweeping out like a skater in a single "bow-bend" that pours all of that energy into an effortless arc easily "rebuff[ing] the big wind." Small wonder that the poet finds himself brought to life by this brilliant exhibition. "My heart in hiding / Stirred for a bird," he writes: "the achieve of, the mastery of the thing!" This is exactly what the crowds would have felt outside the walls of Jerusalem as they waved their palms and shouted for their king.

So stirred is the poet's heart that, in the second stanza, words of praise tumble out of his mouth: "Brute beauty and valour and act, oh, air, pride, plume." He sees, in this "brute" thing, beauty and valor acted out above him on the morning's stage. Sees, as he attempts to catch his breath with "oh," the "air" seemingly lifting itself in "pride," "plume[d]" with a flight so ecstatic that the poet's words tumble across each other in an attempt to keep up. All of that occurs "here," as the poet walks the fields in the morning, thinking and responding. All of that, and then it suddenly "Buckle[s]." The flight breaks off, and the smooth, plumed gliding is shattered, its path shifted in such a way that the dawn's light catches the falcon's wing and flares off the diving, back-lit bird.

And here the poet suddenly lifts his eyes to "Christ our Lord," the broken flight of the bird, splintering in flashes of fire, having "drawn" him (12:32) toward a notion of glory far outside of what he had expected. Hopkins signals the shift by capitalizing the word *AND*: "AND the fire that breaks from thee then," he says to Christ, must be a "billion / Times told lovelier, [and] more dangerous" than the dawn light glinting off the swerving bird. Lovely and dangerous—what sort of fire is that? It is the fire of glory, as John understands it—the fire not of mastery but of breaking off and swerving, the fire not of "air, pride, plume" but of all of that buckling on the cross and ushering in something grander and more lovely. The first buckling opens our eyes to the other, "lovelier [and] more dangerous." The poem works so powerfully on the reader because, like the Gospel, it first fills us with a conventional notion of glory and then shatters it, slinging us forward into something that our eyes can barely take in. It trains us to see.

The last stanza is quieter and deeper somehow. Of course, the poet says to Christ in silent wonder. Of course the falcon's broken flight moved him so deeply: the glory of the cross has been written across the world. The cross is everywhere one looks, underlying and undergirding all things. Even the plodding steps of a farmer, moving across a field and turning up soil in thick, shiny gashes of earth, release glory with each new cut. Even dying embers, falling and galling themselves, "gash" forth "gold-vermillion" sparks, crying out, in their flashing colors, the glory of the blood of Christ—the glory of a brokenness that, "ah my dear," he suddenly sees as an expression of love. This is his body, the world says, broken for you. Do you sense its glory? Can you take it in?

Glory (II), 12:37-50

As we have been saying, however, this notion of glory is hard to make sense of until it is fully expressed on the cross. John steps back from his narrative at this point and muses about those who had seen Jesus' signs and heard his words and yet "were not believing in Him" (12:37). Once again, he draws the reader into his confidence, looking forward to things still before us. He finds an explanation for this inability to see in the prophet Isaiah, who, he reports, "saw His glory, and he spoke of Him" (12:41). This is another extraordinary statement. John seems to have two things in mind here. First, he appears to be remembering Isaiah's famous vision of "the Lord sitting on a throne, lofty and exalted, with the train of His robe filling the temple" (Isa 6:1). What he indirectly "saw" of God's glory—his robe, seraphim calling out to each other, "Holy, Holy, Holy, is the Lord of hosts, / The whole earth is full of His glory" (Isa 6:3), trembling foundations, smoke—was enough to throw him to his knees in despair: "Woe is me, for I am ruined! / Because I am a man of unclean lips, / And I live among a people of unclean lips" (Isa 6:5). But, he goes on, one of the seraphim took a burning coal from the altar and touched it to his lips, proclaiming "your iniquity is taken away, and your sin is forgiven" (6:7). What Isaiah saw was God, in all his glory, being yet willing to forgive sins.

The second vision of glory John seems to be referring to is Isaiah's vision of God's Suffering Servant in Isaiah 52 and 53. There, as Bauckham points out, he would have found, in the Greek text, the terms *hupsoō* (lifted up) and *doxazō* (glorified or exalted) being used to describe this mysterious figure:[6]

> Behold, My servant will prosper;
> He will be high and *lifted up*, and *greatly exalted*.
> Just as many were astonished at you, My people,
> So His appearance was marred more than any man,
> And His form more than the sons of men.
> Thus He will sprinkle many nations,
> Kings will shut their mouths on account of Him;

For what had not been told them they will see,
And what they had not heard they will understand.

(Isa 52:13-15)

What John is suggesting, then, is that what Isaiah saw, in both instances, was Christ, the Son of God. The coal on the altar that touched his lips and burned away his sin was Christ—God's glory burning away all that was unclean and unable to stand in his presence. And the Suffering Servant, marred more than any man, was also Christ—God's glory expressing itself in a form never before anticipated, and in that form, "sprinkling" many nations clean. Because Isaiah "saw" God's glory in this way, John writes, he understood in advance how extraordinarily difficult it would be for people to take in what Jesus was saying.

Their refusal to believe, then, is for John (12:38) a simple fulfillment of Isaiah 52 and 53:

Who has believed our message?
And to whom has the arm of the Lord been revealed?
For He grew up before Him like a tender shoot,
And like a root out of parched ground;
He has no stately form or majesty
That we should look upon Him,
Nor appearance that we should be attracted to Him.
He was despised and forsaken of men,
A man of sorrows, and acquainted with grief;
And like one from whom men hide their face,
He was despised, and we did not esteem Him.
Surely our griefs He Himself bore,
And our sorrows He carried;
Yet we ourselves esteemed Him stricken,
Smitten of God and afflicted.
But He was pierced through for our transgressions,
He was crushed for our iniquities;
The chastening for our well-being fell upon Him,
And by His scourging we are healed.

(Isa 53:1-5)

His message was not believed, John writes, because this notion of God's glory was simply too hard to take in on one's own. God would have to make someone's sin as clear to him as Isaiah's in order for him to be able to respond to the notion of God himself, in all his glory, descending to bear his humiliation and chastening for him. This is exactly what the leaders in chapters 5–10 were unable to see, and without that desperate flash of insight, God's self-giving makes no sense.

This, in fact, was what Isaiah was called to proclaim, John goes on. After his vision and cleansing, God called him to "Render the hearts of this people insensitive, / Their ears dull, / And their eyes dim, / Lest they see with their eyes, / Hear with their ears, / Understand with their hearts, / And return and be healed" (Isa 6:10, quoted in John 12:40). Through his proclamation of God's glory and God's response to sin, Isaiah was to drive people away, in incomprehension or disbelief. We have seen this same response to Jesus throughout these central chapters of the Gospel. But why, Isaiah must have asked. And for how long? John must have surely had God's answer to Isaiah in mind when he quoted this charge:

Until cities are devastated and without inhabitant,
Houses are without people,
And the land is utterly desolate,
The Lord has removed men far away,
And the forsaken places are many in the midst of the land.
Yet there will be a tenth portion in it,
And it will again be subject to burning,
Like a terebinth or an oak
Whose stump remains when it is felled.
The holy seed is its stump.

                                                    (Isa 6:11-13)

Isaiah was to preach God's glory until Israel had been reduced to a burned-over, standing stump, its sins fully burned away and punished. Only then would God relent and heal his people.

This sounds terrifying, but what John realized, in looking back at the final week in Jerusalem from his position after the resurrection, was that God had done exactly this. He had allowed people to remain blind until after his judgment had been fully and finally expressed. But he had expressed that judgment, raining devastation down on all things opposed to his nature, by "crush[ing] *Him*," his Servant, "putting *Him* to grief" (Isa 53:10) at the end of that week. There his judgment was "finished" (19:30). And there his glory was visible in all its fullness, a glory "full of grace and truth." Not until that "holy seed" bore the wrath of God and was "pierced through for our transgressions," falling into the earth and dying, could it "bear much fruit." Only then would the fullness of God's glory be manifest and visible.

6

Looking Forward (John 13:1–17:26)

Now we draw the circle even tighter. We move to a private meal, shared by Jesus and the disciples, on the eve of the Passover. Jesus has been pointing to his death—his death as a source of life and victory. God's glory will be revealed. All will be drawn. But it has not happened yet. Now he draws the disciples close to him and prepares them. When it happens, he says, believe—believe that in dying I am in God, doing his will. And then abide, live in what I have done. In doing so, he says, you will be bearing witness to what I have accomplished.

Washing, 13:1-20

We are at the Last Supper, and John comments that, "knowing that His hour had come that He should depart out of this world to the Father" (13:1), and "knowing that the Father had given all things into His hands" (13:3), Jesus deliberately rose from the meal, laid aside his garments, girded himself with a towel, and began to wash the disciples' feet (13:4). John stresses that this was quite deliberate on the part of Jesus. Jesus had "loved His own who were in the world," John writes, and now, almost silently, he pictures what he is about to do to complete that work: "He loved them to the end" (13:1). "To the end" is *eis telos* in the Greek—meaning fully, completely, reaching the limit or goal.[1] The washing is a demonstration of that end. It pictures the full expression of who God is and how he loves that is about to be unveiled.

What we see is the cross. Humbling himself, laying aside his clothing and girding himself with a towel, Jesus does the work of a servant, giving up all that was properly his in order to make them clean. The intimacy of the act is startling. Imagine him pouring water into a basin, kneeling down and washing their feet, one by one, wiping them dry on the towel at his waist. It is like nothing we have seen in the Gospel so far. Imagine each of the disciples staring at him and anticipating his touch as he works his way around the group. The tension must have been unbearable.

Peter, not unexpectedly, is the one who finally reacts when Jesus reaches him, blurting out, "Lord, do You wash my feet?" (13:6). This is not what someone in authority should be doing, he insists, rebuking Jesus for having reversed everything. Peter does not understand what the act is pointing toward, but even if he did, he would have had the same reaction. Accepting such a gift from one so high above him is overwhelming and he cannot bear it. There is no way to pay it back. Jesus understands that this does not make sense yet. "What I do you do not realize now," he says, "but you shall understand hereafter" (13:7). Store this away, he says. After these days, you will understand what I did and why it was necessary. Peter is not satisfied with this explanation. He is embarrassed now, and to protect himself, he forcefully objects: "Never shall You wash my feet!" (13:8). To that, Jesus quietly replies, "If I do not wash you, you have no part with Me" (13:8), beginning to unfold the parable he is enacting before their eyes. On his own, Peter, like the other disciples, is unclean and self-absorbed, continually setting himself apart from the very one he loves. And this will never change until Jesus washes him, overturning every hierarchy Peter knows in order to accomplish something Peter cannot do on his own.

Peter, again not unexpectedly, begins to understand, but then rushes too far ahead: "Lord, not my feet only, but also my hands and my head" (13:9). We laugh, understanding that Jesus has created a picture to illustrate a point, and that Peter does not need more of the picture to receive what it is pointing to. He simply needs to let Jesus wash his feet. One can see, in this, how hard the gift is to accept. There are no degrees about it, no actions one can take to refine or enhance it. One is simply clean or not: "He who has bathed needs only to wash his feet, but is completely clean; and you are clean, but not all of you" (13:10). This is physically true—the disciples need only to have their dusty feet washed to be made entirely clean—but of course the point is a broader one. Jesus is describing a single action through which he will restore everything that had been lost, an action so complete that it cannot be deepened or extended. And it applies to all equally, except "the one who was betraying Him" (13:11), who would not accept the gift. It is, of course, quite striking, as numerous commentators have pointed out, that even though Jesus knew that Satan had already put it into Judas' heart to betray him (13:2), Jesus also washed his feet, extending God's offer of life to him in exactly the same respectful and intimate terms that it was extended to the other disciples.

Having washed their feet, Jesus takes up his clothing again, joins them at the table, and says, "Do you know what I have done to you?" (13:12). I'm not sure that they do, at least not in any full sense, but he continues to explain, in a sense banking instructions for them to return to after his death and resurrection. As their "Teacher and Lord" (13:13), he has given up all that was properly his in order to wash their feet, so great is his love for them. Once that sinks in, they are to do likewise, "wash[ing] one another's feet" (13:14) in extravagant disregard for position or standing in the world, making it clear to all who have eyes to see that life is no longer something one must hoard and protect; it is now something that rains down as a gift. This, in fact, is what they have been called to do—to make visible to the world how deeply they are loved: "Truly, truly, I say to you, he who receives whomever I send receives Me; and he who receives Me receives Him who sent Me" (13:20). But all of this is in the future. They are the ones who have held fast, believing that he had been sent by God and was doing his work, but in a few hours something will occur that will seem to negate everything they have believed. He is preparing them to take it in: "From now on I am telling you before it comes to pass, so that when it does occur, you may believe that I am [He]" (13:19). This explanation and their reactions to it will stretch over the next three chapters.

George Herbert, "Love III"

George Herbert's "Love III," 1633, lets us feel our way more slowly into Peter's struggle, making it clear that the basis for Peter's refusal is his sense that he does not deserve such a gift. What Herbert must have understood, through peering at his own heart, is that our hesitation to believe has something to do with pride. All the more impressive, then, is Love's refusal to take no for an answer, sweetly and persistently overcoming the prideful parries of unbelief:

> Love bade me welcome: yet my soul drew back,
>   Guiltie of dust and sinne.
> But quick-ey'd Love, observing me grow slack
>   From my first entrance in,
> Drew nearer to me, sweetly questioning
>   If I lack'd any thing.
>
> A guest, I answer'd, worthy to be here:
>   Love said, You shall be he.

I the unkinde, ungratefull? Ah my deare,
                    I cannot look on thee.
Love took my hand, and smilingly did reply,
                    Who made the eyes but I?

Truth Lord, but I have marr'd them: let my shame
                    Go where it doth deserve.
And know you not, sayes Love, who bore the blame?
                    My deare, then I will serve.
You must sit down, sayes Love, and taste my meat.
                    So I did sit and eat.[2]

The poem is drawn in part from a number of feasts that Jesus uses to picture his relationship with those he calls to himself. In Luke 12:37, Jesus describes as "blessed" those believers who, eager for the coming of the kingdom, wait like slaves for their master to return home, poised to immediately open the door when he knocks and rewarded in turn with a feast hosted in their honor: "Blessed are those slaves whom the master shall find on the alert when he comes; truly I say to you, that he will gird himself to serve, and have them recline at the table, and will come up and wait on them." Shifting the terms somewhat, Jesus in Matthew 22 again compares the kingdom of heaven to a feast, a feast that, because those who are first invited refuse to attend, is unexpectedly opened to strangers out on the streets. Herbert perhaps draws the master who serves from Luke and the undeserving guests from Matthew, but the speaker's uneasiness and the master's loving persistence, the real focus of the poem, come straight out of Peter's hesitation as Jesus bends over his feet.

Christ, God's Love, is the host in Herbert's poem. He meets and welcomes the soul as it comes dusty to his door. The soul, like Peter, "[draws] back" from Love's welcome because of a crushing sense "of dust and sinne"—that dust and sin made all the more obvious because someone of so high a standing is welcoming him in. Much like Peter watching Jesus bend first to one set of feet and then another, the speaker's first thought is to protect himself, drawing back from a situation in which the inappropriateness of his participation would be apparent to all. He does not want to be exposed. "Quick-ey'd Love" misses none of this, observing his behavior and drawing nearer, "sweetly questioning" him as to what he might lack. Love's eyes, we notice, are always on the guest even as the guest cannot take his own eyes off himself.

When Love asks the shrinking guest what he lacks, he replies, in the second stanza, that he lacks a better self, someone "worthy to be here." No need for that, Love replies, "You shall be he," the worthy one. Impossible, the guest declares, eyes still firmly on himself: "I, the unkinde, ungratefull? Ah my deare, / I cannot look on thee." This is less a touching sense of honesty than it is a refusal to believe. The speaker cannot imagine a situation in which he can be declared worthy and invited in, and so he drops his eyes and clings doggedly to a world in which hierarchies are maintained and masters are separated from servants. "Never shall You wash my feet!" is how Peter put the same idea. But Love persists. Much like Jesus turning Peter's eyes back to him by saying "If I do not wash you, you have no part with Me" (13:8), Love comes closer, takes his hand and offers himself, saying, with a smile, "Who made the eyes but I?"

But that is the very problem, the speaker replies in the third stanza: the eyes you made, "I have marr'd." This close to the one who made him, all he can feel is "shame." All he can imagine is retreating into the separation he "doth deserve." What Herbert makes clear is how powerful the drive is to go it alone, to stay firmly in a world in which one gets what one deserves. Even if what one deserves is being turned away from all one desires, somehow that is less objectionable than having the world turned upside down. But Love persists. Look at me, he says. "And know you not . . . who bore the blame" for those eyes you have marred? Yes, the speaker slowly agrees, he knows. But if he comes in, if he comes to the table, it will be as a servant, with the notions of effort and what one deserves still kept in place.

No, says Love, as he did to Peter, counteracting all the bargaining, you need to believe. Look fully at Love and see yourself as the honored guest, "worthy to be here" simply because Love himself "bore the blame." It is not about deserving. "You must sit down," says Love, "and taste my meat." We realize at this point that the third stanza is in the present tense. Much as in the Mariani poem where the voice of woman who saw the priest cross over into the ward of death came alive as the poet told the story, so here the speaker suddenly hears the invitation now, in the present. The encounter is ongoing and ever present, with Love continually saying to him "Sit and eat," overcoming every retreat into worry or anxiety or fear. "Taste my meat," says Love—take it in and believe, for "Unless you eat the flesh of the Son of Man and drink His blood, you have no life in yourselves" (6:53). To taste is to believe, allowing God himself to be your satisfaction. What Herbert lets us see is that what overcomes the soul's grip on itself is Love's persistence, Love sweetly, smilingly drawing ever nearer, his bodily posture offering the soul the very thing it least deserves, much as Jesus did with the woman at the well and much as he is about to do in the long discourse that follows. The poem's last line shifts back to the past tense and speaks with a kind of quiet, satisfied confidence: "So I did sit and eat." What Herbert imagines in this poem is not only what Love did (bore the blame) and why (so we may sit and eat) but also our difficulty in believing this, how much we would rather resist and return to our own small lives elsewhere. In detailing the lengths God goes in order to draw someone to him, Herbert discovers in Love itself a quiet, smiling persistence, refusing to turn aside in the face of fear or retreat or self-absorption. Eat, says Love. So I did, the poet writes.

Judas, 13:21-30

Of course, one of the disciples does not respond to Love's persistence. Twice, as Jesus unfolds what he had done, he refers to a member of the group whose heart would not turn to him for cleansing. "You are clean, but not all of you" (13:10), he says; "I do not speak of all of you" (13:18), he repeats. This had to happen; Scripture had already anticipated someone close to the Messiah betraying him (13:18), but the actual breaking of the relationship tears at all concerned. Jesus seems almost overwhelmed at the thought of one of those he loved turning his back on him: "Truly, truly, I say to you, that one of you will betray Me" (13:21). The disciples are confused, unable to take this in, and Peter asks the disciple "whom Jesus loved" to tell them of whom he is speaking. Leaning on Jesus' breast, the disciple asks him, and Jesus replies, apparently in a voice that no one else can hear: "This is the one for whom I shall dip the morsel and give it to him" (13:26). And he does so, dipping the morsel and giving it to Judas. This bit of food, bread most likely, triggers a kind of revulsion and Judas draws back, refusing the spiritual food it points to. At that moment, John remarks, "Satan then entered into him" (13:27), fanning his doubts into flame and driving him away loveless. "What you do, do quickly" (13:27), Jesus says, and Judas hurries out into the night. No one else knows what has happened, supposing that Judas has left to give money to the poor or to buy things for the feast. But the reader has seen it all, and shares the sense of heartbreak.

Vassar Miller, "Judas"

In order to think more fully about what we have just seen, Vassar Miller imagines herself into Judas' position, focusing on his silence. The Gospel, for the most part, is silent about Judas' motivation, and Miller finds her way into this scene by imagining that silence, making it come alive inside of her. In doing so, she is called out of herself and into speech:

Always I lay upon the brink of love,
Impotent, waiting till the waters stirred,
And no one healed my weakness with a word;
For no words healed me without words to prove
My heart, which, when the kiss of Mary wove
His shroud, my tongueless anguish spurred
To cool dissent, and which, each time I heard
John whisper to Him, moaned but could not move.

While Peter deeply drowsed within love's deep
I cramped upon its margin, glad to share
The sop Christ gave me, yet its bitter bite
Dried up my ducts. Praise Peter, who could weep
His sin away, but never see me where
I hang, huge teardrop on the cheek of night.[3]

Miller's Judas begins by comparing himself to the man at the Pool of
Bethesda in John 5. Convinced that he had not been made whole because
he had been unable to get himself into the pool when the Angel of the Lord
stirred up its waters, the man languished in his sickness for thirty-eight
years until Jesus saw him lying there and healed him, saying "Arise, take up
your pallet, and walk" (5:8). Judas, as Miller sees him, lay not at the Pool
of Bethesda but "upon the brink of love, / Impotent, waiting till the waters
stirred, / And no one healed my weakness with a word." Impotent, his heart
unable to move out of himself and toward someone else, Judas on his own
was unable to reach the pool that would heal him. Worse than that, he says
sadly, remembering the scene, no healing word ever came to lift *his* heart and
make it whole. He sank into himself, languishing "upon the brink of love."
This, John would suggest, is an impotence natural to us all.

In the fourth line, Judas looks back and tries to explain why he thinks he
was not healed. Unlike the man at Bethesda who, when asked if he wished
to get well, replied (if only with a kind of excuse for his lack of action) that
he did, Judas was unable to speak when events around Jesus asked him the
same question: "For no words healed me without words to prove / My heart."
He was not healed, he says, because he could find no words to "prove" or
display or even probe his heart, so deeply unworded and lost to him were his
own needs and love and desires. Without being able to articulate these needs,
silent, he could find no one to heal his weakness.

Miller's Judas gives a number of examples, mostly drawn from John.
When Mary anointed Jesus for death and wiped his feet with her hair, Judas
responded, "Why was this perfume not sold for three hundred denarii, and
given to poor people?" (12:5). Those unfeeling words, Judas now says, were

produced by a heart "which, when the kiss of Mary wove / His shroud, my tongueless anguish spurred / To cool dissent." Because of anguish at his tonguelessness, or because of an anguish that could not be put into words, perhaps both, his heart moved away from Mary and her expression of love, willing to offer only a "cool," unreadable "dissent."

So, too, when John the Beloved Disciple, in the scene we have just examined, leaned into Christ's breast, Judas' heart "each time I heard / John whisper to Him, moaned but could not move." It moaned because it could not do likewise; unable to move or respond or speak, it moaned and pulled away. He sees the same thing when he compares himself to Peter, someone always ready to blunder into speech:

> While Peter deeply drowsed within love's deep
> I cramped upon its margin, glad to share
> The sop Christ gave me, yet its bitter bite
> Dried up my ducts. Praise Peter, who could weep
> His sin away, but never see me where
> I hang, huge teardrop on the cheek of night.

Peter, in Gethsemane, "drowsed," deep within his love for his Lord while Judas "cramped upon its margin." But Peter, after betraying his Lord, could weep (Luke 22:62, Mark 14:72, Matt 26:75) and be forgiven, while Judas, having found his tears "dried up" by the bitter, accusatory taste of the sop, was unable to speak or move or cry.

And even now, says Judas, turning to the reader, the same thing continues. You "Praise Peter, who could weep / His sin away," but you "never see me where / I hang, huge teardrop on the cheek of the night." Wordless and expressionless in life, he speaks only in his death, but nobody hears—his death by hanging having become a single teardrop, sorrowing over his failure to love. This, it seems clear, is why Jesus was troubled in spirit at the thought of his betrayal. He was in sorrow over this silent, clenched-tight heart. The poet sees this as well, but in imagining these words, which Judas was never able to speak, she breaks her own silence. In inhabiting his anguish, in finding its place in herself, she is driven to do what Judas was unable to do—prove and probe her own heart, tasting its anguish and opening herself through it to the one whom both of them would love.

Believe, 13:31–14:31

As soon as Judas goes out into the night, Jesus declares that his grand work has now begun. What Judas has set in motion will ultimately bring glory to

God: "Now is the Son of Man glorified, and God is glorified in Him" (13:31). And just as God will be glorified in the work Jesus does on his behalf, so Jesus in turn will be glorified at the completion of that work when God raises him up and brings him home to his presence: "If God is glorified in Him, God will also glorify Him [Jesus] in Himself [God], and will glorify Him immediately" (13:32). It is doubtful that the disciples are able to comprehend much of this. Like his washing their feet, the cross and resurrection, which is what he is speaking about now, are something they cannot make full sense of yet but "shall understand hereafter" (13:7). What they do understand is the word "immediately," for rather than celebrating with Jesus the thought of him returning to his Father's presence, they are overcome with anxiety about their own abandonment. Ignoring this for the moment, Jesus presses forward, formalizing his command that in light of the love he is about to display, they are to wash one another's feet, making him visible to the world:

> A new commandment I give to you, that you love one another, even as I have loved you, that you also love one another. By this all men will know that you are My disciples, if you have love for one another. (13:34-35)

Loving one another is not a new command, but loving in response to the way Jesus has loved them, is.[4] It is a love that grows out of loving him, out of believing they are loved—they very thing Peter had struggled to accept and Judas had repudiated.

Peter expresses the anxiety they all feel, brushing aside the commandment to love one another. "Lord, where are you going?" he asks. Jesus repeats that where he is going they cannot follow, at least not now: "Where I go, you cannot follow Me now; but you shall follow later" (13:36). Peter is not satisfied and tries to push his way in: "Lord, why can I not follow You right now? I will lay down my life for You" (13:37). He knows that the Jewish leaders want to kill Jesus. He has heard the talk of betrayal. He wants to do something. Jesus replies that for all Peter's bluster and concern, he will fail when the time for action presents itself: "Truly, truly, I say to you, a cock shall not crow, until you deny Me three times" (13:38).

No, Jesus is not calling them to take action. What he is calling Peter and the others to do is believe: "Let not your heart be troubled; believe in God, believe also in Me" (14:1). Believe that in his departure God is at work, he says. Believe that in leaving he is accomplishing a great work, on their behalf:

> In My Father's house are many dwelling places; if it were not so, I would have told you; for I go to prepare a place for you. And if I go and prepare a place for you, I will come again, and receive you to Myself, that where I am, there you may be also. (14:2-3)

The place he is going to prepare for them is what he has been calling "eternal life"—life in God's presence forever. If that is so, then they can rest assured that he will return, in time, to "receive" them into that place and into God's presence. Can they believe that? In the face of their current anxiety, can they cling to this thought and let him go? Most commentators take this to be a reference to the Second Coming, when earth and heaven will be united and a new kingdom established with God as its center, but Jesus does not spell that out, and the disciples certainly do not take in all of that. What they do hear is his quiet voice, calling them to believe.

You cannot follow now, Jesus goes on, but "you know the way where I am going" (14:4). This seems deliberately riddling, but it is intended to ease their anxiety. Thomas responds in exasperation: "Lord, we do not know where You are going, how do we know the way?" And Jesus replies, in one of the Gospel's more well-known statements, that they do know, and they have known all along. They know him: "I am the way, and the truth, and the life; no one comes to the Father, but through Me" (14:6). He, in his death, is the "way" to God, that death an expression of God's "true" nature. There is "life" nowhere else—not in any action that they might gird themselves to perform and certainly not in anxiety. What he is calling them to do now is to accept that, to believe that this is so. "If you had known Me," Jesus continues, "you would have known My Father also" (14:7). And they do, he reminds them— they do know him. They know, from having spent time with him, that he would never abandon them. They know this, and in knowing this they have seen the Father reaching out to them: "from now on you know Him, and have seen Him." Can they hold on to that? Can they find their way back to that during these next hours?

And at this point Philip jumps in. Like Peter and Thomas, he only half hears what Jesus is saying, swept up in confusion and anxiety. "Lord, show us the Father," he begs, desperate for some tangible reassurance. Quietly, as in the Herbert poem, Jesus brings Philip's eyes back to him, rebuking him but also giving Philip the reassurance that he craves: "Have I been so long with you, and yet you have not come to know Me, Philip? He who has seen Me has seen the Father; how do you say, 'Show us the Father'?" (14:9). They have seen the Father at work on their behalf. Cling to that, he tells them. In their anxiety, with the world about to shift under their feet, "Believe Me that I am in the Father, and the Father in Me" (14:11). Believe that even in his death they will be seeing the Father reaching to them. Believe in that, he says, and be at peace.

To reassure them, he begins to describe the future, asking them to imagine the world he is about to gain for them. "If you love Me," he says, "you will keep My commandments" (14:15)—that is, they will cling to what he has revealed about God's work on their behalf. If they do that, "whatever you ask in My name, that will I do, that the Father may be glorified in the Son" (14:13). But more than that, if they cling to him and keep his words, they will have God himself, nearer than they ever could have imagined.

Jesus says this in a number of different ways, and again it seems likely that, at the time, the disciples would have responded as much to the tone of his voice as to his specifics. But what a world awaits them. First, he says, they will be filled with a sense of God's very presence—his Spirit: "I will ask the Father, and He will give you another Helper, that He may be with you forever; that is the Spirit of truth, whom the world cannot receive, because it does not behold Him or know Him, but you know Him because He abides with you, and will be in you" (14:16-17). This Helper or Advocate (the word in Greek is *Paraklētos*) will come beside them and fill them with the truth of what Jesus has accomplished, out of love, on their behalf. Second, Jesus himself will return, from death, reassuring them by his life that they too now live with God forever: "I will not leave you as orphans; I will come to you. After a little while the world will behold Me no more, but you will behold Me; because I live, you shall live also" (14:18-19).[5] And third, the Father himself will love them. Since "I am in My Father, and you in Me" (14:20), on that day when he is raised to life, they will know that they have been made alive as well—as loved by the Father as he loves his own Son: "If anyone loves Me, he will keep My word; and My Father will love him, and We will come to him, and make Our abode with him" (14:23).

Once that happens, they will never be alone again. Can they cling to that? Can they put aside their anxieties and be at peace, believing that in passing through death he will accomplish all of this on their behalf? Can they take these things in so deeply that they can turn to them, when the events that have even now been initiated occur?

> Peace I leave with you; My peace I give to you; not as the world gives, do I give to you. Let not your heart be troubled, nor let it be fearful. You heard that I said to you, "I go away, and I will come to you." If you loved Me, you would have rejoiced, because I go to the Father; for the Father is greater than I. And now I have told you before it comes to pass, that when it comes to pass, you may believe. (14:27-29)

And with that, he turns to the reclining disciples and says, "Arise, let us go from here" (14:31). Arise, no longer crippled with anxiety. It is just what he said to the man at the pool of Bethesda, and we understand, as with that scene, that all of the power to do so comes from him. They arise, or so I imagine. John does not say. Perhaps they struggle to their feet, perhaps some rise more quickly than others. But finally, it seems, they all stand together, and Jesus begins to speak again and pray.

Elizabeth Bishop, "Squatter's Children"

In a poem written in 1957 during a twenty-year residency in Brazil, Elizabeth Bishop picks up Jesus' reassurance here that, as the King James version puts it, "In my Father's house are many mansions" (14:2) and tests the words out in a new situation, speaking them to a different set of abandoned children. What the poem suggests is that Bishop hears the words, understands the promise behind them, but can only repeat that promise in secular terms. Wrestling with how to respond to human need in a time when, as she sees it, the applicable "documents" offering relief are no longer entirely clear, Bishop transforms the words of Jesus into a flash of quiet inquiry, letting us hear the beauty and power of his words even as she steps back from them:

> On the unbreathing sides of hills
> they play, a specklike girl and boy,
> alone, but near a specklike house.
> The sun's suspended eye
> blinks casually, and then they wade
> gigantic waves of light and shade.
> A dancing yellow spot, a pup,
> attends them. Clouds are piling up;
>
> a storm piles up behind the house.
> The children play at digging holes.
> The ground is hard; they try to use
> one of their father's tools,
> a mattock with a broken haft
> the two of them can scarcely lift.
> It drops and clangs. Their laughter spreads
> effulgence in the thunderheads,
>
> weak flashes of inquiry
> direct as is the puppy's bark.
> But to their little, soluble,
> unwarrantable ark,
> apparently the rain's reply
> consists of echolalia,
> and Mother's voice, ugly as sin,
> keeps calling to them to come in.

Children, the threshold of the storm
has slid beneath your muddy shoes;
wet and beguiled, you stand among
the mansions you may choose
out of a bigger house than yours,
whose lawfulness endures.
Its soggy documents retain
your rights in rooms of falling rain.[6]

The "squatter" whose children Bishop focuses on here is most likely a man named Manuelzinho, the subject of another poem from that period whom she describes in affectionate, exasperated terms as "a sort of inheritance" of the estate she lived on: "Half squatter, half tenant (no rent)."[7] The first stanza observes the squatter's girl and boy from a great distance. They are "specklike," "alone, but near a specklike house" where they would seem to belong. The sun "blinks" as clouds shift and set "gigantic waves of light and shade" moving across the landscape. The children, as they play, seem to "wade" in the "gigantic waves" of light and dark lapping up around them. Their smallness in the oversized landscape makes them seem frail and unprotected. Clouds pile up, and a storm, which perhaps only the speaker can see at first, rises up behind the house. They play with one of their father's tools, but the mattock is broken and the ground is hard. They inhabit a harsh world, but even so, they are playing and laughing.

As the storm approaches, the poet imaginatively reaches out to the small, specklike children, much like Hopkins reaching out to his falcon or Mariani to his dark-clad priest. "Their laughter," she writes, in a sentence joining the third and fourth stanzas, "spreads / effulgence in the thunderheads, // weak flashes of inquiry / direct as is the puppy's bark." It is a very interesting image. They laugh, and their laughter seems, to the poet, to pass through the darkening thunderclouds in "weak flashes of inquiry"—flashes of lightning, but to the poet, flashes of their weak voices laughingly inquiring as to their place in the world and whether anyone is looking out for them. We are reminded, I think, of the anxious disciples in John 14, worried that they are about to be left as orphans and breaking into Jesus' final words to them with a series of nervous questions.

The children make their inquiries, but they receive no sensible reply. They seem to be surrounded by an indifferent universe. The inhabitants of that specklike house certainly think so. Bishop describes the house as a "little, soluble, / unwarrantable ark." It is a shack really, open to the rain, an "ark" only in the sense that it seems to be bobbing on the "gigantic waves of light and shade" with which the poem began. It is "unwarrantable" because it is unlawful—the family is "squatting" on land it does not own. There is nothing that secures or justifies, either legally or physically, this fragile structure in its gigantic world. To those inside the house, "the rain's reply" to the children's inquiry is the maddening drumming of "echolalia," the blank, senseless repeating of sounds or phrases, drop repeating drumming drop on the tin roof—no answer at all. It is no wonder, then, that the Mother's voice cuts through the sound and, "ugly as sin, / keeps calling to them to come in." She is afraid. She knows their vulnerability. They live in a world that will not answer them and because of that, there are no guarantees. Her voice is ugly as sin because it is filled with the knowledge of a threatening, broken world.

And into that world and its adult worries, the poet speaks. "Children," she says, echoing Jesus' "Little children" (14:33) at the beginning of his Farewell Discourse, here is what the world says back to your inquiry, if you could only hear it. That storm, with all its drumming rain, is in fact an immense house whose "threshold" or doorsill has appeared almost miraculously "beneath your muddy shoes," "slid[ing]" into place and inviting you to enter. Do, she says, do enter: nature, my father's house, has many mansions with all the room you can imagine. The children, "wet and beguiled" by the rain, filled with delight and wonder, are in fact "standing among / [numerous] mansions" from which they are free to "choose." The whole natural world is theirs, the poet writes—a "bigger house" than they could ever imagine, filled with mansions. In contrast to their small, unwarrantable, temporary shack, this bigger house is legal and enduring. It is much like the one Jesus describes, and the poet is attempting to adopt his tone. There are legal documents one can turn to, she writes, a "warrant," and what these "soggy documents" (the wind and the rain) say is that the children have "rights" to this dwelling place. They are not squatters but are at home on this earth, known and loved and cared for.

What Bishop visualizes here, as she reworks the words of Jesus, is both our fear of being orphaned and the words that would have to be spoken to calm those fears. The reassurance she offers the children are words of grace, but grace of another sort—a natural grace, based not on the Word but on "soggy documents" always just about to tatter and dissolve and run. The sogginess of those documents, of course, turns the poet's words of comfort into her own "weak flashes of inquiry" as she gazes up at the darkening clouds. Where on earth do we belong, the poem asks, meditating on Jesus' words to his frightened disciples. What words would have to be spoken to restore to us our "rights"? And on what would someone base those words?

Abide, 15:1-17

After inviting his disciples to arise, Jesus returns to his long, final discourse. Because their anxiety over being left behind had seemed to be all they could think about, he had temporarily turned away from his command that they "love one another, even as I have loved you" (13:34), calling them to "believe" and be at peace, even though what was approaching was very dark indeed. Now he returns to that request, calling them to "abide" in his love and reminding them they must first be made alive in that love before offering love to others.

Once again, Jesus uses a metaphor drawn from Scripture—the image of Israel as God's vineyard, rescued from Egypt and planted in a special place, a vineyard at one time tended and loved, but now, having been let go, running wild and producing worthless fruit (Ps 80:8-16; Isa 5:4). "I am the true vine," Jesus says to the disciples, "and My Father is the vinedresser" (15:1). Just as he has described himself as the true bread of heaven, the true temple, and the true Sabbath, he now points to himself as the reality for which Israel herself had been a picture—God's true vine, planted in the world, producing the fruit of lives wholly in step with God. There must have been real comfort in his return to this earlier manner of speaking. If he is the vine, then they, once his work on the cross is done, will be branches drawing life from him and bearing the fruit God had all along desired: "I am the vine, you are the branches; he who abides in Me, and I in him, he bears much fruit; for apart from Me you can do nothing" (15:5). This means that their relationship with him will continue even after his death, for he is not saying to abide or live in their memory of him, but to abide in his life—in his living presence, poured out within them by his Spirit (14:17), who will continually reassure them of God's love and concern. Just as we are changed by spending time with someone who loves us and draws what is deepest in us up to the surface, so they will be changed through abiding in his continuing presence.

Here is what that process will look like, he continues. Branches that do not bear fruit will be "take[n] away" (15:2) by his Father, the vinedresser, for what the lack of fruit will make obvious is that they have no living connection with Jesus, the vine, and if that is the case, no connection with the Father: "If anyone does not abide in Me, he is thrown away as a branch, and dries up; and they gather them, and cast them into the fire, and they are burned" (15:6). Branches that do bear fruit, through their union with the vine, will be "prune[d], that [they] may bear more fruit" (15:2). To be pruned is to be tended, certain tendencies being cut back so that others might flourish.

Though it might feel painful, Jesus reassures his disciples that this will not be the ultimate cleaning or pruning away of a nonbeliever from God's presence but instead will be something to be welcomed: "You are already clean because of the word which I have spoken to you" (15:3).[8] The crucial thing, then, is that they "abide" in that word, as he speaks it from the cross—dwelling in his love for them, continually returning to it for their sense of worth and standing. One of the ways that they will draw life from his vine, for example, is by turning to him in prayer, asking for help, protection, discipline, forgiveness: "Ask whatever you wish, and it shall be done for you. By this is My Father glorified, that you bear much fruit and so prove to be My disciples" (15:7-8). His Father will be glorified because it will ultimately be his Son whom their fruit reveals, the living vine that their dependency glorifies.

What exactly is the fruit he is calling them to bear? D. A. Carson points out that verses 9-16 of chapter 15 function as commentary on the vine metaphor.[9] The verses have a compelling logic. Jesus says that through the cross he will make it possible for them to live as he does. Just as his Father loves the Son and draws him close, celebrating his beauty and giving him all things, so the Son loves and celebrates his disciples: "Just as the Father has loved Me, I have also loved you; abide in My love" (15:9). And just as the loved Son feels great joy in the presence of the one who loves him, wanting what he wants, so will his disciples: "If you keep My commandments, you will abide in My love; just as I have kept My Father's commandments, and abide in His love. These things I have spoken to you, that My joy may be in you, and that your joy may be made full" (15:10-11). The Son's "joy" in his Father's love will be their joy in his. How did the Son "abide" in that love, expressing his joy? By doing what the Father commanded and laying down his life for the world: "Greater love has no one than this, that one lay down his life for his friends" (15:13). And what does the Son now call his disciples to do? To abide in his love and express their joy by laying down their lives for their friends: "This is My commandment, that you love one another, just as I have loved you" (15:12, 17). To abide in the vine, then, is to abide in Christ's love—to draw near and feel exalted; to make that love visible to the world with real joy. In doing so, they will be drawing people to that love, producing fruit that lasts: "You did not choose Me, but I chose you, and appointed you, that you should go and bear fruit, and that your fruit should remain, that whatever you ask of the Father in My name, He may give to you" (15:16). One can imagine them struggling to take all this in, their breath being taken away as he lifts their eyes past this night and the next days, forward to a life with him forever.

Elizabeth Bishop, from "Poem"

Elizabeth Bishop's "Poem," 1976, unfolds this notion of "abiding"—dwelling
in Christ's love, continually returning to it, resting in its living presence—in
a fascinating way. Although she does not mention "abidance" until five lines
from the end, the poem tracks the Gospel so carefully that it seems clear that
John's use of the term lies behind (and is opened up by) her meditation on life
and memory. Bishop once again translates the Gospel into a secular situation,
but in doing so offers us a set of eyes with which to see it freshly.

> About the size of an old-style dollar bill,
> American or Canadian,
> mostly the same whites, gray greens, and steel grays
> —this little painting (a sketch for a larger one?)
> has never earned any money in its life.
> Useless and free, it has spent seventy years
> as a minor family relic
> handed along collaterally to owners
> who looked at it sometimes, or didn't bother to.
>
> It must be Nova Scotia; only there
> does one see gabled wooden houses
> painted that awful shade of brown.
> The other houses, the bits that show, are white.
> Elm trees, low hills, a thin church steeple
> —that gray blue wisp—or is it? In the foreground
> a water meadow with some tiny cows,
> two brushstrokes each, but confidently cows;
> two miniscule white geese in the blue water,
> back-to-back, feeding, and a slanting stick.
> Up closer, a wild iris, white and yellow,
> fresh-squiggled from the tube.
> The air is fresh and cold; cold early spring
> clear as gray glass; a half inch of blue sky
> below the steel-gray storm clouds.
> (They were the artist's specialty.)
> A specklike bird is flying to the left.
> Or is a flyspeck looking like a bird?
>
> Heavens, I recognize the place, I know it!
> It's behind—I can almost remember the farmer's name.
> His barn backed on that meadow. There it is,
> titanium white, one dab. The hint of steeple,

filaments of brush-hairs, barely there,
must be the Presbyterian church.
Would that be Miss Gillespie's house?
Those particular geese and cows
are naturally before my time.

. . . .

I never knew him. We both knew this place,
apparently, this literal small backwater,
looked at it long enough to memorize it,
our years apart. How strange. And it's still loved,
or its memory is (it must have changed a lot).
Our visions coincided—"visions" is
too serious a word—our looks, two looks:
art "copying from life" and life itself,
life and the memory of it so compressed
they've turned into each other. Which is which?
Life and the memory of it cramped,
dim, on a piece of Bristol board,
dim, but how live, how touching in detail
—the little we get for free,
the little of our earthly trust. Not much
About the size of our abidance
along with theirs: the munching cows,
the iris, crisp and shivering, the water
still standing from spring freshets,
the yet-to-be-dismantled elms, the geese.[10]

The poem describes a small painting created by the poet's great-uncle and passed down as a "minor family relic." The first stanza coolly estimates the value of the work. It is small, "About the size of an old-style dollar bill," and, because it has been simply "handed along" from owner to owner, it has "never earned any money in its life." Size and value seem to run in tandem: the painting is "Useless and free," and it is so small that it seems closer to a preliminary sketch than to a finished painting. It is clearly not something that anybody would have "bother[ed] to" look at closely.[11]

But then, in the second stanza, the poet, almost idly, begins to do just that. Now her language becomes the language of interpretation—still a little cool and distanced, but playful and engaged. It is as if we are being treated to a quick lecture on how to see. "It must be Nova Scotia," she says. You can tell by the "awful shade of brown" the houses are painted. That "gray-blue wisp" must be a steeple. And those "two brushstrokes" in the foreground? We can "confidently" identify them as cows. As the stanza goes on, her work with the painted surface becomes more and more pronounced, the poet not only reading wisps and shades and brushstrokes but "squiggles" of paint and "a half inch of blue sky," unfolding in a particularly knowing way the painting's record of the artist's gestures. That wild iris, she says admiringly, for example, seems to have just burst into bloom, "fresh-squiggled from the tube." Those "steel-gray storm clouds" were the artist's "specialty." Once you get the hang of it, she acknowledges, any detail can be read—or over-read. Is that a "specklike bird" or a "flyspeck looking like a bird?"

In the third stanza, however, something quite different occurs, and it is here that we are first reminded of the Gospel of John. Something shifts, and the poet suddenly realizes that she "recognize[s] the place, [she] know[s] it!" All talk of the painting's small size and lack of value vanishes. It now represents not a generalized scene but a particular place she knows and cares about. If we think of Jesus as a kind of painting—a representation or "explanation" (1:17) of his Father—then much of the Gospel can be said to revolve around this moment when people come to "recognize" (1:31) or "know" (17:3) the life within him, being startled out of their initial negative or coolly evaluative impressions and, like the poet here, suddenly being given eyes to see.

What I love about this poem is the way Bishop slows that moment of recognition down and lets us think about it:

Heavens, I recognize the place, I know it!
It's behind—I can almost remember the farmer's name.
His barn backed on that meadow. There it is,
titanium white, one dab.

This is very carefully worked out. She recognizes the place being represented and then finds it for herself, in her memory. The phrase "It's behind" is broken off when she cannot remember the farmer's name, and then is overridden with a vision of his barn and the meadow it backed up on. She seems to have entered her memory, working her way around it, for then, when she returns to the painting, the barn is alive inside of her, and she can say, "There it is." That "titanium white" dab, passed over previously as just a bit of a white house, is his barn. Now it all makes sense. And suddenly everything has a name—the dab, the "filaments of brush hairs" which "must be the Presbyterian church," "Miss Gillespie's house." Even the geese and cows have names, although—another small joke—the poet would not have known the names of these particular ones.

As we have seen, the Gospel is built around a series of similar moments in which the love of God—embodied in Jesus—comes to life, becoming something a person can enter and taste and move around inside. Bishop's unfolding of the life compressed in the painting—working out within herself how the meadow and barn and houses and steeples all fit together—is a version of what happens when the Samaritan woman recognizes that God is welcoming her rather than turning aside. Like Bishop's speaker, she enters into that sense of being loved, finding not a barn backing on a meadow but her own need to draw close to God and worship. She turns back to Jesus with that need alive inside of her and, as in the poem, "there it is," God himself reaching out to her through Jesus. The man born blind, in chapter 9, goes through much the same experience, having his inner eyes opened and tasting more and more of Jesus, so that, when Jesus finally appears before him, he is ready to believe and worship. Each of the poems we have looked at has moved in the same way, unfolding a personal experience of blindness or silence or abandonment and then returning to Christ with inner eyes opened by that experience.

In the poem's last stanza, Bishop muses over the "strange" fact that she and her great-uncle had both been drawn to the same scene. Because of that coincidence, she had seen—or felt—how art and life, life and memory are compressed together:

> Our visions coincided—"visions" is
> too serious a word—our looks, two looks:
> art "copying from life" and life itself,
> life and the memory of it so compressed
> they've turned into each other. Which is which?

She had experienced the world behind the copy coming to life, the memory carried all these years suddenly becoming something that she could move through and experience again. The two worlds are so "compressed"—now we see why the painting's small size was remarked on—that they have "turned into each other": dab and barn; buried memory and felt scene; representation and life itself.

Bishop goes on to celebrate the role of such acts of compression in our daily lives—remembering, representing, giving form to what we know and love—and we suddenly realize that her language for this comes right out of the Gospel's understanding of the incarnation and the way Christ's cramped flesh makes the fullness of his Father visible:

> Life and the memory of it cramped,
> dim, on a piece of Bristol board,
> dim, but how live, how touching in detail

—the little we get for free,
the little of our earthly trust. Not much.

The grace life gives, she says, "the little we get for free," is that our experiences do not simply flow through us but are constantly being shaped and stored and embodied. Because of this, nothing need be lost; all of it waits to be entered and accessed and tasted once again. John makes exactly the same point. Compressed in the flesh of Jesus is life itself, waiting to be recognized and tasted and "abided" in. "Of His fullness we have all received, and grace upon grace," John writes (1:16). Although memory is a smaller, "earthly" version of what has been "[en]trusted" to us in Jesus, the pattern is exactly the same.

With that, we are ready to consider Bishop's turn on Jesus' remarks about abiding in him. I am the vine, you are the branches, Jesus says. Dwell in the life coursing through me. Return to it, making your home in it. Bishop's apparently useless painting offers a secular version of the same thought. Once the life compressed within it has been recognized and entered into, its painted rivulets become moving, living water (4:10), an ever-standing source of renewal. Consider the final turn at the end of the poem. The painting, now, is,

About the size of our abidance
along with theirs: the munching cows,
the iris, crisp and shivering, the water
still standing from spring freshets,
the yet-to-be-dismantled elms, the geese.

No longer squiggles or brushstrokes, the details in the scene, like incidents in the life of Jesus, are now living things—"munching," "shivering," "still standing" after a spring storm. They, in a sense, live eternally, and their life is forever accessible. Of course, this is only true in a sense, as Bishop quietly makes clear with her remark in the poem's last line about the "yet-to-be-dismantled elms." By reminding us of a future in which these elms no longer stand, she makes the space in which we abide a more fragile and momentary one than John has in mind—an "earthly trust" rather than a divine gift. This is "the size of *our* abidance" (emphasis added), she writes, hearing the Gospel's claims with absolute clarity but not being willing to fully rest in them.

Bishop steps back from the words Jesus speaks, and yet, in her exploration and celebration of art and life, life and memory, she offers the most comprehensive unfolding of abiding in his love that I have encountered. What would it mean to abide in his love? It would mean to recognize and taste it, moving around within the landscapes called up by his words, and then, alive to the desires unfolded there, returning to his "painting" and finding its details dense and alive with meaning. "There it is," the man no longer blind said, "titanium white, one dab."

Bear Witness, 15:18–16:33

I am leaving and returning to the Father, Jesus has said. Believe that in my death God is at work. Abide in what I am about to do. And now he adds, bear witness of this to the world. Jesus gets at this idea by first warning them about the opposition they will soon face. "If the world hates you," he tells them, "you know that it has hated Me before it hated you" (15:18). As we have seen, that hatred grew out of Jesus' claim to be speaking for God and acting in accordance with his will. Those who opposed him argued that he was making himself out to be God, claiming an authority that was not his, but Jesus responded that what they were really opposed to was God himself—they were unable to accept the notion of God going to the unimaginable lengths Jesus described in order to break their enslavement to sin and fill their unappeasable hunger to know him. Hating him for making these claims, what they actually revealed was their hatred of God: "He who hates Me hates My Father also. If I had not done among them the works which no one else did, they would not have sin; but now they have both seen and hated Me and My Father as well" (15:23-24). What Jesus tells the disciples is that they will soon be called to carry on his work. "Because you have been with Me from the beginning," he tells them, you will be called to "bear witness" (15:27) to what he said and did and to what those things meant. In that work, he reminds them, they will be guided and instructed by the Helper he has promised to send them: "When the Helper comes, whom I will send to you from the Father, that is the Spirit of truth who proceeds from the Father, He will bear witness of Me" (15:26). Nevertheless, there will be great opposition, and Jesus is preparing them for that now, so "that you may be kept from stumbling" and not be surprised or discouraged.

These words are hard to take, and Jesus realizes that they are no longer curious about where he is going (16:5). Instead, they are overcome with "sorrow" (16:6) about the opposition and hatred soon to be swirling about them. He reminds them about the Helper whom he will send them, saying: "But I tell you the truth, it is to your advantage that I go away; for if I do not go away, the Helper shall not come to you; but if I go, I will send Him to you" (16:7). Why is this such a great advantage? What does it have to do with their sorrow? When the Helper comes, he will "disclose" to them the full import of what Jesus accomplished on the cross, making it clear that in his death he had accomplished all that God had intended. This is too much for them to take in now, before the fact: "I have many more things to say, but you cannot bear them now" (16:12). But after the cross, the Spirit will unveil the full import of all that Jesus had accomplished. He will disclose it to the world, convicting it of the "sin" of "not believing," of the "righteousness" of which it falls short, and the "judgment" that had now been rendered against the world and its "ruler" (16:8-11).[12] But most importantly, he will disclose it to them, to their ever-increasing joy and delight: "But when He, the Spirit of truth, comes, He will guide you into all the truth; for He will not speak on His own initiative, but whatever He hears, He will speak; and He will disclose to you what is to come. He shall glorify Me; for He shall take of Mine, and shall disclose it to you" (16:13-14).

But there is still the issue of the sorrow that they cannot shake. Jesus does not discount it. He simply reassures them that they will pass through it. His metaphor is drawn from childbirth:

> Truly, truly, I say to you, that you will weep and lament, but the world will rejoice; you will be sorrowful, but your sorrow will be turned to joy. Whenever a woman is in travail she has sorrow, because her hour has come; but when she gives birth to the child, she remembers the anguish no more, for joy that a child has been born into the world. Therefore you too now have sorrow; but I will see you again, and your heart will rejoice, and no one takes your joy away from you. (16:20-22)

They will weep at his death, at God's apparent defeat, and the world will rejoice, but that weeping will turn to joy, he tells them, when they see him again, resurrected, and understand what God has done. Like childbirth, the difficult "hour" they are about to pass through will lead to a joyful new event—his return, and their lasting joy at being in God's presence forever.

Most of this is still opaque, Jesus acknowledges, but a day is coming when it will all be made clear. Unlike now, when they are still confused, "in that day you will ask Me no question" (16:23). His resurrection will give them a way to understand his death.[13] On that day, all that was veiled will be unfolded: "These things I have spoken to you in figurative language; an hour is coming when I will speak no more to you in figurative language, but will tell you plainly of the Father" (16:25). Their hearts leap at this news, tasting the joy that will be theirs when it had all been made clear. It must feel in fact, as if they understand it all already, for at his next words they push pass the sorrow and anguish and celebrate something they have not yet attained: "Lo, now You are speaking plainly, and are not using a figure of speech. Now we know that You know all things, and have no need for anyone to question You; by this we believe that You came from God" (16:29-30). They want to believe and abide and bear witness without passing through the hour before them. But that is not possible. Jesus came in order to die, and there will be nothing to believe and abide in until *after* the hour. Jesus says, "Do you now believe? Behold, an hour is coming, and has already come, for you to be scattered, each to his own home, and to leave Me alone" (16:32). Until he passes alone through that hour, God's glory will not be disclosed and their joy will not be full. They will understand, but not yet. We wait with them, peering toward a future that they only dimly make out: "In the world you have tribulation, but take courage; I have overcome the world" (16:33).

T. S. Eliot, from "Burnt Norton"

You cannot bear it all now, Jesus says to his disciples. I am still speaking to you in a figurative way. Despite what they desire, they can take in his glory only after it has fully entered the world and "overcome" that which forever separates them from it. That victory is what the Holy Spirit will disclose to them, after this "hour," guiding them into all truth. T. S. Eliot gets at a similar tension in the following excerpt from the first section of "Burnt Norton," 1936, the first of his post-conversion *Four Quartets*. The scene he describes is based on a visit to the garden of an empty estate with a friend with whom he had been deeply involved years before. It is a kind of real-life vision. Walking with her, the poet has the experience of a "door we never opened" swinging wide and "What might have been" momentarily becoming possible. It is as if time's stranglehold had been broken. Walking down the garden's aisles of roses, he writes, was like entering a long-lost "first world," filled with still-present possibilities moving along with them in a kind of invisible procession. We can hear, in Eliot's voice, just the sort of leaping free of figures of speech the disciples experienced, and, in its coming up short, the same chastening Christ administers:

> There they were, dignified, invisible,
> Moving without pressure, over the dead leaves,
> In the autumn heat, through the vibrant air,
> And the bird called, in response to
> The unheard music hidden in the shrubbery,
> And the unseen eyebeam crossed, for the roses
> Had the look of flowers that are looked at.
> There they were as our guests, accepted and accepting.
> So we moved, and they, in a formal pattern,

Along the empty alley, into the box circle,
To look down into the drained pool.
Dry the pool, dry concrete, brown edged,
And the pool was filled with water out of sunlight,
And the lotos rose, quietly, quietly,
The surface glittered out of heart of light,
And they were behind us, reflected in the pool.
Then a cloud passed, and the pool was empty.
Go, said the bird, for the leaves were full of children,
Hidden excitedly, containing laughter.
Go, go, go, said the bird: human kind
Cannot bear very much reality.[14]

Nothing happens on this walk, and yet everything changes. The unattended garden is "vibrant" and alive. An "unheard music" directs events; "unseen eyebeams" seem to take it all in. What had been put aside has somehow returned, a kind of "dignified, invisible" presence accompanying Eliot's couple as they make their way "in a formal pattern," through the rose garden: "Along the empty alley, into the box circle, / To look down into the drained pond." The drained pool—dry, brown-edged—is reminiscent of the empty, desert landscapes of other Eliot poems, but this time, rather than standing as an image of spiritual dryness and despair, the empty pool is suddenly "filled with water out of sunlight," its "glitter[ing]" "surface" an emanation of the "heart of light."[15] What earlier Eliot poems describe as lost—the "you" of "Gerontion" or the Word uttered into an uncomprehending darkness—is suddenly present, the timeless rising up into the world of time. The couple's wondering progress through this vanished world seems to have brought them into the presence of something far beyond them and their individual desires. For a moment, everything holds its breath. The invisible presences are "reflected in the pool." Time seems to halt. And then "a cloud passed, and the pool was empty" again, a bird quickly leading them away from the scene, proclaiming "human kind / Cannot bear very much reality."

Eliot echoes here Jesus' remark that, although he has "many more things" to say to his disciples, they cannot "bear them now" (16:12). The depth and intensity of what had been glimpsed in the rose garden is not something that humankind can bear. What Eliot struggles with in the remaining sections of "Burnt Norton" is what to do with this vision, how to incorporate it into his life. As he does so, he works his way toward a position very much like that of the Gospel's.

Eliot was obsessed with the problem of time. Time is relentless, unchangeable, woven into everything we see. It is, the first section of "Burnt Norton" remarks, "unredeemable." Once something has been lost or turned aside from, it seems gone forever. Time turns it under. But what if one suddenly caught a glimpse of a world not bound by these restrictions, a world flowing out of and treasured within the "heart of light"? What if one suddenly glimpsed what Eliot goes on to call "the still point of the turning world"? It cannot be grasped directly. That was the bird's point in the garden, and Jesus' to his disciples: "Except for the point, the still point, / There would be no dance, and there is only the dance. / I can only say, *there* we have been: but I cannot say where."[16] But though it could not be grasped directly, perhaps its power could be experienced as it broke time's hold over us.

That, I take it, is what Eliot heard in John's account, pondering it through his experience in the rose garden. In entering time and limitation, what could not be borne embraced us, making all things new, according to an unseen pattern:

> To be conscious is not to be in time
> But only in time can the moment in the rose-garden,
> The moment in the arbour where the rain beat,
> The moment in the draughty church at smokefall
> Be remembered; involved with past and future.
> Only through time time is conquered.[17]

What could not be grasped directly, outside of time—call it reality or the eternal, the moment in the garden—could be approached within time, as the eternal consented to enter it. So Eliot puts it. How this was accomplished on the cross is what John will devote the rest of the Gospel to explaining.

Prayer, 17:1-26

Jesus has washed the disciples' feet, shared a meal with them, and counseled them to believe, abide, and bear witness to the world. Now, finally, he prays, and as the disciples listen in, they feel themselves being drawn into his intimacy with his Father. It is an intimacy, in fact, that the prayer both celebrates and enacts.

Most commentators divide the prayer into three parts. In the first part, Jesus prays to the Father about himself, but he has the lives of his followers uppermost in his mind:

> Father, the hour has come; glorify Thy Son, that the Son may glorify Thee, even as Thou gavest Him authority over all mankind, that to all whom Thou hast given Him, He may give eternal life. And this is eternal life, that

they may know Thee, the only true God, and Jesus Christ whom Thou hast sent. (17:1-3)

Jesus asks his Father to "glorify" him by using his death to "give eternal life" to all whom God has given him. This will glorify Jesus by revealing the splendor and power of his giving of himself, and it will glorify his Father by revealing the depths of his love for mankind. Eternal life, as we have noted in working through the signs and metaphors describing it, is nothing less than "knowing" God, coming near, drinking in the joy and wonder of his presence, resting in an intimacy only possible because of the death of his Son in their place. To overhear these words would have been like listening in as God spoke to himself about his deepest desires, a taste of the very intimacy to which his Son was even now opening a way, an intimacy to which he was even now returning, having accomplished the work he had been sent to do: "And now, glorify Thou Me together with Thyself, Father, with the glory which I had with Thee before the world was" (17:5). "He was in the beginning with God" (1:2), we learned in John's Prologue, and now he is about to return to that intimate union.

Next, Jesus speaks to his Father about the disciples, describing the way they had received his work on their behalf and asking his Father to hold them in that work after he leaves them. Again, one can only imagine the mix of emotions—pride, heart-stopping surprise, wonder—that they would have felt in hearing themselves so described. Jesus begins: "I manifested Thy name to the men whom Thou gavest Me out of the world; Thine they were, and Thou gavest them to Me, and they have kept Thy word" (17:6). He "manifested" God's "name," righteousness and mercy, on the cross, reaching out, at the greatest cost imaginable, to offer life to the undeserving.[18] Looking forward to the disciples grasping and keeping this "word," Jesus describes his followers as having brought great glory to him: "All things that are Mine are Thine, and Thine are Mine; and I have been glorified in them" (17:10). He prays, then, that they will be "kept" in that "name" (17:11) and word, despite his absence and the opposition of the world. If that happens, they will "be one, even as We are" (17:11), their unity a reflection of the unified life of Father and Son into which they have been drawn.

He has real reasons to pray for them, he continues. He has "guarded them" (17:12) while he was with them, but this is about to change. He is praying so that "they may have My joy made full in themselves" (17:13), despite the opposition they will soon face. He wants them to see, in the face of difficulties and his absence, that his joy in knowing his Father is now theirs, purchased for them by the events of this "hour." They "are not of the world" (17:14), they hear Jesus tell his Father. They have been drawn out of it and into a new life in him. "Sanctify them in the truth" of what he has accomplished, he prays: set them apart, make them new, and then "send them into the world," alive to God and testifying through their actions to the possibility of such a life.

Finally, Jesus prays for those who will come to believe in him through the words of those now in the room with him—the readers of this text, for example. He prays, even as he has for his disciples, that these others may also be drawn into the unity of God: "that they may all be one even as Thou, Father, art in Me, and I in Thee, that they also may be in Us; that the world may believe that Thou didst send me" (17:21). Just as the Son is aware of his Father's love and rests in it, so, amazingly enough, may all believers, unified with each other in turning toward and resting in a shared source of life. This is something, Jesus adds, that the world will notice. Their lives—"I in them, and Thou in Me"—will proclaim to the world that "that Thou didst send Me, and didst love them, even as Thou didst love Me" (17:23). Loved even as God loves his own Son—one can imagine the disciples listening to this almost as to a dream being recounted.

Jesus concludes by praying for the very thing they most desire—that they might see him again. But the meeting he describes must have surely taken their breath away: "Father, I desire that they also, whom Thou hast given Me, be with Me where I am, in order that they may behold My glory, which Thou hast given Me; for Thou didst love Me before the foundation of the world" (17:24). This is a picture of eternal life—that they will one day see Jesus in all his glory. What they now behold in glimpses, they will one day behold in full, being drawn out of themselves in rapt wonder before God whose greatest glory was his Son who lowered himself to die for them. There is no way for them to understand this now, Jesus seems to acknowledge, and reduces this grand vision to a simple thought—that he was sent so that God could love them in the same way that he loved his Son: "that the love where-with Thou didst love Me may be in them, and I in them" (17:26). That, the tone of the prayer whispers to them, is enough to rest in forever.

George Herbert, "Clasping of Hands"

In "Clasping of Hands," George Herbert creates a kind of breathless dance in which he spins together two of the key terms of the prayer of Jesus, "mine" and "thine," shifting them back and forth in a series of intricately varied figures. It is as if his speaker had listened in as Jesus described his followers to his Father—"Thine they were, and Thou gavest them to me," "And all things that are Mine are Thine, and Thine are Mine; and I have been glorified in them" (17:6, 10)—and then borrowed that language to speak back to his Lord about the incredible gift he had been given. Herbert recreates the dizzying whirl of Jesus' prayer, in which believers, who are in the Son, are in the Father, who is in the Son, but he does so in order to hear for himself what was gained and lost in the clasping of hands at the cross. Hearing the prayer anew, he is drawn deeply into its energies and implications:

> Lord, thou art mine, and I am thine,
> If mine I am: and thine much more,
> Then I or ought, or can be mine.
> Yet to be thine, doth me restore;
> So that again I now am mine,
> And with advantage mine the more.
> Since this being mine, brings with it thine,
> And thou with me dost thee restore.
> 　If I without thee would be mine,
> 　I neither should be mine or thine.
>
> Lord, I am thine, and thou art mine:
> So mine thou art, that something more
> I may presume thee mine, then thine.
> For thou didst suffer to restore
> Not thee, but me, and to be mine:
> And with advantage mine the more,
> Since thou in death wast none of thine,
> Yet then as mine didst me restore.
> 　O be mine still! still make me thine!
> 　Or rather make no Thine or Mine!¹⁹

The first stanza focuses on what the speaker has gained in being united with Christ. We need to read quite slowly in order to make out the chiming terms. He begins "Lord, thou art mine, and I am thine, / If mine I am," making the point that in being united with his Lord, both taking him in and giving himself to him, he (the speaker) has become more deeply himself than when he was simply his own. Being connected to God, he has become fully himself—the only way he can truly say "mine I am" in the second line. The Gospel makes just this point in arguing that the only way one is truly alive or truly oneself is in the presence of God, calling this experience "eternal life" (17:3). If this is the case, the poem continues in its opening lines, then in being myself, being fully alive, I am "thine much more" than

I "can" or "ought" to "be mine" on my own. He is most fully himself in this connection.

And that connection does not carry with it a loss of freedom or selfhood, the speaker continues, responding to an imagined objection, because "to be thine, doth me restore; / So that again I now am mine, / And with advantage mine the more." The advantage is all his, in this union. To be given God, to be able to give himself to God, is to occupy a position where he feels more deeply, hurts more fiercely, loses himself more fully in wonder than he ever could have imagined possible. It is to glimpse the glory Jesus speaks of in 17:24, an anticipation of what will one day be seen in full. Giving himself to God works to the speaker's "advantage," he continues, because, in gaining himself ("this being mine"), he also gains the one who drew him out of himself: it "brings with it thine." And what is most amazing about the entire process is that it was God who sought *him* out. God himself set out to restore what had been shattered; he desired their relationship to be otherwise: "And thou with me dost thee restore."

The couplet at the end of the first stanza seems to put down a marker. To turn one's back on this union, to go the way of John's religious leaders and insist on the right to create a self out of the self, for the self, would be to return to some half-alive state, neither mine nor thine: "If I without thee would be mine, / I neither should be mine or thine." We might think of Eliot's Gerontion here, windblown and distracted, having been somehow "removed" from the only love that mattered.

In the second stanza, Hebert creates a kind of mirrored reversal of the first stanza, switching out many of the "thines" and "mines" in order to appreciate what this restoration must have cost.[20] His language, in a sense, has taken note of this cost all along, but it takes an artful reordering of the first stanza in order for him to hear these sobering implications. In becoming "mine," the speaker says to his Lord, you gave up something: becoming "something more / . . . mine, then thine." Jesus became human, becoming sin on the speaker's behalf. By taking on the speaker's humanity and the terrible separation from the Father that his deepest self had insisted upon, his Lord had made possible the restoration celebrated in the first stanza, his suffering eliminating the barrier that had kept the speaker from a life he had not even known to desire: "For thou didst suffer to restore / Not thee, but me, and to be mine; / And with the advantage mine the more." The advantage was all mine, he writes, this last line being the only one repeated word for word in each stanza. But now he understands the cost, for in restoring the speaker, God himself had to become nothing, had to become death in order to bring him to life: "Since thou in death wast none of thine, / Yet then as mine didst me restore."

What does the speaker gain in playing out these different implications of mine and thine? What he discovers, I think, is how profound the reversal was that God accomplished on the cross. Restoring the speaker by becoming nothing himself, God turned upside down the universe as we know it. Hearing the prayer of John 17 anew by sounding it out, Herbert comes alive to its implications. He records such a moment of insight in each concluding couplet, marking a direction he did not want to return to in the first stanza (being mine without thee) and stretching forward to a condition still before him in the second: "O be mine still! still make me thine! / Or rather make no Thine or Mine!" As he speaks, he changes inside—drawing back from a life on his own, leaping forward to that unity completed. A true reader, he feels out the inner landscape of this language for himself, just as we are encouraged to do.

7

Seen (John 18:1–20:31)

After praying, Jesus leads the eleven disciples out and over the ravine of the Kidron to a garden where he had often met with his disciples. He does not go there to hide, since Judas would certainly have known the place. He goes there to pray and wait. The next three chapters, recounting the betrayal, trial, crucifixion, and resurrection, are the display of glory John has been building toward. Here we see fully what has been withheld or tucked behind a screen. Interestingly, in the first two chapters, John steps forward in his role as narrator, quite deliberately arranging and interpreting his material, showing us what he has come to see and believe about these events, and then, as he moves to the resurrection narrative, stepping back again and quietly describing what it was like as these insights first started to dawn. It is a very sophisticated approach. The point of these events, withheld for the longest time, is clearly shaped and delineated, and then released to speak on its own, with power.

Twin Strands, 18:1-27

Jesus and his disciples enter the garden, and after some time passes, Judas appears, leading a large group of Roman soldiers and officers of the chief priests and Pharisees. The religious leaders want to put him to death; the Romans want to maintain control. In both cases, a show of force is mounted to make it clear where the power in this confrontation resides. When they arrive, with their "lanterns and torches and weapons" (18:3), Jesus steps out of the dark garden to meet them. "Whom do you seek?" (18:4), he asks, echoing his first words in the Gospel—"What do you seek?" (1:38)—and reminding us that the issue of his identity has been the Gospel's central question. With this question, he immediately takes charge of events. "Jesus the Nazarene," they reply. "I am [He]" (18:5), he responds, and at those words, "they drew back, and fell to the ground" (18:6). John does not say why, permitting us to speculate that something in this single, undefended person advancing toward them, straightforwardly offering himself to them while also using God's name ("I am") takes them aback. Whether it is the force of his divinity or simply that he has startled the soldiers, it is clear that the power in the scene now rests with him, despite the size of the armed body surrounding him. Jesus emphasizes this fact by again asking the men, once they have picked themselves up from the ground, whom they seek, forcing them to acknowledge what they are doing and whom they are arresting. Again he responds "I am [He]," adding "if therefore you seek Me, let these go their way" (18:8), protecting his disciples from a confrontation in which they would be immediately overwhelmed. John steps forward and makes a simple point—that in demonstrating and then relinquishing his authority, Jesus has acted to save those he loved, just as he had promised his Father he would: "Of those whom Thou hast given Me I lost not one" (18:9). This, it seems to me, is something that became important to John only after the cross, when he saw in it an echo of what occurred there: God himself, with his power everywhere apparent, relinquishing that power in order to save those he loved. The cross, it seems, gave John the eyes to see this.

Peter does not understand yet. He sees the power of Jesus, but he cannot comprehend it being relinquished. So he pushes into the middle of things, draws a sword, and cuts off the right ear of the high priest's slave. He wants to harness the power that Jesus so obviously possesses, directing it along physical, defensive lines. Jesus will have none of this, saying to Peter: "Put the sword into the sheath; the cup which the Father has given Me, shall I not drink it?" (18:11). He does not act, but he is utterly in control of events.

At this point, John begins to describe simultaneous strands of the story, cutting back and forth between Peter and Jesus and making it clear, in their differing responses to the world's pressures, what true power looks like in action. Jesus is arrested, bound, and taken to the house of Annas, the father-in-law of the high priest Caiaphas. Some sort of preliminary trial begins. Peter and "another disciple" follow, but only the other disciple, who is known to the high priest, is able to enter into the court of Annas' house. Peter is left outside, and even when the other disciple goes and speaks to the door-keeper and brings him in, Peter remains in an outside courtyard where slaves and officers are standing around and warming themselves at a charcoal fire

(18:18). One can imagine how alone he must feel, a conspicuous newcomer, unable to reach his master, convinced that he has only his own wits to fall back on. Now John allows the two strands of his story to intersect, for at the very moment Jesus is questioned inside, Peter is challenged outside. John quite deliberately moves us from one scene to the other and back again. Our eyes first turn to Peter. The slave-girl who kept the door approaches him and says, "You are not also one of this man's disciples, are you?" (18:17). Surely everyone standing there is listening. Peter hears the way her negative phrasing of the question suggests an answer and follows her lead, trying to protect himself in what has suddenly become a dangerous situation: "I am not" (18:17). He does not hear the way his self-protective "I am not" echoes Jesus' "I am," but the reader does. He is "not" the self-contained "I am," his power arcing free of the world. He is not even "I am's" disciple, turning to him for life.

In contrast, inside the house, Jesus is making it clear that he is not part of the world's order, refusing to follow the lead the high priest's questions hold out to him, even though he too is physically weak and alone. Annas questions him about "His disciples, and about His teaching" (18:19), attempting to get Jesus to lay himself open to charges against him, but Jesus refuses to play along, neither boldly resisting nor attempting to soften or blur his position. Instead, he speaks the truth: "I spoke nothing in secret. Why do you question Me? Question those who have heard what I spoke to them; behold, these know what I said" (18:20-21). It is as if he is speaking from a completely different orientation. Rather than protecting himself by turning the question aside, Jesus simply speaks the truth: everyone knows his teaching; if anyone was truly curious, all he would have to do is ask someone who heard him. What the truth does—it is one of the basic themes of the Gospel, here just lightly rendered, in passing—is expose those who stand before it, in this case Annas, whose motives stand clearly revealed. This is exactly what we saw in the confrontation outside the garden. An officer standing by immediately gives Jesus a blow, understanding that with these simple words he has stripped away a fiction that everyone else was playing along with, saying "Is that the way You answer the high priest?" (18:22). And Jesus again makes the same point, asking the soldier about his own fearful or hate-filled heart: "If I have spoken wrongly, bear witness of the wrong; but if rightly, why do you strike Me?" (18:23). Not making progress, Annas sends Jesus along to Caiaphas, for formal trial.

Meanwhile, Peter is still standing outside, warming himself and trying to sidestep all possible threats. Suddenly, an entire group confronts him, lifting his exposure to another level. "You are not also one of His disciples, are you?" (18:25), they say, again inadvertently offering him a linguistic way out. "I am not," he repeats. And then a third charge, this time from someone who was actually there, a relative of the man whose ear Peter cut off: "Did I not see you in the garden with Him?" Peter denies all of this again, just as had been predicted, and a cock crows, also predicted. Imagine Peter's devastation, realizing that in his desperate self-absorption, struggling, on his own, to keep himself afloat, he had done just what Jesus had said he would, denying him three times, and exposing both his inability to be the kind of person he desired to be and the world's subtle, ever-increasing pressure to abandon all such impulses and flee. What he is overwhelmed by, Jesus calmly endures.

Elizabeth Bishop, from "Roosters"

Much like Gerard Manley Hopkins finding his way to Christ's glory through his experience with the hovering falcon, Elizabeth Bishop, in "Roosters," works her way toward this scene through a confrontation with her own accusing cock crows. As she does so, swinging gradually from one approach to the world to another, she opens up for us the "pivot" of the heart to which both Peter and the Gospel's readers are being called.[1]

"Roosters" is set in Key West, during World War II. Much of the imagery of the long first section, which I will not excerpt here, has military connotations—maps, pins, medals on chests. It is four in the morning, and a couple is awakened by the crow of a rooster, just below their "gun-metal blue window." Its cry is immediately echoed by another and another, until a "senseless order floats / all over town." The speaker associates this order with tradition, militarism, and ego. Each insistent voice seems to crowd out all others, "each one an active / displacement in perspective; / each screaming 'This is where I live!'" It seems at first that the speaker's problem is with the world outside her window, but we gradually realize that the world's insistent self-absorption is also being repeated inside the house where the speaker is furious at being awakened "here where are / unwanted love, conceit and war." Love not being returned, accusations still trembling in the air, self-protective gestures hardening into "conceit"—this is the world the roosters have suddenly brought back to consciousness. The speaker's anger at the roosters, then, is actually displaced anger at being rejected or ignored or hurt by her lover, and she is flailing away at a "senseless order" that seems to have taken dominion everywhere. Like Peter, she fights that order on its terms, not drawing a sword and swinging it wildly about but performing an emotional, imaginative equivalent. Hating the roosters for the ego and self-absorption they wake her to and remind her of, she launches into a surreal fantasy in which the offending roosters rise and fight, tearing at each other in a violent confrontation that leads to "torn-out, bloodied feathers drift[ing] down" above the town.

A section break occurs, and the speaker shifts from the Key West situation to Peter's denial—another story about roosters. She seems to have left her four in the morning anger behind, but we gradually realize that thinking through her own sense of failure is what has brought her to Peter:

St. Peter's sin
was worse than that of Magdalene
whose sin was of the flesh alone;

of spirit, Peter's,
falling, beneath the flares,
among the "servants and officers."

Old holy sculpture
could set it all together
in one small scene, past and future:

Christ stands amazed,
Peter, two fingers raised
to surprised lips, both as if dazed.

But in between
a little cock is seen
carved on a dim column in the travertine,

explained by *gallus canit*;
flet Petrus underneath it.
There is inescapable hope, the pivot;

yes, and there Peter's tears
run down our chanticleer's
sides and gem his spurs.

Tear-encrusted thick
as a medieval relic
he waits. Poor Peter, heart-sick,

still cannot guess
those cock-a-doodles yet might bless,
his dreadful rooster come to mean forgiveness,

a new weathervane
on basilica and barn,
and that outside the Lateran

there would always be
a bronze cock on a porphyry
pillar so the people and the Pope might see

that even the Prince
of the Apostles long since
had been forgiven, and to convince

all the assembly
that "Deny deny deny"
is not all the roosters cry.

Bishop is drawing from both John's version of Peter's denial (the quoted phrase "servants and officers" is from 18:18) and Matthew's (Peter following the crowd into the courtyard of the high priest "to see the end" is quoted from Matthew 26:58). Peter's tears appear in all three Synoptic Gospels.

Peter's sin, Bishop writes, was worse than that of Mary Magdalene (in her traditional identification as a prostitute). Her sin was "of the flesh alone." His sin, in the high priest's garden, standing over the charcoal fire "among the 'servants and officers,'" was "of spirit." The speaker, we realize, is quietly identifying with Peter—whatever the sin against her, it was "of the flesh alone," paling in comparison to hers, "of the spirit." Turning to the Gospel with her own failure sharply etched in her mind, however, she imagines how "Old Holy sculpture" might have approached this denial: "Christ stands amazed, / Peter, two fingers raised / to surprised lips, both as if dazed." But then she goes on and imagines something more—the tormenting rooster, "between" the two, set on a column, on which is written *gallus canit; flet Petrus*, or "the rooster crowed, Peter wept." Those tears mark the moment he turned from furiously resisting and reproducing the world's order to acknowledging his own failure. They are the speaker's tears as well, and as she reads them in light of the Gospel, she sees them as marking the possibility of turning outside of oneself for life. It is a moment of "inescapable hope, the pivot," and although "Poor Peter, heart-sick" could not yet guess what would happen, "his dreadful rooster" would in time "come to mean forgiveness." A "bronze cock" would always stand outside the Lateran in Rome, reminding the Pope and all who see it that "'Deny deny deny' / is not all the roosters cry."

Peter's roosters have allowed the speaker to feel her way through to the moment when railing against a world of "unwanted love, conceit and war" exhausts itself, exposing her self-protective willingness to abandon even what she most loves in order to defend herself. Then the Gospel whispers to her that a new life might rise out of this failure. Her own internal roosters, insistently proclaiming "deep from raw throats / a senseless order," have led her to this whisper, bringing her to the moment when one order collapses in on itself and another order beckons—the "pivot."

Having freed herself by working her way through Peter's denial, the speaker, in the third and final section of the poem, returns to the scene in Key West:

In the morning
a low light is floating
in the backyard, and gilding

from underneath
the broccoli, leaf by leaf;
how could the night have come to grief?

gilding the tiny
floating swallow's belly
and lines of pink cloud in the sky,

the day's preamble
like wandering lines in marble.
The cocks are now almost inaudible.

The sun climbs in,
following "to see the end,"
faithful as enemy, or friend.

The morning has advanced. The "gun-metal blue" of four o'clock has broken down, and "a low light is floating / in the backyard, and gilding // from underneath / the broccoli, leaf by leaf." The senseless order of the night has come undone, replaced by something brighter and freer to wander: "lines of pink cloud in the sky, // the day's preamble / like wandering lines in marble." The oppositions, both internal and external, which had seemed fixed forever, have now been erased. The speaker, along with Peter, has pivoted from an acknowledgment of her failure outward toward life. She is not there yet, but clearly something has changed. Christ is not named directly in this section; Bishop is too much of a skeptic for that. But clearly, the "hope" of another order breaking into a senseless one, an order whose dominant notes are tears and "forgiveness," is derived from the Gospel, however down to earth its enactment in her backyard. What she is sure about, a point she makes by linking Matthew's language about Peter following the crowd to the high priest's house "to see the end" with the sun "climb[ing] in" to her Key West yard, is that even with the end of her story not yet written, another order has begun. "How could the night have come to grief?" she asks in wonder, her eyes now fixed on the light's relentless march against the darkness, momentarily lifting us past the dark night we are about to enter in the Gospel.[2]

Pilate, 18:28–19:15

We pick up again after Peter's denial, skipping with John over the formal trial before Caiaphas and moving directly to Jesus being taken to the palace of the Roman governor Pilate for judgment and sentencing. Just as John kept our eyes on Peter, uneasily suspended between the world and Jesus, so he now focuses on Pilate, placing him in a similar position and watching him move back and forth between the two realms. Pilate has great skills, but as we saw with Peter and with Bishop, the two worlds are different and cannot be reconciled. Light has broken into darkness, and, as throughout the Gospel, Pilate is forced into a position where he must move toward the light or back away from it. Like Peter, his sometimes frantic movements chart the space of decision into which the Gospel seems more and more intent on drawing its readers. John's narrative hand is everywhere apparent as he brings out this drama.

John begins by noting that Jesus' accusers lead him into Pilate's official residence, the Praetorium, but refuse to enter themselves, "that they might not be defiled, but might eat the Passover" (18:28). As many commentators have noted, their commitment to remaining ritually pure and thus not entering into a pagan residence before the feast is strikingly at odds with the larger action they are engaged in—putting an innocent man to death. Pilate is forced to come out to meet the crowd, and when he does so, he asks them "What accusation do you bring against this Man?" (18:29). Carson makes the point that a kind of gamesmanship is going on here. Pilate already knows what their accusations are, since he would have had some part in sending the Roman soldiers to arrest Jesus the night before.[3] The leaders seem to have expected Pilate to support their position and render judgment, but instead he forces them to spell out a formal charge. He is making it clear that he is in charge and not simply doing the crowd's bidding. Not wanting to lose face, the leaders give Pilate a non-answer, demanding that he do what they all know is expected of him: "If this Man were not an evildoer, we would not have delivered Him up to you" (18:30). Refusing to be manipulated, Pilate counters, "Take Him yourselves, and judge Him according to your law" (18:31). He knows that they are seeking a penalty that they are not permitted to impose if they do the judging, and by this statement, he forces them to publicly declare that fact: "We are not permitted to put anyone to death" (18:31), they say. This is how the "world" works. Each party attempts to establish and defend a position, constantly seeking secure grounds to inhabit, a view that John deftly undercuts by once again pointing to a larger order, outside of their struggle, where neither party has standing or stability. The leaders brought Jesus to Pilate, John remarks, alluding to this larger order, not only because they needed his assistance in putting this man to death, but so that "the word of Jesus might be fulfilled, which He spoke, signifying by what kind of death He was about to die" (18:32)—that is, death through crucifixion, being "lifted up" or "exalted" on a Roman cross.

Not yet aware of that larger world and flush from his "victory" over the Jewish leaders, Pilate goes inside to deal with Jesus. The leaders, out of our earshot, must have made an accusation against Jesus worthy of the death penalty, for once inside Pilate immediately asks Jesus "Are you the King of the Jews?" (18:33). That is, have you set yourself up as a rival to Rome's power? If so, death would indeed be the penalty. Just as he had with Annas and with the soldiers outside the garden, Jesus responds by stripping Pilate of the protection of his office and forcing him to acknowledge what he is doing: "Are you saying this on your own initiative, or did others tell you about Me?" (18:34). Are these your words? Will you stand behind them? Pilate, wise in the ways of the world, refuses to have his own motives examined and steps away from the light's exposure: "I am not a Jew, am I? Your own nation and the chief priests delivered You up to me; what have You done?" (18:35). I take no responsibility for sifting through this arcane religious debate, Pilate says. You are the vulnerable one. You have been accused. But Jesus refuses to be intimidated. Instead, he reaches back to Pilate's use of the term *King* and uses it to give Pilate a glimpse of another world, beyond this one, where Pilate's own motives in fact *are* at issue: "My kingdom is not of this world. If My kingdom were of this world, then My servants would be fighting, that I might not be delivered up to the Jews; but as it is, My kingdom is not of this realm" (18:36). Imagine how unsettling this must be. Flush with power, Pilate has brushed up against a realm where he seems to have no standing at all. Although he does not fall to the ground as the soldiers did in the presence of this deeply secure figure, he is clearly knocked off his feet. "So you are a king?" he asks, trying to gain time. "You say correctly that I am a king," Jesus replies. "For this I have been born, and for this I have come into the world, to bear witness to the truth. Everyone who is of the truth hears My voice" (18:37). This is the claim Jesus has been making throughout the Gospel. He represents a world beyond this one—call it "truth" or "life." He has come as a king to bear witness to that world and to sweep this one up into it. Can you sense that world? his quiet presence before Pilate asks. Are you "of" it? Light has broken into darkness—are you able to respond?

We might imagine a pause here as Pilate tries to sort out what has just happened, but then, instead of saying something like "No, I can't see. Help me," he responds defensively: "What is truth?" (18:38). He closes his eyes. There is no other world for him save this one, where people struggle and advance and shore up what is theirs. What is truth in such a world, he says, and turns away from its king, judging himself, as John put it earlier (3:18-20), by recoiling from its light. It is not something with which he is willing to deal.

Pilate goes back outside, trying to ignore what he has brushed up against. Clearly, Jesus is not claiming to be a political king, and this is not a case of sedition. So he says to the leaders "I find no guilt in Him," but in a cunning ploy he offers them a way to save face while still acknowledging his superior position. He says, essentially, that he is willing to pretend that Jesus is guilty, thus delivering the judgment they desire, if they will go along with releasing him as a Passover observance, which is what he desires. They both will win: "But you have a custom, that I should release someone for you at the Passover; do you wish then that I release for you the King of the Jews?" (18:39). Pilate, remember, is not interested in the truth. He is interested in staying in charge. But he has gone too far, for in making it obvious that "King of the Jews" is just some combination of words, something someone has said with no real truth to it, Pilate has insulted them, manipulating something that they are absolutely serious about. They refuse his offer. "Not this Man, but Barabbas," they say, insisting, as many have noted, that an innocent man take the place of a clearly guilty one. The crowd wins, but once again, quietly, John has called our attention to the larger pattern unfolding.

So Pilate tries something else, shutting his ears to Jesus' claims about himself, but inadvertently bringing his claims into greater and greater prominence. He has Jesus violently scourged, then lets his soldiers crown him with thorns, array him in a purple robe, hail him as king, and strike him in the face. Why? This is not random cruelty. Rather, Pilate is mocking the leaders' charge that Jesus is a political threat by turning him into a kind of cartoon king and thereby demonstrating that he is no threat to anyone. I'll show you what sort of king he is, Pilate's actions say—none at all. At the same time, at a deeper level, he is also attempting to counter Jesus' claim to be the king of another, more powerful realm. How could that be? Pilate is now able to say. Look at what I am able to get away with! No, this is the only realm that counts, and Pilate is the one in charge. He takes the beaten Jesus outside, convinced that he has outwitted both the crowd and Jesus, and presents the bloody, crowned figure to them with the simple statement "Behold, the Man!" (19:5), or in the well-known Latin translation, *"Ecce Homo."* He announces that what he has done shows that he has found no guilt in him, an odd thing to say after punishing him so severely, until we realize that Pilate thinks that his abuse has proven that Jesus presents no threat to Rome and thus is not guilty. Look at this man, he says—how could such a "king" matter to someone like me?

Pilate seems to have won, holding his position against the crowd's attack and countering the unsettling vision he had glimpsed inside his palace. But John hears the statement "Behold, the Man" quite differently. Like Caiaphas before him (11:51), he notes, Pilate has spoken a truth he does not understand, essentially saying "Behold, in this broken and humiliated figure, man in all his glory. " This is true in at least two senses. On the one hand, this is who man is, and this is the "glory" he deserves. But this is also true glory—embodied in this man who, having put aside all power and authority in order to gain back the world, is now being exalted in his humiliation. Can you see this? Pilate says to all those with eyes to see, completely unknowingly.

In fact, no. Where Pilate expects the crowd to agree that this bloody mock-king is no king at all, the chief priests and officers are enraged. "Crucify, crucify," they cry. Why? The beating confirms the charge they have been unwilling to make up until this point. Jesus' obvious weakness proves he cannot be the Son of God as he has claimed. He cannot be the Messiah, for God would never permit his messianic king to undergo such treatment, making this scene conclusive proof that this man is a liar and a fraud. Crucify him as a blasphemer, they cry. Remove him from our presence. Nail him up and prove, once and for all, that he is cursed and not who he said he was.

But Pilate will not back down. Now that they have shown what their charge really is, he has them where he wants them and takes back the upper hand. "Take Him yourselves, and crucify Him, for I find no guilt in Him" (19:6), he says. They cannot do this, as Pilate knows, forcing them once again to be explicit about their desires: "We have a law, and by that law He ought to die because He made Himself out to be the Son of God" (19:7). He "made Himself out" to be something he was not, an old charge that we saw in the Gospel's earlier chapters—Jesus "making himself equal with God" (5:18) or attempting to "make [Him]self out to be God" (10:33). It is a powerful charge, and Jesus' condition seems to prove that he has indeed spoken blasphemously. No Son of God would stand before them arrayed like this.

Pilate goes back inside, one last time, obviously shaken. He has not forgotten Jesus' claim to be from another world after all, and at the leaders' charge that Jesus had claimed to be the Son of God, "he was the more afraid" (19:8), John tells us. That other "realm" (18:36), whose presence he had sensed all along, has just been named. "Where are You from?" he demands, when he is alone with Jesus. But now Jesus gives him no answer. He stands before him in silence, light breaking into the world, and waits. Here, the Samaritan woman responded. Here, the blind man opened his inner eyes. Here, Peter saw what he had done and wept. But Pilate cannot, or will not. Instead, he blusters: "You do not speak to me? Do You not know that I have the authority to release You, and I have the authority to crucify You?" (19:10). To which Jesus calmly replies, You do not. Your authority has been given to you from above, the very realm you are trying so hard to avoid: "You would have no authority over Me, unless it has been given you from above; for this reason he who delivered Me up to you has the greater sin" (19:11).

Pilate understands and makes efforts to release him, but, having refused to fully come to grips with who Jesus is, he finds himself unable to withstand the world's pressure. Back outside, the crowd cries "If you release this Man, you are no friend of Caesar; everyone who makes himself out to be a king opposes Caesar" (19:12), and this breaks him. Both Pilate and the crowd understand how power works. The leaders have recast their actual charge—Jesus has blasphemously "made himself out" to be the Son of God—in political terms. He has made himself out to be a king and thus an opponent of Caesar's. Now Pilate is suddenly vulnerable. If he can be "made out" to be no friend of Caesar's, then his own standing, his own life, might be at risk. And so the world wins, just as it had with Peter, by relentlessly exerting its power. There seems to be nothing else to be done. Pilate brings Jesus out again and hands him over. He sits in his judgment seat on this "the day of preparation for the Passover; it was about the sixth hour" and hands over the lamb to be sacrificed, with the words "Behold, your King!" (19:14). Perhaps he is still hoping to dissuade the crowd, but they roar again, at the blasphemous insult, "Away with Him, crucify Him!" and when Pilate asks, one last time, "crucify your King?" the chief priests answer, "We have no king but Caesar" (19:15). "The only emperor is the emperor of ice-cream," the poet Wallace Stevens wrote, echoing this cry and making much the same point.[4] The world they live in, despite what they would like to say, is a physical one. Its emperor is Caesar—power, advantage, self-assertion. But Caesar's kingdom is also ice cream—a taste and then gone. Pilate understands this, but cannot act on his sense that it could be otherwise and is undone. The decision is taken out of his hands, and he "deliver[s] Him to them to be crucified" (19:16).

John Berryman, "Ecce Homo"

John Berryman's "Ecce Homo" powerfully takes up Pilate's call to "Behold the Man!" Turning to a photograph of a Renaissance-era sculpture, Berryman suddenly finds himself confronting what John saw—Pilate's beaten, bloody mock-king, no conceivable threat to any of the world's powers, who was simultaneously man at his lowest and God at his most glorious. What is interesting about the poem is the journey it describes the poet making in order to arrive at this insight. Berryman lets us actually experience the shift in vision that would have to occur in order to take all of this in:

> Long long with wonder I thought you human,
> *almost* beyond humanity but not.
> Once, years ago, only in a high bare hall
> of the great Catalan museum over Barcelona
> I thought you might be more—
>
> a Pantocrator glares down, from San Clemente de Tahull,
> making me feel you probably were divine,
> *but* not human, thro' that majestic image.
> Now I've come on something where you seem both—
> a photograph of it only—
>
> Burgundian, of painted & gilt wood,
> life-size almost (not that we know your Semitic stature),
> attenuated, your dead head bent forward sideways,
> your long feet hanging, your thin long arms out
> in unconquerable beseeching—[5]

Berryman begins by describing the response to Christ he held through most of his life: "Long long with wonder I thought you human, / *almost* beyond humanity but not." I thought of you as extraordinary but human, he says—awestruck by accounts of Christ's love and tenderness and humility, his heart leaping in wonder at Christ's almost inhuman display of compassion. "Once," he adds, "years ago," I had the sense that "you might be more," describing a moment in the National Museum of Art of Catalonia, in Barcelona, when he stared up at a twelfth-century fresco from the Church of San Clemente de Tahull displayed there. The image he saw was of Christ as Judge, raised to glory and enthroned in heaven, his face stern, his feet resting on the globe of the earth. (*Pantocrator* is the Greek translation of the Hebrew name for God, *El-shaddai*, a term eventually applied to representations such as this of "Christ in Glory" or "Christ in Majesty.") Through "that majestic image," Berryman writes, I had, at least for the moment, the sense that "you probably were divine, / *but* not human."

But "Now," he adds, in the manner of most of the poets we have been considering, I have come across another, fuller representation, "where you seem both" human *and* divine. And what he describes is not unlike the broken, yet glorious figure that John saw Pilate presenting to the crowd, which is why he titles his poem, "Ecce Homo." This Christ, a Renaissance-era, painted wood sculpture, "life-sized almost," hangs dead. His head droops, "bent forward sideways," his "long feet" hang, and his "thin long arms" are stretched out. His body seems broken and attenuated, almost pulled apart by its terrible, human weight. And yet, the poet adds, his arms are outstretched "in unconquerable beseeching." Even in death his figure seeks to embrace the world and take it in. That is where his true divinity is expressed, the poet realizes—in being conquered by death he conquered death for all those who behold and take him in. As John saw in the scene with Pilate, Jesus' glory is expressed in his brokenness. Christ conquers by being conquered, rules by being humiliated.

The "now" that the poem turns on in line nine seems crucial—a version of Bishop's "pivot." For a "long" time I thought you were human, Berryman writes. "Once" I glimpsed your divinity, high and exalted. But "now" I see that you are both—that the two must work together for your shattered "beseeching" to be a living, "unconquerable" gesture. What strikes us suddenly is that for this speaker Christ *is* living. Despite approaching him through various forms of representation, the Christ he speaks so intimately to—"your long feet," "your dead head"—lives and listens, draws near and understands, having passed through death in order to love him forever, just as Jesus suggested he would in his Farewell Discourse. One can sense the poet, by the way he addresses the one he speaks to, being drawn toward an unconquerable embrace. It is a remarkably subtle gesture, exactly the sort of response that John's text, another representation, is even now seeking to encourage.

Crucifixion, 19:17-30

When we turn to the crucifixion, what is most striking about the way John takes us through it is that he focuses not so much on the glory or horror of the event as on its meaning, what he has understood (1:18). Much as Elizabeth Bishop did in "Poem," returning to the painting after having worked out its landscape within herself, John sees not dabs of color or generic details but living markers, woven together in such a way that each of them can be read and entered into. It is that web of significance, each of its elements crying out what had been accomplished, that he takes the reader through. This is what I saw, he finally says.

The soldiers take Jesus to Golgotha, "the Place of a Skull," and crucify him between two other men. John, however, focuses initially not on the body of Jesus but on the sign Pilate put on the cross, identifying the broken figure as "Jesus the Nazarene, the King of the Jews" (19:19). He notes that the inscription is in three languages, addressed to the entire world. The chief priests object, wanting Pilate to write "He *said* 'I am King of the Jews.'" They are convinced that his broken, humiliated body would be all that was needed to prove that he was not who he said he was and thus had been properly executed for blasphemy—for "saying" such a thing. Pilate refuses. He is still smarting from being so nakedly forced into this situation. For him, this torn body says that if the Jews had a king, this is what he would look like. But what John sees is God, through these human schemers, reaching out to the entire world with the news that he has sent his king to Israel, and that in being broken, his king has ascended to his throne and begun his reign, just as had been predicted in 3:14, 8:28, and 12:32.

What happened when the King, Israel's Messiah, ascended his throne? He was forsaken. Another detail that John focuses on makes this clear. The soldiers at the foot of the cross, after they had crucified Jesus, divided his outer garments into four parts, each taking a portion, but deciding to cast lots for his seamless tunic, so as not to have to tear it. David had imagined a similar scene in Psalm 22, crying out "My God, my God, why hast Thou forsaken me?" (22:1) and comparing life outside of God's love and protection to death itself—an agonizing death by torture, made infinitely worse because God had "laid" him in it:

> I am poured out like water,
> And all my bones are out of joint;
> My heart is like wax;
> It is melted within me.
> My strength is dried up like a potsherd,
> And my tongue cleaves to my jaws;
> And Thou dost lay me in the dust of death.
> For dogs have surrounded me;
> A band of evildoers has encompassed me;
> They pierced my hands and my feet.
> I can count all my bones.
> They look, they stare at me;
> They divide my garments among them,
> And for my clothing they cast lots.

(Ps 22:14-18)

What John realizes is that Jesus had completed or "fulfilled" (19:24) Psalm 22 by literally embodying David's despairing vision. His clothing had been removed and divided up; his hands and feet had been pierced as he was nailed to the wooden beams; his strength had drained away as enemies gathered to watch and jeer. But deeper than that, he sees that Jesus had been forsaken in a way that David, who ends his great lament confident that God will not hide his face forever, could not have imagined. "Therefore the soldiers did these things" (19:25), John writes. They did them so that this could be seen.

To this point, John has not looked directly at the cross. Now he turns his attention to the followers of Jesus standing nearby, a group that includes Jesus' mother and "the disciple whom He loved" (19:26). If we assume that the narrator and this disciple are one and the same, then what happens here is that Jesus reaches out to John from the cross and draws his eyes to him. "Woman," Jesus says to his mother, "behold, your son!" and to the disciple, "Behold, your mother!" (19:26-27). We remember, of course, the last time Jesus spoke to his mother, at Cana, saying, "Woman, what do I have to do with you? My hour has not yet come" (2:4). The hour has now come, and what it has accomplished is made visible in the new family he establishes here. His mother and the Beloved can be made one because he and his Father are one; in turning to Jesus for life, they are turning together to the Father, and united in him. Behold how you are loved, Jesus says to both of them from the cross. In light of that, behold one another.

With that, Jesus completes his work on the cross, his last words seared into John's memory. He records two sentences. The first, spoken by Jesus when he knew "all things had already been accomplished, in order that the Scripture might be fulfilled," was the simple statement "I am thirsty" (19:28), leading the soldiers to put a "sponge full of sour wine upon a branch of hyssop" (19:29) and lift it to his mouth. John seems to have heard Psalm 69 again in this statement, although there are other references in Scripture to thirst, including the words from Psalm 22 I have just mentioned.[6] In Psalm 69, David calls on God to rescue him from unjust persecution. He is "hated without a cause," "weary with my crying, my throat . . . parched," bearing the reproaches of those who would reproach God. There is no one but God to comfort him: "I looked for sympathy, but there was none, / And for comforters, but I found none. / They also gave me gall for my food, / And for my thirst they gave me vinegar to drink" (Ps 69:20-21). John would have seen the details of David's abandonment echoed in what Jesus had just gone through. But even more powerfully, I think, he must have eventually realized that David's prayer for God to pour out his indignation and anger on those who had turned their backs on him had also been fulfilled on the cross.

"Pour out Thine indignation on them, / And may Thy burning anger over-take them," David writes in the verses that immediately follow. "And may they not come into Thy righteousness. / May they be blotted out of the book of life" (Psalm 69:24, 27, 28). What John eventually saw was that God *had* blotted his enemies out of the book of life, just as David had asked, but he had done so by blotting out his own Son, denying him, who was righteous, a place with the righteous, so that those turning to him might be enemies no longer.

John must have felt confirmed in sensing Psalm 69 at play in these last words when he remembered the detail about the branch or stalk of hyssop used to lift the sponge to the lips of Jesus.[7] Hyssop was the plant used to shake the blood of the sacrificed lamb over the door at Passover, and its presence in this scene must have indicated to John that Jesus was sacrificed so that death would pass over and those he loved would be released from bondage forever (see Lev 14:4, Exod 12:22). This is what Jesus' second and final sentence, after he had received the sour wine, refers to: "It is finished" (19:30). God's anger had been fully poured out; the work of reconciliation had been completed. Jesus, as he had promised, had "loved them to the end" (13:1)—*finished* and *end* both being variations of *telos*, indicating that the goal had finally been achieved, fully and completely. With that, he dies. Taking it all in, however, making sense of what had taken place—that had just begun.

Kathleen Norris, "La Vierge Romane"

Kathleen Norris was also struck by the brief words Jesus speaks in John's version of the crucifixion—"Woman, behold your son," "I am thirsty," "It is finished." In "La Vierge Romane," from a collection of poems written from 1987 to 1999, she unfolds what Jesus did on the cross by meditating on his quiet words to his mother and silence itself, following John's lead by taking in the crucifixion indirectly, reminding us of the unexpected power of such an approach. "La Vierge Romane" is "the Romanesque Virgin," a twelfth-century representation of mother and child:

Her face long
and plain, impossibly
serene, has prayed
through blood
and water,
childbirth and death,
these eight centuries past.

She has let her hands fall
open, the child secure
on her lap, old
beyond his years.

"There is your son," Jesus says
from the cross—his stretched hands
powerless—"there, your mother."
And here, during Easter,
the two-months infant nurses
beside me, in the monk's choir,
knowing only mother,
the milk
of all promise,
hands kneading greedily
at the breast. The man
in the choir stall before me, whose mother
has just died, holds his hands
behind his back,
as if a prisoner
being led to a fearful place.

I think I will go
where words are neither hard
nor loving,
but blaze unseen in bones
that grieve, in bones that thrive
and grow. And all that binds
the child to the mother will be
sweet food, like sun in wood,
on the wood of the Virgin's face.

She prays for us,
but silently. Her hands hold on
by letting go. From her
the child learns
to give us to each other.[8]

As the poem begins, the speaker, on Easter morning, is meditating on a version of the statue. What most strikes the poet about the mother of Jesus is her serenity. Without a change in expression, she has prayed without speaking for both her son and those who gaze at her "through blood / and water, / childbirth and death, / these eight centuries past." Her calm gaze is echoed by the position of her body, at ease with the miraculous child: "She has let her hands fall / open, the child secure / on her lap."

The speaker then moves to Jesus' words from the cross. It is Easter, and the statue of mother and child has prompted her to think about the new relationship between mother and son created through the cross. She is sitting in the "monk's choir," surrounded by others—the "here" of the poem, in contrast to the "there" of the Gospel: "'*There* is your son,' Jesus says / from the cross—his stretched hands / powerless—'*there*, your mother.'" She then describes two of the people around her: a nursing infant, "knowing only mother, / the milk / of all promise," and a man in front of her who has just lost his mother and "holds his hands / behind his back, / as if a prisoner / being led to a fearful place." Mothers and children, birth and death—this series of loose, associative connections seems to have been prompted by the statue and the remembered words from the cross, as if something in the scene was tugging at the poet and she was trying to unfold it.

With the third stanza, something snaps into place. "I think I will go," she says, and with these words we realize she had been slowly coming to a decision. "I think I will go / where words are neither hard / nor loving, / but blaze unseen in bones / that grieve, / in bones that thrive / and grow." She will go, or give herself, to situations in which her words will no longer be "hard" or "loving," attempting to grasp or force or hold close, but "unseen" and silent, spoken forth in an entirely different way. We do not know to what specific situation she is referring—perhaps it is a relationship with a spouse or an aging relative—but it seems clear that she is turning her back on using words to pin down and know for sure, "bind[ing]" us to one another. She is turning toward something riskier and more intimate and more open. Her examples are the deeply expressive wordlessness of the grieving man with his prisoner-like hands behind his back ("bones that grieve") or the busy, equally wordless hands of the eager infant ("bones that thrive and grow").

That is to say, she is turning toward the Virgin's quiet serenity, hands open, the child secure on her lap: "She prays for us, / but *silently*. Her hands hold on / by *letting go*" (emphasis mine). It was from her, she speculates, that the child Jesus "learn[ed] / to give us to each other." What she hears now in the words Jesus speaks from the cross—"There is your son; there, your mother"—is him loving the world by letting it go. Letting the world go by dying for it, his unspoken words "blaze" with power, creating life where there was none, creating a new family where there was only grief. By means of the silent statue and the wordlessly expressive figures in the choir stall around her, Norris has heard the very words of Jesus, spoken to her from the cross. Like Mary and John, she has heard him giving her to the world and "us to each other." Embrace those around you, he says; speak to them as I speak to you, by laying your strength down. Speak not through the sound of your words, he says, but through their silence. In doing so, you will speak, as I do, the very words of life.

Pierced, 19:31-42

In his description of the crucifixion, John has focused on details that eventually became significant to his understanding of what had been accomplished there—that on the cross, Jesus was enthroned as king; that he was forsaken and poured out (Ps 22), the recipient of God's indignation (Ps 69); and that, with that work "finished," a new community, based on his love for them, had been established. This, he eventually understood, was what Jesus had been anticipating when he healed the broken or fed the hungry—this is what he had been calling people to believe. In the second part of his account of the crucifixion, John turns to the body on the cross, now dead, and focuses on two more details. Although it seems likely that he did not understand the significance of these two details until later, what he stresses is what he came to see when he himself had been awakened to his own great need.

It is late afternoon on Friday, and so that the bodies will not hang on the cross through the Sabbath, which begins on Friday night, the Jewish leaders ask Pilate to have the legs of the condemned men broken, so that they might no longer support themselves and their death would be hastened. The soldiers break the legs of the other two men, but when they come to Jesus they find that he is already dead and they do not need to disable him. Instead, one of them pierces his side with a spear, confirming that there is no response. Blood and water gush out. At that, John bursts out, "And he who has seen has borne witness, and his witness is true; and he knows that he is telling the truth, so that you also may believe" (19:35). This has been read a number of different ways, but the most straightforward way of taking it is that the narrator is talking about himself—he saw this, he is bearing witness to what he saw, and he knows (as no one else would) that what he is saying is true. He wants the reader to see what he has seen and believe.[9]

What did he see here, and why does he stake his reputation on testifying to it? He saw two things. First, he saw that the bones of Jesus were not broken, so "that the Scripture might be fulfilled, 'Not a bone of him shall be broken'" (19:36). That is, he saw that God had set Jesus aside as the true Passover lamb. As recorded in Exodus 12:46 and Numbers 9:12, the Passover lamb, whose blood was placed on the doorways of houses as a yearly reminder of the way God freed Israel from Egypt and brought her home, was required to have none of its legs broken. John saw this and understood that the death of Jesus was what the Passover lamb had been pointing to all along. He saw that through the death of the Lamb of God, he himself had been spared and brought out of slavery and given a new life. He understood what God had "said" through the soldiers' actions, and he believed.

Second, John saw that when Jesus' body was pierced by a soldier's spear, another Scripture had been fulfilled: "They shall look on Him whom they pierced" (19:37). As with the Passover lamb, John saw this as no casual echo. In the prophet Zechariah's vision of the last days, when God would defeat Israel's enemies who were envisioned as laying siege to the capital city Jerusalem, John saw a second and corroborating explanation of the crucifixion:

> And it will come about in that day that I will set about to destroy all the nations that come against Jerusalem. And I will pour out on the house of David and on the inhabitants of Jerusalem, the Spirit of grace and of supplication, so that they will look on Me whom they have pierced; and they will mourn for Him, as one mourns for an only son, and they will weep bitterly over Him, like the bitter weeping over a first-born. . . . In that day a fountain will be opened for the house of David and for the inhabitants of Jerusalem, for sin and for impurity. (Zech 12:9-10, 13:1)

Zechariah said that God would destroy Israel's enemies and give new life to Jerusalem. What John saw is that through the death of Jesus, God had accomplished both of these things. By bearing sin's penalty, Jesus had conquered Israel's true enemy, and in doing so, he had made it possible for God's people to turn back and enter into his presence, to be filled there with his own Spirit, flooding them with a sense of his "grace" and making them eager to "supplicate" or call on him for mercy.

Seeing Jesus' torn body in light of Zechariah's prophecy would have made clear to John what Zechariah's slippery pronouns had been pointing to—that it was God himself who was pierced in the death of his Son: "they will look on *Me* whom they have pierced, and they will mourn for *Him*." He would have understood, because it happened to him, that after his great victory, when God poured out life on Jerusalem, that life was first experienced as "mourning." Because God, in victory, had poured out on Jerusalem "the Spirit of grace and of supplication," John had seen and believed. *He* had been flooded with a sense of God's grace, and *he* had been stirred to turn to him in supplication. This is what John is testifying to now, as he writes. He had looked in faith on him whom they had pierced and understood— "mourned" the fact—that it was his sins Jesus had died for. He saw the true cost of his rebellion—that it had cost God everything, his "first born," his "only son"—but also saw, because he saw in faith, that God was offering him mercy. God had turned his eyes toward him who had been pierced in order to offer him life.

To see and believe, then, a phrase John uses throughout the Gospel, means to "mourn" or acknowledge one's willful failings—one's blindness, say, or enslavement to something that is not life—and then to turn, through the power of "the Spirit of grace and of supplication," toward the one pierced in one's place. It is to trust that mourning is not the end of the story—that, as Zechariah saw in the unfolding of this vision and the children of Israel saw in looking toward the serpent raised up on the pole, those who "look on Me" will drink and live. Zechariah describes that life in terms that have echoed throughout John's Gospel: "In that day a fountain will be opened for the house of David and for the inhabitants of Jerusalem, for sin and for impurity" (Zech 13:1). This is the living water of God's presence, opened up now, in mercy, to all of the world. One can just imagine all of these things coming together when John looked, in faith, at the body on the cross in light of Zechariah's vision. No wonder he burst out that he himself had seen these things and that he knew he was telling the truth.

But as I have been stressing, John would not have understood all of this at the time, for the Spirit of grace and supplication had not yet been poured out on him. We sense this in the way he describes the subsequent handling of Jesus' body, returning to the feelings of sadness and regret that those who had lost such a great master would have felt. Joseph of Arimathea and Nicodemus, whom we now see for a third time, remove the body. They bind it and a great weight of spices in linen wrappings and then place it in a new tomb in a nearby garden. All seems hurried and hushed. The Sabbath is near, a period in which dead bodies should not be handled. The reader knows by now that something more is to come, but the participants in the scene do not. We enter a great pause. John has passed back and forth across this gap a number of times, the reader with him, but the narrative itself is now about to radically shift. One can almost sense it gathering itself.

George Herbert, "Holy Baptisme I"

George Herbert reads Jesus' pierced side very much along the lines we have just sketched. If, from Zechariah, John understood faith as both "mourning" and "drinking"—acknowledging the true nature of his sin as it was made visible in the broken body of Jesus and then drinking from the fountain of God's mercy, Herbert lets us see more clearly how the two work together. For

Herbert, mourning *is* drinking; seeing more of his sin shows him more of his
need for mercy, and more of God's willingness to provide it. Like all of the
poets we have been examining, Herbert looks first to his own experience—in
this case, his sins, rather than a falcon or a painting or New Year's Eve story,
but his own experience nonetheless—and then, stirred to life by exploring
that landscape, returns to the Gospel with ears to hear. It seems clear that
John must have gone through a similar spiritual and imaginative awakening:

> As he that sees a dark and shadie grove,
>   Stayes not, but looks beyond it on the skie;
>   So when I view my sinnes, mine eyes remove
> More backward still, and to that water flie,
>
> Which is above the heav'ns, whose spring and vent
>   Is in my deare Redeemers pierced side.
>   O blessed streams! either ye do prevent
> And stop our sinnes from growing thick and wide,
>
> Or else give tears to drown them, as they grow.
>   In you Redemption measures all my time,
>   And spreads the plaister equall to the crime:
> You taught the Book of Life my name, that so
>
> > What ever future sinnes should me miscall,
> > Your first acquaintance might discredit all.[10]

Herbert begins by comparing his experience with sin to a person in a
"dark and shadie grove" who notices light flickering through thick leaves
and finds himself powerfully drawn to that bright sky outside the grove. In
just the same way, he writes, "when I view my sinnes," his eyes move greedily
past them to the bright sky breaking through their tented canopy—to what
he calls "that water . . . / Which is above the heav'ns, whose spring and rent /
Is in my deare Redeemers pierced side." Moving "backward" suggests he is
thinking about baptism and what is pictured there—God's Spirit, pouring
out from his Redeemer's side, washing him clean and giving him new life. It
is a packed, powerful image. What Herbert sees is that the cleansing waters
of baptism "spring" from the "vent" in his Savior's side, the death he suffered
in the speaker's place. This is just what John the Baptist proclaimed: Jesus,
the "Lamb of God who takes away the sin of the world," is "the one who bap-
tizes in the Holy Spirit" (1:29, 33). When I view my sins, the poet says, when
I mourn them, I see as well the sky beyond them and "flie" to that light,
drinking in more and more of the life flowing from Christ's pierced side, the
life in which I have been baptized.

The second and third stanzas describe two different things that happen when the speaker flies in faith to those "streams" of life. "O blessed streams!" he writes, presumably thinking of the twin streams of blood and water gushing forth at the soldier's thrust, "either ye do prevent / And stop our sinnes from growing thick and wide, // Or else give tears to drown them, as they grow." Again, the language is very dense, as if the poet had passed this way repeatedly. Drinking of those living streams, being filled with Christ's Spirit even while he is wrestling with sin, the speaker is given either a new life inside which "stop[s] our sinnes from growing thick and wide" or an increased mourning and repentance—"tears to drown them, as they grow." In both cases, as he says in line three, his eyes "remove": they move twice, toward that sin and then back again to "that water." This is the way faith moves, Herbert realizes—mourning and drinking, forward and back, always alive to the light flickering just beyond the grove.

He can confidently examine his sin, Herbert adds in the third stanza, because Christ's work has been completed or "finished" (19:30). Despite the darkness of the grove, that bright, life-giving sky is permanently there. "In you Redemption measures all my time," the poet writes, no longer addressing the "blessed streams" of life but, like Berryman in "Ecce Homo," speaking now to Christ himself, as if Christ had come alive to him as he was working through the inner landscape of his sins. Your redemption applies to or "measures" all my time, he writes—nothing will shake it or cause it to no longer apply. The healing "plaister" spread by the cross across his wounds is "equall" to all his "crime." Because Christ has "taught the Book of Life" the poet's name, naming him as a child of God, he will always be recognized, never turned away.

As the last couplet has it, even when his future sins attempt to rename him (to "miscall" him) in terms God would seem not recognize—thief, murderer, hater of God—his "first acquaintance" with his Savior, established when he turned in faith to the life streaming from his pierced side, would never be broken. He will always be recognized, that "first acquaintance . . . discredit[ing] all" future charges against him. Staring at his sin, working through its dark and shady grove, the poet's questions grow deeper and broader. What about the future? What about his repeated failings? But as his questions deepen, his Redeemer does as well, the endless reach of God's love plumbed and "measure[d]," if only in part, by the poet's particular need.

Resurrection, 20:1-10

John has just taken us through the arrest and death of Jesus, quite consciously writing from the perspective of someone on whom the "Spirit of grace and of supplication" had been poured out and who was looking in faith "on Him whom they pierced." Now, in his account of the resurrection, he pulls back from that perspective. Rather than, as with the crucifixion, interpreting and unfolding a grand drama whose import he now understands, calling our attention to certain tensions and moments of revelation, he now returns us to the position of those on whom the import of what had been accomplished was still dawning. It is as if he is presenting us with the door through which we must enter. This is the moment of recognition, variously and individually shaded for each reader. The questions raised here are intended to generate new ways of thinking and feeling. The poets we will examine each walk us through, in quite different ways, that moment of awakening.

Jesus has been buried, his body bound in linen and spices and placed in a new tomb in a nearby garden. Saturday passes. Sunday, the first day of the week arrives, and, while it is still dark, Mary Magdalene and others come to the place where his body had been laid. They expect to find a body, but instead they find the stone blocking the entrance to the tomb already moved and the body missing. Mary runs back to Peter and the Beloved and tells them that something has been done to the body, perhaps some sort of desecration: "They have taken away the Lord out of the tomb, and we do not know where they have laid Him" (20:2). She is entirely focused on his body, his remains. Peter and the Beloved run to the tomb, the Beloved getting there first. Hesitant, he stoops and looks, sees the linen wrappings the body had been bound in, but does not go in. Peter arrives and immediately enters the tomb. He sees the wrappings and "the face-cloth, which had been on His head, not lying with the linen wrappings, but rolled up in a place by itself" (20:7). The Beloved follows Peter in, and "he saw and believed. For as yet they did not understand the Scripture, that He must rise again from the dead" (20:8-9). And with that, the two of them "went away again to their own homes" (20:10).

This is a riddling, perhaps deliberately so. What John describes—and if he is the Beloved, remembers—is the flash of insight when he realized that the body had not been taken away. No one would have removed the linen wrappings or calmly rolled up the facecloth if he were stealing the body or carrying it off elsewhere. Something else had happened, and John had no words for it. He had not yet experienced Scripture falling into place around the event and making it clear. He had as yet no way of describing the Messiah's suffering as a victory and not a defeat. And yet, he "believed." Standing in the tomb, overwhelmed with grief, John felt the balance tip and understood that the crushing of the Messiah was not the end of things. He understood that God had somehow acted to restore the one he had sent. He does not speak of this to Peter, as far as we can tell. Perhaps he does not know how to. He and Peter go their separate ways, but a first moment of recognition has occurred. John saw something, and believed.

R. S. Thomas, "The Answer"

The Welsh poet R. S. Thomas, an Anglican clergyman who died in 2000, wrote poem after poem wrestling with the absence of God, remarking once that "I never thought other than / That God is that great absence / In our lives, the empty silence / Within, the place where we go / Seeking, not in hope to / Arrive or find."[11] Remarkably, that empty silence became for Thomas the space where God's presence, utterly different from him, was most piercingly felt—that silence "the shadow of your steep mind / on my world."[12] In "The Answer," 1978, wrestling once again with God's absence, Thomas powerfully uses that to unfold what the Beloved must have gone through when he entered the tomb, saw the rolled-up facecloth, and "believed":

Not darkness but twilight
in which even the best
of minds must make its way
now. And slowly the questions
occur, vague but formidable
for all that. We pass our hands
over their surface like blind
men, feeling for the mechanism
that will swing them aside. They
yield, but only to re-form
as new problems; and one
does not even do that
but towers immovable
before us.
            Is there no way
other than thought of answering
its challenge? There is an anticipation
of it to the point of
dying. There have been times
when, after long on my knees

in a cold chancel, a stone has rolled
from my mind, and I have looked
in and seen the old questions lie
folded and in a place
by themselves, like the piled
graveclothes of love's risen body.[13]

Thomas begins by describing the half-light, "Not darkness but twilight," in which "even the best / of minds" in the modern world "must make its way / now." It is a world in which everything is shaded, nothing is firm. Questions occur, "vague but formidable / for all that." With no clear way of answering them, "We pass our hands / over their surface like blind / men, feeling for the mechanism / that will swing them aside"—a brilliant image, both tactile and intellectual at once, getting at the way we touch and touch a problem, unable to address it directly, but unwilling to leave it alone. Sometimes, "They / yield, but only to re-form / as new problems," the moment of release not a moment of respite but simply an opportunity for the issues to shift about and shape themselves into new versions of the same problem. All of us know this pattern; as Thomas suggests, it is the rhythm of the modern world. But one problem, he chillingly remarks, "does not even do that." It simply "towers immovable / before us." He is almost certainly thinking of God's silence, his seeming abandonment of the earth, but by leaving the problem unnamed, Thomas allows its hulking intractability to darken and thicken.

And darken it does. Once it has been admitted into the poem, that towering problem is all the poet can think about, even though he knows, as he has just argued, that even the best of minds, in this twilight world, can make no real progress against such an impasse. Almost in desperation, he cries out in the second stanza, "Is there no way / other than thought of answering / its challenge?" Well, he responds to his own question, "There is an anticipation / of it," the problem, "to the point of dying." One would not call what he has in mind thinking, exactly—feeling one's way into the problem; going deeper and deeper, anticipating the way abandonment, for example, spreads itself everywhere; taking it in through the body's imagination; coming as close to it as we can without dying. One might imagine the disciples, on Sunday morning, finding themselves in just such a position—unable to think, exhausted, bone-weary and alone, their dashed hopes having brought them to a state not unlike death.

Imagining himself there, calling back the exhaustion of his body and the darkening of his soul on some lonely occasion, Thomas goes on. He unfolds one of those moments of dark "anticipation," thinking set aside, bearing the weight of some insoluble problem in the body's very joints, and realizes that darkness is where answers come. John called this belief—that moment of recognition, below the level of words, when the looming questions, as familiar and nearby as one's own body, simply dissolve and are replaced with what we can only call life, or love. Thomas' version of this is extraordinary:

> There have been times
> when, after long on my knees
> in a cold chancel, a stone has rolled
> from my mind, and I have looked
> in and seen the old questions lie
> folded and in a place
> by themselves, like the piled
> graveclothes of love's risen body.

Thomas takes the Beloved's focus on the folded facecloth, testimony somehow, at a level far below thought, that the body had not been moved, and turns it into his own gaze as his own questions inexplicably drop away. The mystery of the body has not been solved, the problem still remains, but its death-like grip has been set aside, replaced with life and breathing. Thought comes later. This is as precise an account of the way belief occurs as I know. It is what we have been hungering to see dramatized throughout the Gospel—what does recognition look like?—and now that we are ready, John provides an example. This is his first account—three more follow.

Mary, 20:11-18

The second moment of recognition is Mary's. Peter and the Beloved leave, and Mary Magdalene, who seems to have followed them and waited outside the tomb while they slowly emerged, steps forward: "But Mary was standing outside the tomb weeping, and so, as she wept, she stooped and looked into the tomb" (20:11). Through her tears, she sees two angels sitting where the body had been laid, but even that is not enough to overcome her sadness about the missing body. "Woman, why are you weeping?" they say, implying that she should not be. "Because they have taken away my Lord, and I do not know where they have laid Him" (20:13), she responds.[14] Nothing will break her focus on the missing body. Turning around, going back outside, she sees Jesus standing there but does not recognize him. Even when he speaks, repeating the question about her tears, Mary, "supposing Him to be the gardener," thinks of nothing but the body: "Sir, if you have carried Him away, tell me where you have laid Him, and I will take Him away" (20:15).

Perhaps someone had objected to his being laid here. Perhaps this had been only a temporary resting place. Whatever the case, she wants the body back and is prepared to take the steps necessary to obtain it. Jesus must not have replied, because she turns away from him and returns to her frantic seeking, only to hear, from behind, her name: "Mary!" As several commentators note, she has become one of the sheep described in chapter 10. She knows the voice that calls her name, turning and saying, in recognition, "Rabboni!" (20:16) or "Teacher." The Beloved responded to a detail that did not fit with what he had expected to see, his heart suddenly lifting up; Mary responds to the sound of her name. Both, in their own ways, hear themselves addressed.

As when John stared at the linen wrappings, Mary's initial moment of recognition is raw, charged, and not fully sorted out. We can sense a whole new way of viewing the world shifting and groaning into place. Somehow, she finds herself clinging to Jesus. The narrator does not tell us how, and perhaps she herself does not know, consumed as she is in wonder. Jesus' response at first seems quite abrupt, even unsettling: "Stop clinging to Me, for I have not yet ascended to the Father; but go to My brethren, and say to them, 'I ascend to My Father and your Father, and My God and your God'" (20:17). These are much-debated lines, with much thought having been given to the "for" between the two initial clauses. What is there about his having not yet ascended that should keep Mary from touching or clinging to him? There have been many answers, some quite speculative. But perhaps this is not the right question to ask. Ascending to the Father and preparing a place for believers to live with God is what Jesus promised to do during his last hours with his disciples (14:1-4). His death would seem to have made this impossible, but Jesus is now sending Mary to his disciples to assure them that this is not so. As he had promised, he is in the process of ascending to the Father, having passed through a death that, rather than being a disaster, has now removed the barriers between God and humanity. His Father has become their Father, and his God their God. This is extraordinary news. Mary is not to cling to his physical body, then, because, although he has not yet ascended he *is* ascending—he has brought into being a new world in which she, and all believers, will be united with him not through physically clinging to a body but through faith. This is great good news. Bodies are not permanent, however deeply they are loved, but this new relationship is, which is not to say that it is easily understood, either by Mary or anyone else who wrestles with these unsettling, world-changing words: "Don't cling to me. Believe." But, like the Beloved, she does believe, returning to the disciples with the news that she has "seen the Lord" (20:18), just as he had promised.

Jorie Graham, "Noli Me Tangere"

Jorie Graham's "Noli Me Tangere"—the Latin translation of 20:17: "Don't touch me"—approaches these words of Jesus by way of a meditation on a scene in a fresco cycle by Giotto on the life of Christ, in the Scrovegni Chapel, Padua. Recognizing something of herself in Mary's attempt to hold onto her Lord, Graham works her way deeper and deeper into Christ's words by hearing for herself what it would mean to believe and not to cling:

1

You see the angels have come to sit on the delay
    for a while,
they have come to harrow the fixities, the sharp edges
    of this open
sepulcher,
    they have brought their swiftnesses like musics

down
    to fit them on the listening.
Their robes, their white openmindedness gliding into the corners,
    slipping this way then that
over the degrees, over the marble

flutings.
    The small angelic scripts pressing up through the veils.
The made shape pressing
    up through the windy cloth.
I've watched all afternoon how the large
    red birds here

cross and recross neither for play nor hunger
    the gaps that constitute our chainlink fence,
pressing themselves narrowly against the metal,
    feeding their bodies and wings
tightly in.
    Out of what ceases into what is ceasing.
Out of the light which holds steel and its alloys,

into the words for it like some robe or glory,
    and all of this rising up into the deep blue unbearable thinness,
the great babyblue exhalation of the one God
    as if in satisfaction at some right ending
come,

then down into the dustyness that still somehow holds
    its form as downslope and new green meadow

through which at any moment
    something swifter
might cut.
    It is about to be
Spring.
    The secret cannot be

kept.
    It wants to cross over, it wants
to be a lie.

2

Is that it then? Is that the law of freedom?
    That she must see him yet must not touch?
Below them the soldiers sleep their pure deep sleep.
    Is he light
who has turned forbidding and thrust his hand up
    in fury,

is he flesh
    so desperate to escape, to carry his purpose away?
She wants to put her hands in,
    she wants to touch him.
He wants her to believe,
    who has just trusted what her eyes have given her,

he wants her to look away.
    I have listened where the words and the minutes would touch,
I've tried to hear in that slippage what
    beauty is—
her soil, his sweet tune like footsteps
    over the path of

least resistance. I can see
    the body composed
of the distance between them
    I know it is ours: he must change, she must
remember.
    But you see it is not clear to me why she

must be driven back,
    why it is the whole darkness that belongs to her
and its days,
    why it is these hillsides she must become,
supporting even now the whole weight of the weightless,
    letting the plotlines wander all over her,

crumbling into every digressive beauty,
    her longings all stitchwork towards his immaculate rent,
all alphabet on the wind as she rises from prayer. . . .

3

It is the horror, Destination,
    pulling the whole long song
down, like a bad toss
    let go
in order to start again right,
    and it is wrong

to let its one inaudible note govern our going
    isn't it, siren over this open meadow
singing always your one song of shape of
    home. I have seen how the smoke here
inhabits a space
    in the body of air it must therefore displace,

and the tree-shaped gap the tree inhabits,
    and the tree-shaped gap the tree
invents. Siren,
    reader,
it is here, only here,
    in this gap

between us,
    that the body of who we are
to have been
    emerges: imagine:
she lets him go,
    she lets him through the day faster than the day,

among the brisk wings
    upsetting the flowerpots,
among the birds arranging and rearranging the shape of
    the delay,
she lets him
    slip free,

letting him posit the sweet appointment,
    letting out that gold thread that crazy melody
of stations,
    reds, birds, dayfall, screen-door,
desire,

until you have to go with him, don't you,

until you have to leave her be
    if all you have to touch her with
is form.[15]

The poem begins, in the first three stanzas of section 1, with the Giotto fresco, focusing not on Christ and Mary but on the two angels sitting on the "open sepulcher" on the painting's left. As Graham notes, the angels seem to break up the "fixities, the sharp edges" of the opened marble enclosure, "Their robes, their white openmindedness gliding into the corners, / slipping this way then that." Incongruously perched on the corners of the raised vault, they introduce a note of "delay" or what the poem later calls "slippage" to the lines and angles ("the degrees") that dominate this portion of the painting.[16]

The poet then turns to her own backyard and a parallel scene, continuing her investigation of the painting by examining and turning over a similar arrangement just outside her window. Something in the painting calls out to her, and she draws on the living scene before her to try to take it in. She has been watching "red birds" all afternoon "cross[ing] and recross[ing] . . . / the gaps that constitute our chainlink fence." The birds echo the winged angels, and the delay the angels inhabit becomes the gap in the fence the birds press themselves repeatedly through. Who knows why, she seems to say, taking note of the ease with which the birds, like the angels before them, move back and forth between realms: between "what ceases" and "what is ceasing"; "light" and "the words for it"; the high "unbearable thinness" of the sky and the dusty forms of "downslope and new green meadow." She is letting her language run here, allowing the scene before her to suggest multiple ways to enter the delay marked out by Giotto's windblown angels. Although Graham does not touch on this directly, Jesus' description of himself as Jacob's ladder in 1:51 comes to mind here. Some connection between the realms is about to be made, the birds suggest. "It is about to be / Spring," the poet guesses. "The secret cannot be // kept." And yet, what is to appear has not appeared yet—we see only the birds crossing and recrossing the open space where the two realms are poised to touch.

The second section of the poem turns to Christ and Mary, as if the poet has now been prepared to take in that scene. In the painting Mary is kneeling, hands outstretched. Christ is moving away from her, his head turned back as he speaks, an arm outraised as if to hold her off. "Is that it then?" the poet asks. She "must see him yet must not touch?" What could his words to her mean? the poet asks. Her interpretation is close to the one we have just sketched in our examination of the Gospel: "She wants to put her hands in, /

she wants to touch him. / He wants her to believe." Mary wants to hold Christ, to possess him physically, but he wants something more: he wants her to believe. Graham returns to the angels (and birds) marking or holding open the space between in order to picture what belief might look like if we thought of it as letting go rather than touching or clinging. Is that what he meant? she asks. I have tried to hold myself there, she writes—or at least in its secular equivalent: "I've listened where the words and the minutes would touch, / I've tried to hear in that slippage what / beauty is—." I have heard my words fumble before what they wanted to hold, felt the moment slide by unmarked, she writes, and yes—there was a kind of beauty in that openness, a kind of faith involved in not clamping my language down.

"I can see / the body composed / of the distance between them," she remarks, returning to the painting and the gap between Christ and Mary. That body is our body, she now sees—the human condition, the finite space we inhabit: "I know it is ours: he must change, she must / remember." He draws away and we remain—longing, remembering, believing. And yet, the poet persists, turning on the "openminded" angels, why does this have to be so? "But you see it is not clear to me why she // must be driven back, / why it is the whole darkness that belongs to her." The words of Jesus seem to ring in the poet's ears, seemingly thrusting her back to darkness and "wander[ing]" and the kind of "crumbling . . . digressive beauty" that can only taste and never have: "her longings all stitchwork towards his immaculate rent, / all alphabet on the wind as she rises from prayer." The tension is almost palpable here, the poet having fully found herself, down on her knees in her own struggle with words, in Mary's situation.

An interesting turn occurs in the third section of the poem. It is as if Graham returns to the bad taste in her mouth from the end of section 2— Why must she be driven back? Why?—and realizes that she had been in the grip of a dangerous longing to arrive, to have it all settled. Mary Magdalene must have been driven by this as well. Graham calls that longing "the horror." It is the desire to reach a "Destination" and rest. Desired deeply enough, it renders every action simply "a bad toss," a failure to reach the "one song of shape of / home" that you know you must somehow deserve. Faith does not work this way, the poet quietly admits. It lets go, waits, makes something out of the space of delay. Like "smoke . . . / inhabit[ing] a space / in the body of air," faith comes alive in the gap, the waiting, the not-yet.

What, then, would such faith look like? It would look very much like this poem, Graham suggests. In reaching out to Giotto's rendering of the scene, she has not been able to "put her hands in" or "touch him," the painter. She has had to guess, revise, always being willing to be turned away. But she

has made something out of the space between them, embodying the painting's (and the Gospel's) tensions in her own words and world.[17] So too her
readers. As with the poets we have turned to in this book, in entering her
words, in using our experiences to flesh out hers, we have not rendered her
fully or held her words stable. But we have trusted there was life in her words
and acted on that belief. Such an expectation is much like faith. It is Mary
letting go of his physical body while yet looking forward to another sort of
embrace—Mary discovering herself in the delay, coming alive in the distance
between them. "Siren, / reader, / it is here, only here, / in this gap // between
us, / that the body of who we are / to have been / emerges." This applies to
both reader and believer. In each case, as the ending of the poem suggests
with its rapid imagining of Mary letting him slip free, "letting him posit the
sweet appointment" and its "crazy melody / of stations" along the way, none
of which ever, in this life, quite signals arrival—in each case, the faith that
is willing to let go and embrace the tension inherent in waiting is the faith
through which new life emerges.

Thomas, 20:19-31

A third recognition scene occurs that evening. The disciples have gathered
together, talking about these things. The doors are shut because they are still
at risk and afraid. Jesus suddenly appears in their midst, not affected by the
doors, and speaks to their fears, as he had before his death: "Peace be with
you." He shows them his hands and side, the marks of death on his body,
and they "rejoice," understanding that their Lord has passed through death
and stands now in their presence. He died, but death is not the end of the
story—new life, standing before them, is. In their joy, they see and believe,
and as he had promised, he now sends them out to witness to this belief:
"Peace be with you; as the Father has sent Me, I also send you" (20:21;
see 17:18-20). One can sense how carefully John has thought about these
things. The Beloved saw a physical detail that did not fit and believed that
the old world had been set aside. Mary Magdalene heard her name and
knew that Jesus had been restored to her in a way never before possible.
The disciples see that he has not been bound by death and are sent into the
world as witnesses to this fact, proclaiming that death will bind no one who
believes. The moments of recognition are different and grow out of particular circumstances, and yet they make the same point: that with the death
and resurrection of Jesus the world has changed, a closeness with God which
is life itself has now been restored.

Before sending them out, Jesus, as he promised in 15:26-27, breathes on them the Holy Spirit who will testify in their hearts to that restored relationship, making real to them the living Messiah they are to offer to the world. "Receive the Holy Spirit," he says. "If you forgive the sins of any, their sins have been forgiven them; if you retain the sins of any, they have been retained" (20:23).[18] They will forgive sins by pointing to the crucified and resurrected Messiah, offering the world his death in its place. And they will retain sins through the same offer, for some hearts will clutch and turn away. They will not be the ones doing this; God will, or God will through them. However we phrase this, they will be out in the world, their locked doors a thing of the past.

These three recognition scenes are complicated and extended by a final scene involving Thomas who was not there when Jesus came to the others. His initial refusal to believe echoes the refusals of many in the central chapters of the Gospel, and the patient way Jesus draws him toward himself demonstrates his power to overcome such hesitation.

Thomas meets up with the other disciples, and they tell him they have "seen the Lord." His reply is of course quite famous: "Unless I shall see in His hands the imprint of the nails, and put my finger into the place of the nails, and put my hand into His side, I will not believe" (20:25). This is often taken as skeptical and pragmatic—I need to see for myself. But there is something else going on here as well. Thomas is visualizing Christ's dead body, returning in his imagination to the imprint of the nails, touching that place with his finger, and then thrusting his entire hand into the wound in his side. It is as if he were saying that he cannot get over the fact that the Messiah, the one he loved and had been willing to follow into death (11:16), had died—that his kingship had come undone in such a shocking and grotesque way. He was there. For him to believe, death itself—and those specific wounds—would have to be overcome. It would have to be transformed, all of it. Receiving Christ's spirit back or sensing his presence would not be enough. No, what Thomas cannot free himself from is what would have to be transformed—death itself. Think how different this is from the Beloved sensing his intellectual/spiritual underpinnings shift or forlorn Mary hearing her name spoken. Thomas would have to see the very thing that had crippled him and broken his spirit undone.

And that is what happens. Eight days later the disciples gather again, Thomas with them this time, and Jesus again appears in their midst, speaking "Peace" to their anxious hearts. He says to Thomas, "Reach here your finger, and see My hands; and reach here your hand, and put it into My side; and be not unbelieving but believing" (20:27). See and believe, Jesus says.

See that what you most fear has been turned into life, in me. And Thomas does, believing without ever touching the wounds, already knowing what he would find there. Thomas' next words are what the entire Gospel has been pointing toward, for what he sees is that only God himself could have over-turned death in this manner. Jesus is not only his Lord and Master, returned to him, he is God himself, in human form, overcoming our gravest enemy. "My Lord and my God" (20:28), he says, recognizing and worshipping. It should come as no surprise that it is the one most deeply weighed down by sin and death who sees most clearly the power that overcame them.

This suggests, then, that when Jesus responds to Thomas' act of adora-tion, "Because you have seen Me, have you believed? Blessed are they who did not see, and yet believed" (20:29), he is not criticizing Thomas but is, instead, looking forward to future believers who will hear his words and believe even though they are not in a position to see. Even without seeing, John suggests in the way he has structured these scenes, readers to come will, in their own ways, sense the ground shifting, hear their names called, rejoice at life restored, and marvel at their deepest wounds transformed. He has arranged this text, in fact, to make such recognitions possible:

> Many other signs therefore Jesus also performed in the presence of the disciples, which are not written in this book; but these have been written that you may believe that Jesus is the Christ, the Son of God; and that believing you may have life in His name. (20:30-31)

What John wants readers to see is that Jesus was in fact the Messiah, the long-expected king. Not only did his death not disprove this claim, it was the crucial work he performed in conquering Israel's enemies and inaugurat-ing God's new and final kingdom. Because he lives and overcame death, all of those who unite themselves with him will live as well—will drink living water, eat living bread, dwell with him forever. John has drawn these signs together to proclaim this. Belief is recognizing life and turning to it, finding life not in an idea but in a person—someone who can be known, approached, visualized, and loved. It is turning to a recognizable voice, to someone who knows you.

Thomas Gardner, from "Running Journal"

The final poem I want to turn to in bringing out the power of John's text is one of my own—the fourth poem in a sequence that grew out of a year my family and I spent in Finland, written in 1997. The poems in the sequence focus on daily runs I did on trails near our house and attempt to capture what

passed through my mind, first as I ran and then later as I reflected on the run
in my journal. This section is set in late September and slowly works its way
around to Thomas' encounter with his risen Lord:

> Coolish damp runs.
> Birch leaves down, H. D.'s *blackened stalks of mint.*
> Half awake across a creek today,
> I caught a thick smell off its surface,
> and looked back at the wheat field it skirted,
> newly plowed-down.
> Torn stalks showing, flecks of yellow.
> I hadn't seen a thing.
>
>   Thought of Turku
> and its wounded birch Christs,
> paint gone, dark as roots in time's steady soaking.
> Thought of forearms and hands,
> pieced-on once, now split off and missing.
>
>   Thinking now
> of palms all but visible, palms everywhere implied:
> flecks of red showing in the folds of a robe,
> spatters in a beard's tight rings.
> Open palms: earth's body lifted,
> Sacred head now wounded.[19]

The poem begins with the speaker looking back over the morning's "cool-
ish damp run," so typical of the Finnish fall. I say "speaker" here, as I have
throughout the book, to make the point that he is not me exactly—some version of me, of course, but heightened, focused, perhaps partly invented. He
thinks back on the run, recreating the landscape—"Birch leaves down"—
and remembering a fragment of the poet H. D. that passed through his
mind in response to the dying-back landscape. A story slowly begins to take
shape—the moment during the run when his almost automatic processing
of details was broken into by the "thick smell" of turned earth lifting off the
surface of a creek. That smell caught his attention and snapped him awake,
focusing him on the "newly plowed-down" field he had been running alongside without noticing. Looking back, he had noticed "torn stalks" and "flecks
of yellow" still showing against the thick, turned earth, the run having suddenly come alive, the unmarked fall morning having been torn open and
made fully present.

    In the second stanza, the speaker, still thinking back, attempts to recre-
ate the hold that the dark field and torn stalks had on him as he continued

running. Something in that field had spoken to him, but what? When he surfaced into awareness, he found himself thinking of the cathedral in the city of Turku and its carved birch Christs. The torn stalks and fallen leaves had reminded him of those worn-away figures, so darkened by time that they looked like "roots" turned under the soil or soaking in a bog. They were broken and battered—their "forearms and hands, / pieced-on once, now split off and missing." Running, thinking about the plowed-under field, his mind had jumped to those wounded Christs, finding in them an image for brokenness of things—a lament, perhaps, for the wounds of the season. When I gave this sequence to a friend to read, she described this as my "Thomas" poem. "Of course," I thought, "Thomas refusing to believe because he had not seen those wounds himself." When my mind leaped to those broken Christs, I had, like Thomas, visualized what was missing, what had gone wrong with the world. What's interesting, however, is that I have no memory of deliberately turning to this scene from John's Gospel, even though I know it quite well and have often thought about it. This suggests that when we write our words are often more alert than we are, for clearly, at some level, my poem had indeed worked its way back to the words of the Gospel, filling itself with that Finnish landscape in order to prepare itself to hear.

Be that as it may, Thomas clearly comes into the poem at this point. With the third stanza, however, something different occurs. After Jesus came to Thomas and called him to himself, showing, by his wounds, that all had been transformed, he looked forward, as we have noted, to those who "did not see, and yet believed" (20:29). That is the position my speaker finds himself in. He is not Thomas—he will never see those broken-off hands and forearms restored. And yet, his world has changed as well. This is signaled first of all by the change of tense: "now," as he writes and thinks, those missing hands and palms are "all but visible," broken off but somehow deeply present. He sees them in his imagination, having worked his way back to them through what he *had* seen—the posture of the body, the way the carved folds fell on the robe, the red in those folds echoing the same red, in spatters, in his beard. Something in all of that "implies" the missing palms and gives them back to the speaker, "open."

What had happened? It appears that, in visualizing the statue and thinking of those "flecks of red," the speaker had been reminded of the "spatters" of blood from the thorns pushed down on Christ's head. Thinking of that blood, he had suddenly understood the orientation of Christ's body—that, even with its arms missing, the figure was reaching out to him, having shed that blood in order to "lift" him up. He was the one in whom all had gone wrong. He was the broken one. And not only him; through the wounds of that "Sacred head," "earth's body" itself, the entire world, far beyond the Finnish countryside, was being lifted. Visualizing those flecks of red, the speaker understood the price that was paid when those hands were lost, and through that price, understood how much he, himself, was loved. Like Thomas, he can see the hands he loves—he sees them everywhere implied. Christ is present for him, recognized through what he has accepted and transformed. The speaker sees though he does not see. As do all of the poets we have examined. As do all believers.

8

Epilogue (John 21:1-25)

What's most striking about the Epilogue is how quiet and personal it is. Juxtaposed to the Prologue's inspired and impassioned theology about the light coming into the world and the Word becoming flesh is a quiet story about a group of disciples recognizing Jesus and being fed by him. It is intimate, as if to remind us that the Gospel's grand story works itself out on a human scale. What we see here is what being loved by God looks like—a picture of eating, one that looks forward to a grander, eternal feast.

Sent, 21:1-25

Seven of the disciples, after the resurrection, leave Jerusalem and return to the Sea of Galilee. Peter, restless perhaps, declares that he is going fishing, and the others decide to go with him. They spend the night fishing and catch nothing. As dawn breaks, they see a figure standing on the beach but do not recognize him. He calls out to them, "Children, you do not have any fish, do you?" and they answer "No" (21:5). The man directs them to cast their nets on the right side of the boat, and when they do, they make a remarkable catch, so large they are not able to haul it in.[1] This is enough to open the eyes of the Beloved Disciple, who, much as when he peered into the empty tomb and saw the linen wrappings and folded facecloth, senses a hand at work disrupting the expected and recognizes the hard-to-make-out figure. "It is the Lord," he says, and Peter, knowing by now to trust the Beloved's response, acts. He pulls on a garment, perhaps out of modesty or respect, and throws himself into the sea, anxious to see the one he loves. One recognizes first, one acts first; neither is praised or criticized. Both are responding, in their own ways, to life.

As he swims, Peter drops out of the narrator's sight. The rest of them struggle in with the great haul of fish trailing behind them in the net. They make it to shore, get out, and see a charcoal fire already going with fish placed on it, and bread. Jesus invites them to add some of the fish they have caught to the meal. Peter comes back into view, his initial embrace (we assume) of the one he loves having taken place outside of our line of sight; he hauls in the net and its one hundred and fifty-three fish. Jesus invites them all to eat, and gives them the bread and fish he has prepared in a way that clearly recalls the feeding of the 5,000. This, the narrator concludes, is how Jesus "manifested" himself to his disciples for a third time "after He was raised from the dead" (21:14). What's remarkable is how quiet it all is. Clearly this is a story with a point, rounding off the Gospel. But unlike the earlier scenes where Jesus fed or healed people or raised someone from the dead, there seems no need now to interpret or look beyond the story. The disciples already believe. They have been made alive in their connection with Jesus. We might say this is a picture of an ordinary but completely new life: abiding in Jesus, being fed by him, recognizing his presence in normal activities, trusting what he says, going to him out of love. It is only the rest of the Gospel that lets us see what has made this possible—his death, God coming to earth in human form. If, in believing and turning to him, they have eaten his flesh, then any meal echoes that act and offer and communion. This intimate little scene, then, holds its own with all of the theology. It does not replace it, but it enacts it, on the scale of individual lives. "Heaven in ordinarie," as George Herbert puts it about communing with God in prayer.[2]

So then we turn to two such lives—Peter and the Beloved—both of them central figures and both crucial for the church that will grow from their witness. In a way, this is how they abide in the life of Jesus. After the meal is finished, Jesus speaks to Peter. Three times, he asks him "Do you love Me?" As many commentators note, the setting, with the charcoal fire recalling a similar fire outside the high priest's palace, and the three questions echoing Peter's three denials, returns Peter to his earlier failure. This seems quite deliberate on the part of Jesus. Earlier, acting on his own inadequate strength, Peter had quickly bent to the world's pressure and denied knowing, much less loving, Jesus. Now, having recognized in Jesus his only source of life, he quietly responds "Yes, Lord; You know that I love you" (21:15, 16), expanding that the third time to "Lord, You know all things; You know that I love you" (21:17). One has to listen carefully to the tone of voice here. It is not frustration: "Of course! You know I do." Rather, it is quietly matter-of-fact: "You know everything about me, my failures, my return, my continuing need for you. And you recognize that as love." He is mourning and drinking, as we saw in Herbert's "Holy Baptisme." Even when Jesus offers him the chance to compare himself to others and lift himself up just a bit, asking "Do you love Me more than these?" (21:15), Peter refuses to follow that lead. Even when the third question throws him into grief at the memory of his denial (21:17), he still understands that the new life he has been offered is able to stand up to such an assault: "Lord, You know all things" (21:17).

Jesus responds by commissioning Peter: feed my lambs, shepherd my sheep, giving him the job of speaking the good news of a restored relationship with God into the broken lives of others, just as it had been spoken into his own. And further, Jesus tells Peter about the "kind of death" he would undergo, a death "glorify[ing] God" (21:19). That death, in which he would be brought low and made dependant, would glorify God because these were precisely the things Peter had tried so hard to avoid, before the crucifixion. Now, Jesus says, God will receive great glory in Peter's testimony that his true standing and exaltation lie outside of this world, in his relationship with God. At this, Jesus quietly says "Follow Me," repeating the invitation to come with him into his Father's presence that he has issued throughout the Gospel, and Peter does.

The invitation was probably both a literal and a spiritual one, for, as they start to walk, Peter turns and notices the Beloved, also following behind. Peter is curious about him, and his curiosity allows John to quickly sketch a second response, his own, to the life they had been given. Peter says, "Lord, and what about this man? (21:21), and Jesus responds, "If I want him to remain until I come, what is that to you? You follow Me!" (21:22). We notice, of course, that Peter's tendency to notice and compare himself to others has not vanished. Surely he will be dealing with this his entire life. But also important is what John has been called to do—to remain, or "abide," as the word could also be translated (15:4). Peter is to shepherd and die, John is to remain or abide—not "not die" as John quickly explains (21:23), but to testify or witness to others as to what he has seen and where he has turned for life.[3]

This, of course, is what he has been doing throughout the Gospel. He has been abiding and testifying. The last verses in the text seem to confirm this line of thought. Echoing John's words at the crucifixion—"And he who has seen has borne witness, and his witness is true" (19:35)—the Gospel closes with these words: "This is the disciple who bears witness of these things, and wrote these things; and we know that his witness is true" (21:24). This has been taken a number of ways, but it suggests that the Beloved, who has been called to remain, has borne witness to the events narrated in the Gospel and has, in fact, written them.[4] We might say that he remains and abides in the words he has written—that they have a life beyond him. It is hard to know for sure who the "we" is that certifies that the Beloved's witness is true. It may be a group of elders, writing after the fact. It may be the narrator himself, using "we" much as he had in 1:14: "we beheld his glory." In any case, his witness is living and true. Interestingly, whoever the "we" is, in the very last verse in the Gospel, as his words fall away into charged silence, the narrator uses "I" for the first time: "And there are also many other things which Jesus did, which if they were written in detail, I suppose that even the world itself would not contain the books which were written" (21:25). How odd and moving. The I, effaced throughout the Gospel, quietly shows itself, though only as a pointer or witness or reflection, and then winks out, only the portrait of Jesus remaining behind.

NOTES

Introduction

1   I will be using the New American Standard translation throughout, copyright 1960. References to the Gospel of John will be cited by chapter and verse. Other biblical references will be by book title, chapter, and verse.

2   Marilynne Robinson, *The Death of Adam: Essays on Modern Thought* (New York: Houghton Mifflin, 1998), 228.

3   Wallace Stevens, "Of Modern Poetry," in *Wallace Stevens: Collected Poetry and Prose*, ed. Frank Kermode and Joan Richardson (New York: Library of America, 1997), 218.

4   There are a number of texts to consult for suggestions concerning other poems one might examine. Mark Edwards' *John Through the Centuries*, Blackwell Bible Commentaries (Oxford: Blackwell, 2004), a reception history of the Gospel, includes poets, novelists, and playwrights in his verse-by-verse examination of responses to John. Anthologies, many linking poems and specific biblical texts, include Robert Atwan and Laurance Wieder, eds., *Chapters into Verse: Poetry in English Inspired by the Bible*, vol. 2, *Gospels to Revelation* (Oxford: Oxford University Press, 1993); David Curzon, ed., *The Gospels in Our Image: An Anthology of Twentieth-Century Poetry Based on Biblical Texts* (New York: Harcourt Brace, 1995); David Impastato, ed., *Upholding Mystery: An Anthology of Contemporary Christian Poetry* (Oxford: Oxford University Press, 1997); David Craig and Janet McCann, eds., *Contemporary Poetry by People of Faith* (Wheaton, Ill.: Harold Shaw, 1994); Diana Culbertson, ed., *Invisible Light: Poems about God* (New York: Columbia University Press, 2000); James H. Trott, ed., *A Sacrifice of Praise: An Anthology of Christian Poetry in English from Caedmon to the Mid-Twentieth Century*, 2nd ed. (Nashville: Cumberland House, 2006); Kevin Hart, ed., *The Oxford Book of Australian Religious Verse* (Melbourne: Oxford University Press, 1994); Donald Davie, ed., *The New Oxford Book of Christian Verse* (Oxford:

Oxford University Press, 1981). See also David Jasper and Stephen Prickett, eds., *The Bible and Literature: A Reader* (Oxford: Blackwell, 1999).

5   Robinson, *The Death of Adam*, 231.

6   Robinson, *The Death of Adam*, 234.

7   Robinson, *The Death of Adam*, 236, 234.

8   Robinson, *The Death of Adam*, 235–36.

9   Robinson, *The Death of Adam*, 243.

10   Robinson, *The Death of Adam*, 240.

11   Robinson, *The Death of Adam*, 240.

12   I am drawing here on Kenneth Burke's 1943 essay "Symbolic Action in a Poem by Keats," in *A Grammar of Motives* (Berkeley: University of California Press, 1969), in which he argues that a poem is a "mode of action," "the symbolic act of the poet who made it," recording the series of steps a poet takes in moving from one set of images to another. Close reading, for Burke, becomes an attempt to re-enact the dramatic arc of those steps. I am not arguing that the Gospel of John is a poem, but I am employing the way I read poems in reading the Gospel. For more on Burke and reading poetry see my entry "Close Reading," in *The Princeton Encyclopedia of Poetry and Poetics* (Princeton, N.J.: Princeton University Press, forthcoming).

13   Richard Bauckham, *The Testimony of the Beloved Disciple: Narrative, History, and Theology in the Gospel of John* (Grand Rapids: Baker Academic, 2007), 121, 123.

14   Bauckham, *The Testimony of the Beloved Disciple*, 118.

15   Bauckham, *The Testimony of the Beloved Disciple*, 120.

16   Bauckham, *The Testimony of the Beloved Disciple*, 120.

17   Bauckham, *The Testimony of the Beloved Disciple*, 120, 121.

18   Alan Culpepper, *The Gospel and Letters of John* (Nashville: Abingdon, 1998), 71. See his entire chapter, "The Gospel as Literature" for a quick survey of the different questions on which literary-oriented biblical scholars have focused. His *Anatomy of the Fourth Gospel: A Study in Literary Design* (Philadelphia: Fortress, 1983) is generally regarded as the major early introduction of these matters into critical discussions.

19   Culpepper, *The Gospel and Letters of John*, 70.

20   Culpepper, *The Gospel and Letters of John*, 15. For an example of how Culpepper's work has been built upon, see Mark W. G. Stibbe, *John* (Sheffield, UK: Sheffield Academic, 1993). Stibbe's "narrative-critical" commentary stresses the elusiveness of Christ in John's presentation, a variation on Culpepper's focus on recognition/nonrecognition scenes. Craig R. Koester's *Symbolism in the Fourth Gospel: Meaning, Mystery, Community*, 2nd. ed. (Minneapolis: Fortress, 2003) is a thorough treatment of the symbolic language and action through which Jesus makes his Father known, valuably unfolding connections between scenes employing similar language or situations. Adele Reinhartz's "The Gospel of John," in *The Oxford Handbook of English Literature and Theology*, ed. Andrew Hass, David Jasper, and Elisabeth Jay (Oxford: Oxford University Press, 2007), 323–41 offers a useful account of "literary-critical" approaches to John, "some

twenty or more years" after the publication of Culpepper's book. D. A. Carson in *The Gospel According to John*, 63–68, discusses a number of problems that he sees in Culpepper's transferral of methods of reading developed in examining the novel to the reading of the Gospel.

21 Robert Alter, *The Art of Biblical Narrative* (New York: Basic Books, 1981). David Jasper's introductory chapter "The Study of Literature and Theology," in *The Oxford Handbook of English Literature and Theology*, ed. Andrew Hass, David Jasper, and Elisabeth Jay (Oxford: Oxford University Press, 2007), 15–32 offers a fine survey of work in this field.

22 Frank Kermode, "John," in *The Literary Guide to the Bible*, ed. Robert Alter and Frank Kermode (Cambridge, Mass.: Harvard University Press, 1987), 443, 441.

23 Kermode, "John," 444.

24 Kermode, "John," 464.

25 Kermode, "John," 445.

26 Kermode, "John," 445.

27 Kermode, "John," 447.

28 Kermode, "John," 452, 453.

29 Kermode, "John," 453.

30 D. A. Carson, *The Gospel According to John* (Grand Rapids: Eerdmans, 1991). I have also regularly consulted George R. Beasley-Murray's *John*, 2nd ed., Word Biblical Commentary 36 (Nashville: Nelson, 1999); Craig S. Keener's *The Gospel of John: A Commentary*, 2 vols. (Peabody, Mass.: Hendrickson, 2003); and Tom Wright's *John for Everyone*, 2 vols. (Louisville: Westminster John Knox, 2004). This last volume, in which N. T. Wright is writing for a popular audience, has helped me see the usefulness of a scene-by-scene account of the Gospel. A series of sermons on John, taped in 1980–81, by Max Harris at Grace Covenant Presbyterian Church in Blacksburg, Virginia, helped me hear more clearly the resonances of words such as "life," "light," and "sight" in John. His *Theatre and Incarnation* (London: Macmillan, 1990) contains a number of important readings of the theatrical manner in which God reveals himself in his "Word made flesh."

31 Alfred Corn's *Incarnation: Contemporary Writers on the New Testament* (New York: Viking, 1990) is a striking collection of essays by contemporary writers about individual books of the Bible. Years ago, its demonstrations of the way poets and novelists think about the Bible started me on the path that led to this book. *Acts* by Larry Woiwode (San Francisco: HarperSanFrancisco, 1993) and *Three Gospels* by Reynolds Price (New York: Scribner, 1996) are book-length expansions of essays in the Corn book. See also David Rosenberg, ed., *Congregation: Contemporary Writers Read the Jewish Bible* (New York: Harcourt Brace, 1987) and *Communion: Contemporary Writers Reveal the Bible in Their Lives* (New York: Anchor, 1996). Peggy Rosenthal's *The Poet's Jesus: Representations at the End of a Millennium* (Oxford: Oxford University Press, 2002) and *Praying the Gospels through Poetry* (Cincinnati, Ohio: St. Anthony Messenger Press, 2002), using two different approaches, offer useful models for linking poems and biblical texts.

32 I draw this notion of "re-enacting" from Kenneth Burke's "Symbolic Action in a Poem by Keats."

33 Emily Dickinson, Poem 1715, in *The Poems of Emily Dickinson: Reading Edition*, ed. R. W. Franklin (Cambridge, Mass.: Harvard University Press, 1999), 616.

34 For a thorough defense of the traditional position, see Carson, *The Gospel According to John*, 68–81. For a general survey of positions taken by a number of modern scholars, see Culpepper, *The Gospel and Letters of John*, 29–41. For important arguments about the author's anonymity, see Richard Bauckham, "The Beloved Disciple as Ideal Author," in *The Testimony of the Beloved Disciple*, 73–91. See also Bauckham's discussion of the author's portrayal of himself as an eyewitness, in *Jesus and the Eyewitnesses: The Gospels as Eyewitness Testimony* (Grand Rapids: Eerdmans, 2006), 358–411.

Chapter 1

1 See Richard Bauckham's chapter "The Audience of the Gospel of John," in *The Testimony of the Beloved Disciple*, 113–23, for a survey of various approaches to John's audience. In particular, see his remark about the way the narrator, on occasion, puts "his readers in a better position than any of the characters in the story for understanding a major theme in the words of Jesus" while also not "giving too much help too soon" (121).

2 See Bauckham's discussion in *The Testimony of the Beloved Disciple*, 240–42, of the ties between Genesis 1:1-4 and John 1:1, in particular his claim that the opening verses of the Prologue "include Jesus in the unique divine identity by identifying him with the Word that was God in the beginning and that as God's agent created all things" (242).

3 I've drawn this phrasing from Craig R. Koester's *The Word of Life: A Theology of John's Gospel* (Grand Rapids: Eerdmans, 2008), 48. His discussion of the difference between physical and spiritual birth is quite valuable.

4 Robert Hass, "The First, Second, and Third Epistles General of John," in *Incarnation: Contemporary Writers on the New Testament*, ed. Alfred Corn (New York: Viking), 326–27. Hass points out here that W. B. Yeats, in "Crazy Jane Talks with the Bishop," echoes this sense of tenting among us in the lines "A woman can be proud and stiff / When on love intent; / But Love has pitched his mansion in / The place of excrement."

5 T. S. Eliot, *Collected Poems 1909–1962* (New York: Harcourt Brace, 1970), 29–31.

6 Lancelot Andrewes, *Sermons of the Nativity and of Repentance and Fasting. Works of Lancelot Andrewes*, vol. 1, ed. John Henry Parker (Oxford: Oxford University Press, 1841), 204.

7 This is what *The Waste Land*, the poem for which Eliot considered using "Gerontion" as an introduction, is all about. The image of the violated, tongueless Philomel, turned into a nightingale, is the poem's clearest expression of what seemed for Eliot an impossible yearning not to be bound and silenced by the body and language.

8   See, e.g., "A Song for Simeon" (1928) in Eliot, *Collected Poems 1909–1962*, 101: "Now at this birth season of decease, / Let the Infant, the still unspeaking and unspoken Word, / Grant Israel's consolation / To one who has eighty years and no to-morrow."

9   Eliot, *Collected Poems 1909–1962*, 92.

10 I am picking up both senses of 1:5 here: "the darkness did not comprehend [or overcome] it." See Carson's discussion in *The Gospel According to John*, 119–20 for the way the Gospel deliberately keeps in play both senses of the verb *katalaben*.

Chapter 2

1   See "Baptism," in *Dictionary of Biblical Imagery*, ed. Leland Ryken, James C. Wilhoit, and Tremper Longman III (Downers Grove, Ill.: InterVarsity, 1998).

2   See Koester, *The Word of Life*, 91–107, for a survey of the various uses (and implications behind) the term *Son of God*. Carson, *The Gospel According to John*, 151, discusses support for translating the title in 1:34 as "the Chosen One of God," which would make a direct link to Isaiah 42:1, declaring Jesus to be "chosen as the suffering servant, the Lamb of God who takes away the sin of the world."

3   Denise Levertov, "Work that Enfaiths," in *New and Selected Essays* (New York: New Directions, 1992), 250.

4   Levertov, "Credo," in "Mass for the Day of St. Thomas Didymus," in *Candles in Babylon* (New York: New Directions, 1982), 110.

5   Levertov, "Work that Enfaiths," 250.

6   Denise Levertov, "A Poet's View," in *New and Selected Essays*, 241.

7   Levertov, "Work that Enfaiths," 250.

8   Denise Levertov, from "Mass for the Day of St. Thomas Didymus," 113–15.

9   Denise Levertov, "St. Thomas Didymus," in *A Door in the Hive* (New York: New Directions, 1989), 101–3.

10 See Koester's discussion in *The Word of Life*, 187–91, of the connection between the call to "come and see" and "walking in the light."

11 Both phrases are variations on the term *Messiah*. See Koester, *The Word of Life*, 91–92, and Bauckham, *The Testimony of the Beloved Disciple*, 228–31.

12 N. T. Wright, *Jesus and the Victory of God* (Minneapolis: Fortress, 1996), 513–19. See also Carson, *The Gospel According to John*, 162–65.

Chapter 3

1   A number of commentators have taken note of this shape. See, e.g., Francis J. Moloney, *The Gospel of John: Text and Context* (Boston: Brill, 2005), 9–10, and Culpepper, *The Gospel and Letters of John*, 128–29.

2   On the term *Woman*, see Keener, *The Gospel of John*, vol. 1, 504–9.

3   Carson, *The Gospel According to John*, 170–71.

4   See, e.g., Koester, *The Word of Life*, 197–98.

5   Richard Wilbur, *The Mind-Reader* (New York: Harcourt Brace, 1976), 12.

6   Richard Bauckham, *The Testimony of the Beloved Disciple*, 120, remarks that "As in many later instances, what Jesus says has an obvious, literal meaning, referring to a physical reality, and a metaphorical meaning that turns the physical image into a symbol of Jesus' salvific activity or the salvation he brings." He goes on and notes that John explains the meaning this time to the reader, as an "illustrative example," showing them how to do it.

7   Bauckham, *The Testimony of the Beloved Disciple*, 121.

8   Dickinson, *The Poems of Emily Dickinson*, 166.

9   Dickinson, *The Poems of Emily Dickinson*, 406. "Opon" is Dickinson's variant.

10   See Carson's discussion of the doubleness of this phrase in *The Gospel According to John*, 189.

11   Carson usefully surveys various views on "water and the Spirit," in *The Gospel According to John*, 191–96.

12   Ray Monk, *Ludwig Wittgenstein: The Duty of Genius* (New York: The Free Press, 1990), 170.

13   Charles Wright, "Indian Summer II," in *Negative Blue: Selected Later Poems* (New York: Farrar, Straus & Giroux, 2000), 163.

14   Charles Wright, "A Journal of the Year of the Ox," in *The World of the Ten Thousand Things: Poems 1980–1990* (New York: Farrar, Straus & Giroux, 1990), 164–65.

15   Dickinson, *The Poems of Emily Dickinson*, 171. I discuss Wright's use of Dickinson, and this image in particular, in *A Door Ajar: Contemporary Writers and Emily Dickinson* (New York: Oxford University Press, 2006), 84–93.

16   Carson, *The Gospel According to John*, 198.

17   Bauckham, *The Testimony of the Beloved Disciple*, 121.

18   See, e.g., Carson, *The Gospel According to John*, 203–4.

19   Henry Vaughan, *The Complete Poetry of Henry Vaughan*, ed. French Fogle (New York: New York University Press, 1965), 323–25.

20   In a remarkable essay on this poem, "A Pharisee to Pharisees" in *Style and Faith* (New York: Counterpoint, 2003), 71–87, the poet Geoffrey Hill remarks that Vaughan brings together in "The Night" "that which is above understanding-by-reason (theology) and that which dips below the process of understanding-by-reason (the contingent nature of sensory material)" (87).

21   John uses the expression "the Jews" about seventy times in the Gospel, often when dealing with opponents of Jesus, which has led to a good bit of discussion about anti-Semitism in the Gospel. Quite often, the term refers to the Jewish leaders based in Jerusalem. At other times, it refers to people from Jerusalem or Judea. Sometimes, it refers to the Jewish nation as a whole. Not all of the references are negative, though certainly a majority are. Carson, *The Gospel According to John*, 142, surveys these uses and concludes that anti-Semitism or even anti-Judaism seem to miss the mark, "for the Evangelist is not motivated by a desire to destroy what he understands to be right and good in Judaism, but to convert those who have so failed to appreciate their own heritage that they have failed to

see its fulfillment in Jesus Christ." For an important account by a Jewish scholar working from a reader-response perspective of the issues raised for her when responding to the Beloved Disciple's friendship and offer of a gift, see Adele Reinhartz, *Befriending the Beloved Disciple: A Jewish Reading of the Gospel of John* (New York: Continuum, 2001), 17–80.

22   It is also possible to read this as the Father giving the Spirit to his Son, without measure. See Carson, *The Gospel According to John*, 213–14.

23   As we will see, Jesus uses the formulation "I am [something]" seven times in the Gospel. He also uses the formulation "I am" [in Greek, *egō eimi*] seven times in what is called the absolute sense. The most striking of these is in 8:58 when Jesus uses the term to claim divine identity: "Before Abraham was, I am." This statement in 4:26 is the first of the absolute formulations. The others are: 6:20, 8:24, 8:28, 8:58, 13:19, 18:5, 6, 8. Richard Bauckham has a thorough discussion of both sets of sayings and their links to God's self-identification in Exodus 3:14 and Isaiah 43:9-10. See *The Testimony of the Beloved Disciple*, 243–50. Bauckham concludes that the seven "signs" and these two sets of seven "I ams" are all related, with the statements making explicit what the signs signify—that "To reveal the glory of God's unique identity, to give the eternal life that God alone has in himself, Jesus must himself belong to God's own unique identity" (250).

24   Robert Frost, "Directive," in *Robert Frost: Collected Poems, Prose, & Plays*, ed. Richard Poirier and Mark Richardson (New York: Library of America, 1995), 341–42.

25   Robert Frost, "The Figure a Poem Makes," in *Collected Poems, Prose, & Plays*, 777.

26   Robert Frost, "Letter to 'The Amherst Student,'" in *Collected Poems, Prose, & Plays*, 740.

27   Robert Frost, "Education by Poetry," in *Collected Poems, Prose, & Plays*, 721–22.

Chapter 4

1   See, e.g., James F. McGrath, *John's Apologetic Christology* (Cambridge: Cambridge University Press, 2001), 89.

2   Wendell Berry, "Preface" to *A Timbered Choir: The Sabbath Poems 1979–1997* (Washington: Counterpoint, 1998), xvii, xviii.

3   Wendell Berry, "The Sabbath Poems 1979, II," in *A Timbered Choir*, 6–7.

4   Behind this, we can hear Frost's "Spring Pools": "The trees that have it in their pent-up buds / To darken nature and be summer woods— / Let them think twice before they use their powers / To blot out and drink up and sweep away / These flowery waters and these watery flowers," *Collected Poems, Prose, & Plays*, 224.

5   Wendell Barry, "The Sabbath Poems 1983, IV," in *A Timbered Choir*, 59.

6   See note 23 chapter 3.

7   Brett Millier, *Elizabeth Bishop: Life and the Memory of It* (Berkeley: University of California Press, 1993), 79–80.

8   Elizabeth Bishop, "A Miracle for Breakfast," in *The Complete Poems 1927–1979* (New York: Farrar, Straus and Giroux, 1983), 18–19.

9   Bonnie Costello, *Elizabeth Bishop: Questions of Mastery* (Cambridge, Mass.: Harvard University Press, 1991), 98–100. Two recent books on Bishop discuss the way her poems approach and swerve away from belief, although the authors come to different conclusions. See Cheryl Walker, *God and Elizabeth Bishop: Meditations on Religion and Poetry* (New York: Palgrave Macmillan, 2005), and Laurel Snow Corelle, *A Poet's High Argument: Elizabeth Bishop and Christianity* (Columbia: University of South Carolina Press, 2008). Corelle's discussion of "A Miracle for Breakfast" (41–45) focuses on the power of religious tradition even after "energizing faith departs."

10   Dickinson, *The Poems of Emily Dickinson*, 616.

11   See Carson, *The Gospel According to John*, 297, where he notes: "Verses 54 and 40 are closely parallel: 'Whoever eats my flesh and drinks my blood has eternal life, and I will raise him up on the last day' (v.54); '. . . everyone who looks to the Son and believes in him shall have eternal life, and I will raise him up on the last day' (v.40). The only substantial difference is that one speaks of eating Jesus' flesh and drinking Jesus' blood, while, the other, in precisely the same conceptual location, speaks of looking to the Son and believing in him. The conclusion is obvious: the former is the metaphorical way of referring to the latter."

12   See the thorough account of the connection between the elements of the Feast of Booths and Jesus' description of himself as the light of the world and the source of living water in Koester, *Symbolism in the Fourth Gospel*, 152–60, 192–200.

13   Koester, *Symbolism in the Fourth Gospel*, 192–200.

14   Price, *Three Gospels*, 144–49. The entire essay "The Strangest Story: A Preface to the Good News According to John," in which Price describes Jesus as a "lyric visionary poet" is quite valuable.

15   John Donne, *The Complete Poetry of John Donne*, ed. John T. Shawcross (New York: New York University Press, 1968), 344.

16   Dickinson, *The Poems of Emily Dickinson*, 150.

17   George Herbert, "The Collar," in *The Works of George Herbert* (London: Oxford University Press, 1941), 153.

Chapter 5

1   Carson, *The Gospel According to John*, 415–16.

2   Paul Mariani, "Pietà," in *Deaths and Transfigurations: Poems* (Brewster, Mass.: Paraclete Press, 2005), 51–52.

3   See Carson, *The Gospel According to John*, 429–30, for a survey of various ways this verse has been taken.

4   Richard Bauckham, *Jesus and the God of Israel: God Crucified and Other Studies on the New Testament's Christology of Divine Identity* (Grand Rapids: Eerdmans, 2008), 49–51.

5   Gerard Manley Hopkins, "The Windhover," in *Gerard Manley Hopkins: Poems and Prose*, ed. W. H. Gardner (Middlesex, UK: Penguin, 1953), 30.

6   Bauckham, *Jesus and the God of Israel*, 46–50.

Chapter 6

1   We will see a version of this in the cry "It is finished" on the cross (19:30).

2   Herbert, "Love (III)," in *The Works of George Herbert*, 188–89.

3   Vassar Miller, "Judas," in *If I Had Wheels or Love: Collected Poems of Vassar Miller* (Dallas: Southern Methodist Press, 1991), 110.

4   Carson, *The Gospel According to John*, 484–85.

5   I take Jesus to be referring to the resurrection here, when they will "behold" him, but there has been debate about this. See Carson, *The Gospel According to John*, 501–2.

6   Bishop, "Squatter's Children," in *The Complete Poems 1927–1979*, 95.

7   Bishop, "Manuelzinho," in *The Complete Poems 1927–1979*, 96–99.

8   "Prune" and "clean" are versions of each other in Greek. See Carson, *The Gospel According to John*, 515.

9   Carson, *The Gospel According to John*, 520.

10   Elizabeth Bishop, "Poem," in *The Complete Poems 1927–1979*, 176–77.

11   I am expanding a reading of this poem that I first presented in *Regions of Unlikeness: Explaining Contemporary Poetry* (Lincoln: University of Nebraska Press, 1999), 69–72.

12   These verses have been read in many different ways. See Carson's summary of various views in *The Gospel According to John*, 534–39. Koester, in *The Word of Life*, 153–55 offers a fuller version of what I have just summarized here.

13   Carson, *The Gospel According to John*, 545.

14   Eliot, "Burnt Norton," in *Collected Poems*, 176.

15   In *The Waste Land*, a similar experience of staring into "the heart of light, the silence," leads to desolation when nothing can be made of the experience— "*Oed' und leer das Meer.*" See "The Burial of the Dead," section I of the poem, in Eliot, *Collected Poems*, 54.

16   Eliot, "Burnt Norton," in *Collected Poems*, 177.

17   Eliot, "Burnt Norton," in *Collected Poems*, 178.

18   Bauckham, *Jesus and the God of Israel*, 50.

19   Herbert, "Clasping of Hands," in *The Works of George Herbert*, 157.

20   See an article by Esther Gilman Richey that quite powerfully unfolds the notion of mirroring in this poem: "The Intimate Other: Lutheran Subjectivity in Spenser, Donne, and Herbert." *Modern Philology*, 108.3 (2011): 1–32.

Chapter 7

1   Bishop, "Roosters," in *The Complete Poems 1927–1979*, 35–39.

2   I am reworking a reading of this poem first presented in *Regions of Unlikeness*, 44–46.

3   Carson, *The Gospel According to John*, 590.

4   Stevens, "The Emperor of Ice-Cream," in *Wallace Stevens*, 50.

5   John Berryman, *Collected Poems 1937–1971*, ed. Charles Thornbury (New York: Farrar, Straus and Giroux, 1989), 251–52.

6   "My strength is dried up like a potsherd, / And my tongue cleaves to my jaws; / And Thou dost lay me in the dust of death" (Psalm 22:15).

7   On the debate over "hyssop," see Carson, *The Gospel According to John*, 620–21.

8   Kathleen Norris, "La Vierge Romane," in *Journey: New and Selected Poems 1969–1999*, 121–22.

9   It is also possible to read this as distinguishing between the narrator and the eyewitness on which his account is based. See Keener, *The Gospel of John*, vol. 2, 1154–55 for this debate. Bauckham's chapter "The Beloved Disciple as Ideal Author," in *The Testimony of the Beloved Disciple*, 73–91, offers a thorough analysis of the importance of eyewitness testimony here.

10 Herbert, "Holy Baptisme I," in *The Works of George Herbert*, 43–44.

11 R. S. Thomas, "Via Negativa" in *Collected Poems 1945–1990* (London: Phoenix, 2000), 220.

12 Thomas, "Shadows," in *Collected Poems 1945–1990*, 343.

13 Thomas, "The Answer," in *Collected Poems 1945–1990*, 359.

14 I would cite again the Marilynne Robinson essay "Psalm Eight," which I discussed in the "Introduction" for its subtle work with this series of exchanges between Jesus and Mary Magdalene. See *The Death of Adam*, 227–44.

15 Jorie Graham, "Noli Me Tangere," in *The End of Beauty* (New York: Ecco, 1987), 40–44.

16 The fact that she is responding to a painting is actually never directly addressed in the poem, but when one examines the details of Giotto's fresco, the focus of her meditation becomes obvious.

17 I have addressed Graham's manner of finding the tensions embodied in paintings or memories or myth alive within herself in "Jorie Graham's Incandescence," in *Regions of Unlikeness*, 168–213.

18 The "breathing" of the Spirit in 20:22 has been read many different ways. Carson in *The Gospel According to John*, 649–55, offers a summary. I disagree with his view that this is a "symbolic" act.

19 Thomas Gardner, "Running Journal (Finland)," in *Roots and Renewal: Writings by Bicentennial Professors,* ed. Mark Shackelton and Maarika Toivonen (Helsinki: Renvall Institute, 2001), 182–88.

Chapter 8

1   Reynolds Price, in "The Strangest Story: A Preface to the Good News According to John," writes movingly about the "intense air of personal recall" (163) he notes here. See his reading of the final scene, 171–77.

2   Herbert, "Prayer I," in *The English Poems of George Herbert*, 71.

3   See Bauckham's account of the Beloved as "ideal witness" in *The Testimony of the Beloved Disciple*, 82–91.

4   See Bauckham, *The Testimony of the Beloved Disciple*, 78–82.

BIBLIOGRAPHY

Alter, Robert. *The Art of Biblical Narrative*. New York: Basic Books, 1981.

Alter, Robert, and Frank Kermode. *The Literary Guide to the Bible*. Cambridge, Mass.: Harvard University Press, 1987.

Andrewes, Lancelot. *Sermons of the Nativity and of Repentance and Fasting. Works of Lancelot Andrewes*, vol. 1. Edited by John Henry Parker. Oxford: Oxford University Press, 1841.

Atwan, Robert, and Laurance Weider, eds. *Chapters into Verse: Poetry in English Inspired by the Bible*, vol. 2, *Gospels to Revelation*. Oxford: Oxford University Press, 1993.

Bauckham, Richard. *Jesus and the Eyewitnesses: The Gospels as Eyewitness Testimony*. Grand Rapids: Eerdmans, 2006.

———. *Jesus and the God of Israel: God Crucified and Other Studies on the New Testament's Christology of Divine Identity*. Grand Rapids: Eerdmans, 2008.

———. *The Testimony of the Beloved Disciple: Narrative, History, and Theology in the Gospel of John*. Grand Rapids: Baker Academic, 2007.

Beasley-Murray, George R. *John*. 2nd ed. Nashville: Nelson, 1999.

Berry, Wendell. *A Timbered Choir: The Sabbath Poems 1979–1997*. Washington: Counterpoint, 1998.

Berryman, John. *Collected Poems 1937–1971*. Edited by Charles Thornbury. New York: Farrar, Straus & Giroux, 1989.

Bishop, Elizabeth. *The Complete Poems 1927–1979*. New York: Farrar, Straus & Giroux, 1983.

Bloom, Harold, and Jesse Zuba, eds. *American Religious Poems*. New York: Library of America, 2006.

Burke, Kenneth. "Symbolic Action in a Poem by Keats." In *A Grammar of Motives*. Berkeley: University of California Press, 1969.

Carson, D. A. *The Gospel According to John*. Grand Rapids: Eerdmans, 1991.

Corelle, Laurel Snow. *A Poet's High Argument: Elizabeth Bishop and Christianity*. Columbia: University of South Carolina Press, 2008.

Corn, Alfred. *Incarnation: Contemporary Writers on the New Testament*. New York: Viking, 1990.

Costello, Bonnie. *Elizabeth Bishop: Questions of Mastery*. Cambridge, Mass.: Harvard University Press, 1991.

Craig, David, and Janet McCann, eds. *Contemporary Poetry by People of Faith*. Wheaton, Ill.: Harold Shaw, 1994.

Culbertson, Diana, ed. *Invisible Light: Poems about God*. New York: Columbia University Press, 2000.

Culpepper, Alan. *Anatomy of the Fourth Gospel: A Study in Literary Design*. Philadelphia: Fortress, 1983.

————. *The Gospel and Letters of John*. Nashville: Abingdon, 1998.

Curzon, David, ed. *The Gospels in Our Image: An Anthology of Twentieth-Century Poetry Based on Biblical Texts*. New York: Harcourt Brace, 1995.

Davie, Donald, ed. *The New Oxford Book of Christian Verse*. Oxford: Oxford University Press, 1981.

Dickinson, Emily. *The Poems of Emily Dickinson: Reading Edition*. Edited by R. W. Franklin. Cambridge, Mass.: Harvard University Press, 1999.

Donne, John. *The Complete Poetry of John Donne*. Edited by John T. Shawcross. New York: New York University Press, 1968.

Ecclestone, Alan. *The Scaffolding of Spirit: Reflections on the Gospel of St. John*. London: Darton, Longman & Todd, 1987.

Edwards, Mark. *John Through the Centuries*. Blackwell Bible Commentaries. Oxford: Blackwell, 2004.

Eliot, T. S. *Collected Poems: 1909–1962*. New York: Harcourt Brace, 1970.

Frost, Robert. *Robert Frost: Collected Poems, Prose, & Plays*. Edited by Richard Poirier and Mark Richardson. New York: Library of America, 1995.

Gardner, Thomas. "Close Reading." In *The Princeton Encyclopedia of Poetry and Poetics*. Princeton: Princeton University Press, forthcoming.

————. *A Door Ajar: Contemporary Writers and Emily Dickinson*. Oxford: Oxford University Press, 2006.

————. *Regions of Unlikeness: Explaining Contemporary Poetry*. Lincoln: University of Nebraska Press, 1999.

————. "Running Journal (Finland)." In *Roots and Renewals: Writings by Bicentennial Professors*, edited by Mark Shackelton and Maarika Toivonen, 182–88. Helsinki: Renvall Institute, 2001.

Graham, Jorie. *The End of Beauty.* New York: Ecco, 1987.

Harris, Max. *Theatre and Incarnation.* London: Macmillan, 1990.

Hart, Kevin, ed. *The Oxford Book of Australian Religious Verse.* Melbourne: Oxford University Press, 1994.

Hass, Robert. "The First, Second, and Third Epistles General of John." In *Incarnation: Contemporary Writers on the New Testament,* edited by Alfred Corn. New York: Viking, 1990.

Herbert, George. *The Works of George Herbert.* Edited by F. E. Hutchinson. London: Oxford University Press, 1941.

Hill, Geoffrey. *Style and Faith.* New York: Counterpoint, 2003.

Hopkins, Gerard Manley. *Gerard Manley Hopkins: Poems and Prose.* Edited by W. H. Gardner. Middlesex: Penguin, 1953.

Impastato, David, ed. *Upholding Mystery: An Anthology of Contemporary Christian Poetry.* Oxford: Oxford University Press, 1997.

Jasper, David. "The Study of Literature and Theology." In *The Oxford Handbook of English Literature and Theology,* edited by Andrew Hass, David Jasper, and Elisabeth Jay, 15–32. Oxford: Oxford University Press, 2007.

Jasper, David, and Stephen Prickett, eds. *The Bible and Literature: A Reader.* Oxford: Blackwell, 1999.

Jeffrey, David Lyle. *A Dictionary of Biblical Tradition in English Literature.* Grand Rapids: Eerdmans, 1992.

Keener, Craig S. *The Gospel of John: A Commentary.* 2 vols. Peabody, Mass.: Hendrickson, 2003.

Kermode, Frank. "John." In *The Literary Guide to the Bible,* edited by Robert Alter and Frank Kermode, 440–66. Cambridge, Mass.: Harvard University Press, 1987.

Koester, Craig R. *Symbolism in the Fourth Gospel: Meaning, Mystery, Community.* 2nd ed. Minneapolis: Fortress, 2003.

———. *The Word of Life: A Theology of John's Gospel.* Grand Rapids: Eerdmans, 2008.

Levertov, Denise. *Candles in Babylon.* New York: New Directions, 1982.

———. *A Door in the Hive.* New York: New Directions, 1989.

———. *New and Selected Essays.* New York: New Directions, 1992.

Mariani, Paul. *Deaths and Transfigurations: Poems.* Brewster, Mass.: Paraclete, 2005.

McGrath, James F. *John's Apologetic Christology.* Cambridge: Cambridge University Press, 2001.

Miller, Vassar. *If I Had Wheels or Love: Collected Poems of Vassar Miller.* Dallas: Southern Methodist Press, 1991.

Millier, Brett. *Elizabeth Bishop: Life and the Memory of It.* Berkeley: University of California Press, 1993.

Moloney, Francis J. *The Gospel of John: Text and Context.* Boston: Brill, 2005.

Monk, Ray. *Ludwig Wittgenstein: The Duty of Genius.* New York: Free Press, 1990.

Norris, Kathleen. *Journey: New and Selected Poems 1969–1999.* Pittsburgh, Penn.: University of Pittsburgh Press, 2001.

Price, Reynolds. *Three Gospels.* New York: Scribner, 1996.

Reinhartz, Adele. *Befriending the Beloved Disciple: A Jewish Reading of the Gospel of John.* New York: Continuum, 2001.

————. "The Gospel of John." In *The Oxford Handbook of English Literature and Theology*, edited by Andrew Hass, David Jasper, and Elisabeth Jay, 323–41. Oxford: Oxford University Press, 2007.

Richey, Esther Gilman. "The Intimate Other: Lutheran Subjectivity in Spenser, Donne, and Herbert." *Modern Philology* 108.3 (2011): 1–32.

Robinson, Marilynne. *The Death of Adam: Essays on Modern Thought.* New York: Houghton Mifflin, 1998.

Rosenberg, David. *Communion: Contemporary Writers Reveal the Bible in Their Lives.* New York: Anchor, 1996.

————, ed. *Congregation: Contemporary Writers Read the Jewish Bible.* New York: Harcourt Brace, 1987.

Rosenthal, Peggy. *The Poet's Jesus: Representations at the End of a Millennium.* Oxford: Oxford University Press, 2002.

————. *Praying the Gospels through Poetry.* Cincinnati, Ohio: St. Anthony Messenger Press, 2002.

Ryken, Leland, James C. Wilhoit, and Tremper Longman III, eds. *Dictionary of Biblical Imagery.* Downers Grove, Ill.: InterVarsity, 1998.

Stevens, Wallace. *Wallace Stevens: Collected Poetry and Prose.* Edited by Frank Kermode and Joan Richardson. New York: Library of America, 1997.

Stibbe, Mark W. G. *John.* Sheffield, UK: Sheffield Academic, 1993.

Thomas, R. S. *Collected Poems 1945–1990.* London: Phoenix, 2000.

Trott, James H., ed. *A Sacrifice of Praise: An Anthology of Christian Poetry from Caedmon to the Mid-Twentieth Century.* Nashville: Cumberland House, 2006.

Vaughan, Henry. *The Complete Poetry of Henry Vaughan.* Edited by French Fogle. New York: New York University Press, 1965.

Walker, Cheryl. *God and Elizabeth Bishop: Meditations on Religion and Poetry.* New York: Palgrave Macmillan, 2005.

Wilbur, Richard. *The Mind-Reader.* New York: Harcourt Brace, 1976.

Williams, Rowan. *Christ on Trial: How the Gospel Unsettles Our Judgment.* Grand Rapids: Eerdmans, 2000.

Woiwode, Larry. *Acts.* San Francisco: HarperSanFrancisco, 1993.

Wright, Charles. *Negative Blue: Selected Later Poems.* New York: Farrar, Straus & Giroux, 2000.

———. *The World of the Ten Thousand Things: Poems 1980–1990.* New York: Farrar, Straus & Giroux, 1990.

Wright, N. T. *Jesus and the Victory of God.* Minneapolis: Fortress, 1996.

———. *John for Everyone.* 2 vols. Louisville: Westminster John Knox, 2004.

Yeats, W. B. *Selected Poems and Three Plays.* Edited by M. L. Rosenthal. New York: Macmillan, 1986.

Scripture Index

GENERAL INDEX